Black & Decker
POWER TOOL
CARPENTRY

Marshall Cavendish London & New York

Edited by Sarah Parr
Consultant editors: Tony Mason & Alec Limon
Designed by Graham Beehag

Published by Marshall Cavendish Books Limited,
58 Old Compton Street,
London W1V 5PA

© Marshall Cavendish Limited 1972, 1973,
    1974, 1975, 1976, 1977, 1978
Some of this material was first
published by Marshall Cavendish Limited
in the partwork *Golden Homes*.

First printing 1978

Printed in Great Britain by Redwood Burn Limited

ISBN 0 85685 373 9

INTRODUCTION

Trying your hand at home carpentry is something of a gamble,
but *power-tool* carpentry virtually guarantees you success –
even with the most exciting and ambitious of projects.
This book has been specially written to enable *anyone* to quickly
master the basic power-tool techniques and put them into
practice on projects chosen for their qualities
of design and simplicity of construction.
In fact, the only difficulty you are likely to come across is
deciding which project to start first, since the choice includes
virtually everything from a garden gate to a 4-poster bed!

CONTENTS

Techniques
Basic tool kit **8**
Woodworking joints **11**
Workmate **16**
Power tool safety **19**
The drill **20**
Sanders **25**
Power sawing **27**
The jointer **36**
The router **37**
The bench grinder **37**
The lathe **39**
Spray painting **43**

Projects
Hall stand **46**
Telephone table **51**
Victorian butler's tray **55**
Coffee table **59**
Dinette trolley **61**
Sofa-bed **66**
Studio couch & chair **71**
Mix-and-match living room suite **76**
Round table **87**
Table with a rural look **91**
Dining chairs **99**
Fold-down table with cupboard **105**
Made-to-measure kitchen unit **108**
Kitchen unit with oven and hob **114**
Kitchen wall cupboard **119**
Bunk beds **123**
Bed platform **128**
Fitted wardrobe **133**
Fitted dresser **137**
Four-poster bed **141**
Linen chest **145**
Garden bench **150**
Garden seat/planter **154**
Garden gates **160**
Tree house **165**
Climbing frame **169**
Gazebo **174**

Index 182

Publisher's note
The timber for the projects in this book has been selected for its relatively easy availability. If you have difficulty obtaining a particular size stock, it is suggested that you buy the next largest size and have it trimmed down by your timber merchant (they should do this for a nominal fee) or trim it yourself.

Techniques

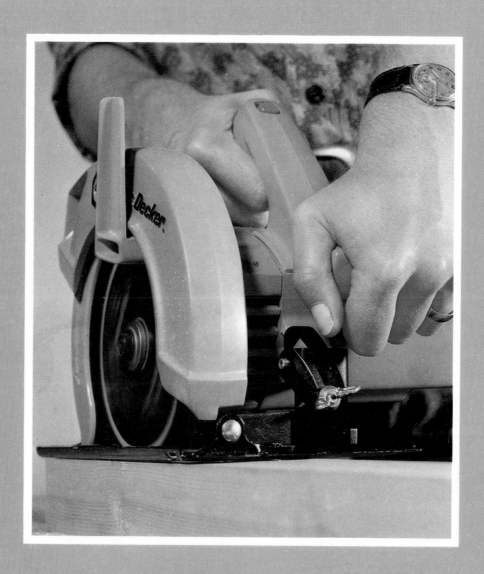

Basic tool kit

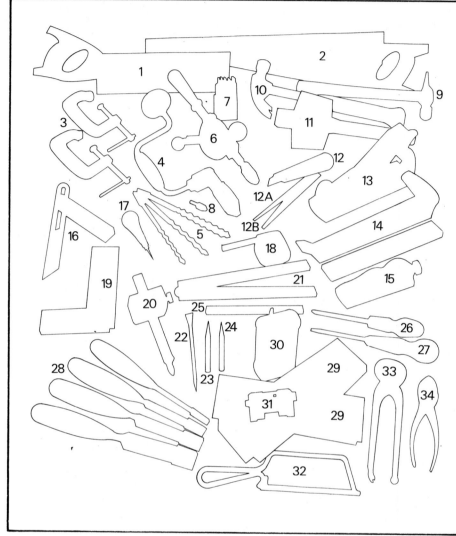

One of the dullest and slowest jobs in carpentry is making a large number of identical pieces—sawing the same shape repeatedly, hand-drilling row after row of holes, sanding to shape and so on. Power tools take the routine and heavy labour out of many of these tasks so that your enthusiasm and energy are not diminished and your work will be of a better standard. Power tools will also enable you to complete a better looking product, because you can achieve greater accuracy of line not only when sawing long edges but also when making strong, durable joints.

However, the power tool kit will need to be complemented by a hand tool kit, consisting of the following:

1. Tenon or back saw. These saws are available in blade lengths of between 8in and 14in (203mm and 356mm) with 13, 14, 15, 16 or 20 points per inch (ppi). This is used for jointing and cutting across the grain on small pieces. The back of the blade may be of brass or steel. The saw with 20 points per inch (25mm) is for cutting dovetails and it has a thin blade to give greater accuracy. The dovetail saw performs a ripping action, so cut along the grain when using it.

2. Handsaw. This is used for cutting larger pieces of timber. There are three types of handsaw. The one shown here is a panel saw. It is 20in to 22in (508mm to 559mm) long with 10 ppi. Its specialist purpose is for fine cross cut and jointing work and for cutting plywood, block-board and hardboard. The other types of handsaw (not shown) are the rip saw and the crosscut saw. The rip saw is 26in (660mm) long with 5 ppi. Its specialist

purpose is for cutting softwoods, working with the grain. The crosscut saw is 24in to 26in (610mm to 660mm) long with 6, 7 or 8 ppi and is specially used for cutting across the grain of hardwoods and softwoods and for working with the grain on very hard woods.

3. G cramps. These are used for a range of cramping purposes. These cramps are available in a 1in to 18in (25mm to 457mm) range of opening and between 1in to 8in (25mm to 203mm) depth of throat. When using G cramps always place a waste scrap of timber between the piece to be cramped and the shoes of the cramps. This prevents bruising.

4. Rachet brace. This has spring loaded jaws in a screw tightened chuck. It is specially designed for holding wood auger bits (**5**). The brace is available with or without a reversible rachet in a sweep (the arc described by the turning handle of the brace) ranging from $5\frac{7}{8}$in (148mm) to 14in (355mm).

5. Wood auger bits. These are used with a rachet brace.

6. Hand drill. This is used for holding wood and metal twist drill bits (**7**) and countersink or rose bits (**8**). The example shown here has a double pinion (cogged drive wheel).

7. Twist bits. These are commonly available in sizes ranging from $\frac{1}{64}$in (0.4mm) to $\frac{1}{2}$in (13mm). The type of steel used depends on the use to which the bit is to be put.

8. Countersink or rose bit. This is used for countersinking drilled holes so that countersunk screw heads will fit flush with the surface of the piece you are working with.

9. Warrington pattern or cross pein hammer. This is used for general nailing and joinery and can be used for planishing and beating metal. Weights of these hammers range from 6oz (170g) to 16oz (450g).

10. Claw hammer. This is used for general purpose carpentry, in particular, for driving and removing nails. When taking out nails, make sure that the nail head is well into the claw of the hammer and, if it is necessary to protect the surface of the wood, place a scrap piece of timber between the claw and the wood. Exert even pressure to lever the nail out. Claw hammers are available in weights ranging from 16oz (450g) to 24oz (570g).

11. Carpenter's or joiner's mallet. This is used for general carpentry and cabinet work and is available in head lengths of between 4in (102mm) and $5\frac{1}{2}$in (140mm).

12. Handyman's knife. This useful carpentry knife can be fitted with a variety of blades to suit specific purposes. The blades include angled concave, convex, linoleum and hooked blades. Wood and metal saw blades (**12A** and **12B**) can also be fitted to this tool as can a blade for cutting plastic laminate.

13. Bench plane. There are various types of bench plane and they are available in a range of lengths and widths. The smooth plane (shown here) comes in lengths of between $9\frac{1}{2}$in and $10\frac{1}{4}$in (241mm to 260mm) and widths of between $1\frac{3}{4}$in and $2\frac{3}{8}$in (45mm to 60mm). The Jack plane (not shown) is available in lengths of between 14in (356mm) and 15in (381mm) and widths ranging from 2in (51mm) to $2\frac{3}{8}$in (60 mm). The Fore plane (not shown) is 18in (457mm) long and $2\frac{3}{8}$in (60mm) wide. The Jointer or Try plane (not shown) is 22in (561mm) long and $2\frac{3}{8}$in (60mm) wide. When working with resinous or sticky woods, a plane with a longitudinally corrugated sole makes the job of planing easier because friction between the timber and the plane is reduced. If you do not have such a plane, apply a spot of vegetable oil to the sole of your ordinary plane—this will perform much the same function.

14. Surform plane. This is one of a range of open rasp/planing tools, all of which are useful and versatile. They are primarily used for rough work but with care some reasonably fine craftsmanship can be produced. Each tool in this range has replaceable blades.

15. Block plane. This small plane is particularly useful for fine cabinet work and for planing end grain. Available in lengths of between 6in and 7in (152mm to 178mm) and cutter widths of between $1\frac{15}{16}$in (49mm) and $1\frac{5}{8}$in (41mm).

16. Sliding bevel. This tool is used for setting out angles or bevels. Available in blade sizes of 9in (239mm), $10\frac{1}{2}$in (267mm) and 12in (305mm).

17. Bradawl. This is a chisel pointed boring tool used for marking screw positions and counterboring for small size screws.

18. Adjustable steel rule. The pocket size variety, when fully extended, range in length from 6ft (1.83m) to 12ft (3.66m). The larger varieties are available in either steel, glassfibre or fabric in lengths of up to 100ft (30.5m).

19. Carpenter's square. This is used for setting out right angles and for testing edges when planing timber square. The tool has a sprung steel blade and the stock is protected by a thin strip of brass or other soft metal. Available in blade lengths of $4\frac{1}{2}$in (114mm), $7\frac{1}{2}$in (190mm), 9in (239mm) and 12in (300mm).

20. Marking gauge. This is used to mark one or more lines on a piece of timber, parallel to one edge of that timber. The type shown here is a mortise gauge which has a fixed point on one side and one fixed and one adjustable point on the other. Its specific use is for marking out mortise and tenon joints but it can be used in the same way as an ordinary marking gauge.

21. Folding boxwood rule. This tool is also available in plastic. Primarily for joinery and carpentry use, it should be used narrow edge onto the timber for the most accurate marking. These rules are available in 2ft (600mm) and 3ft (1m) sizes.

22. Scriber marking knife. One end of this tool is ground to a chisel shaped cutting edge for marking timber. The other end is sharpened to a point and can be used for scribing metal.

23. Nail punch or set. This tool is used for tapping pin and nail heads below the surface of timber. A range of head sizes is available to suit pin and nail sizes.

24. Centre punch. This is used for spot marking metal to give a guide for drilling. The point is marked by tapping the wide end of the tool with a hammer. Automatic centre punches (not shown) are available. These are spring loaded so you do not have to tap the end of the tool.

25. Carpenter's pencil. This has an oblong shaped lead which is sharpened to a chisel edge so that it can be used to black in lines scribed on timber.

26. Pozidriv type screwdriver. This tip is designed for use with Pozidriv type screws which are increasingly replacing screws with the conventional blade head. The crosshead screw head allows far greater contact between the screwdriver tip and the screw head—providing, of course that the correct size of screwdriver tip is used. This makes for greater torque (twisting power) and reduces the likelihood of tool slip and consequent damage to the work.

27. Cabinet screwdriver. This tool is available in blade lengths of between 3in (76mm) and 18in (457mm) and tip widths of between $\frac{3}{16}$in (4.8mm) to $\frac{1}{2}$in (13mm). The screwdriver tip should fit the screw slot completely and the risk of tool slip will be further reduced if the screwdriver tip has been cross ground.

28. Carpenter's chisels. These are available in several shapes and sizes of both handles and blades. The firmer bevel edge chisels shown here are probably the most useful all round chisels to have in a basic tool kit. Chisel handles are either of ash, boxwood or plastic (shown here). Plastic handles are virtually unbreakable on quality chisels but timber handles should be treated with care and should only be hit with a wooden mallet. Blade widths vary from $\frac{1}{8}$in (3mm) to 2in (51mm).

29. Oilstones. These are used for sharpening the cutting edges of such tools as planes and chisels. There are two main kinds of oilstone, natural and artificial. Natural stone comes in several types. *Washita* gives a good finish and cuts well. *Arkansas* is an expensive stone but it is of high quality and produces a very fine edge. These are the most commonly used natural oilstones. Artificial stones come in three grades—coarse, medium and fine—and have the advantage of maintaining their quality. They are available in a selection of sizes including 5in × 2in (127mm × 51mm), 6in × 2in (152mm × 51mm), 8in × 2in (203mm × 51mm), 10in × 2in (254mm × 51mm) and 8in × $1\frac{7}{8}$in (203mm × 46mm).

30. Fine machine oil. This has many lubricating uses in the workshop and is a reasonable substitute for Neatsfoot oil when using an oilstone.

31. Honing gauge. This is a useful device for holding bladed tools at the correct angle for sharpening on an oilstone. The disadvantage of this tool is that it tends to cause wear in the centre of the oilstone rather than distributing the wear evenly over the whole stone.

32. Junior hacksaw. This is a general purpose saw for light metalworking jobs.

33. Shoulder pincers. These are used for pulling nails and pins from timber. If possible, always place a scrap of waste timber between the jaws of the pincers and the work piece to avoid bruising.

34. Slip joint pliers. This tool has a thin section so that the jaws can reach into tight places. It has two jaw opening positions and shear type wire cutter.

1. Butt joint

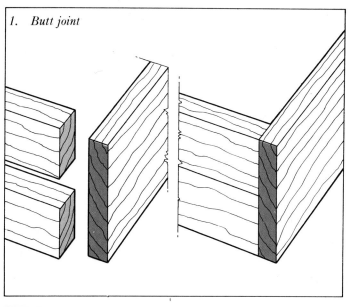

1. The butt joint is the simplest of all joints in carpentry. It may be made straight or right-angled, and needs nails or screws, sometimes with the addition of glue, to hold it firmly joined together.

2. The dowelled joint is basically a butt joint reinforced with dowels – lengths of wooden rod. Both halves of the joint are often drilled at once to make the holes line up.

3. The secret dowelled joint is better-looking because the end of the dowels do not show. The two rows of holes are drilled separately, so great accuracy is essential.

4. The 45° mitred joint has a very neat appearance, because no end grain is visible. Unfortunately, it is a very weak type of joint unless it is reinforced in some way, for instance, with a corrugated staple.

5. The halving joint is used at the corners of a rectangular frame. It is simple to make, has a reasonably neat appearance, and is quite strong if glued together.

2. Dowelled joint

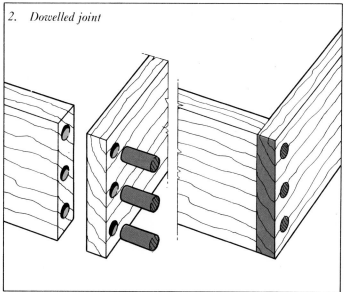

4. The mitred joint

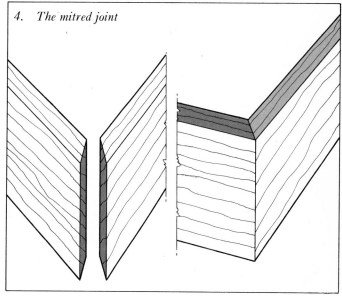

3. Secret dowelled joint

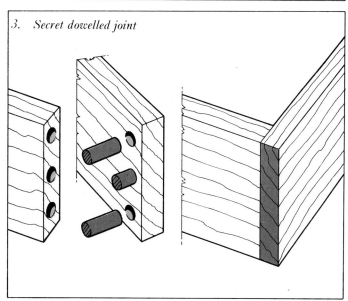

5. Halving joint

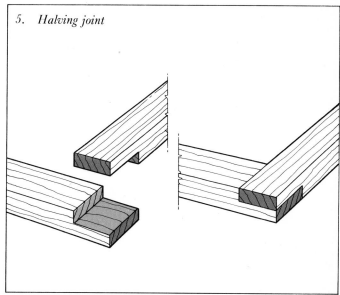

Woodworking joints

6. The T-halving joint is a variant of the usual L-shaped halving. It is generally used in conjunction with the previous type of halving, for instance in the construction of simple frameworks.

7. The cross-halving joint is the third member of this versatile family. This type of joint should be used where two pieces of timber have to cross without increasing the thickness of the frame.

8. The dovetail halving joint is an extra-strong halving. Its angled sides make it impossible to pull apart in a straight line, though it still needs glue to hold it together.

9. The through housing joint is used for supporting the ends of shelves, because it resists a downward pull very well. It, too, must be reinforced with glue or screws.

10. The stopped-dado joint has a neater appearance, but is harder to make because of the difficulty of cutting out the bottom of the rectangular slot neatly.

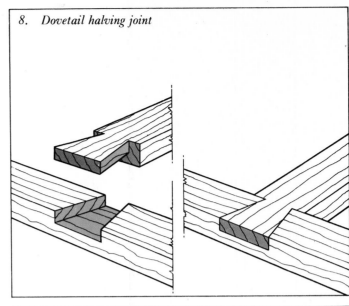

8. *Dovetail halving joint*

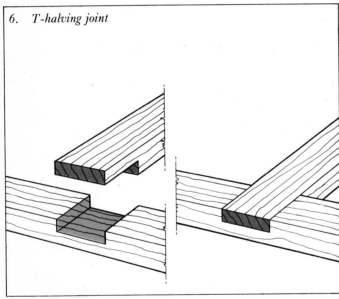

6. *T-halving joint*

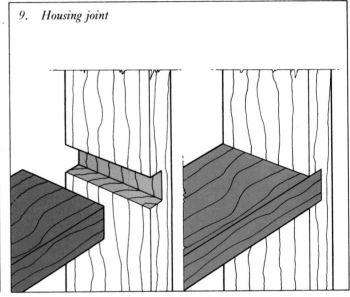

9. *Housing joint*

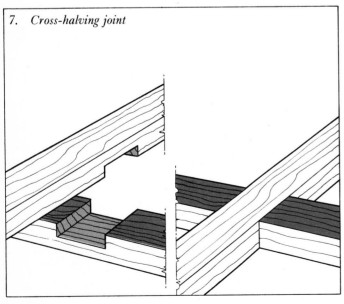

7. *Cross-halving joint*

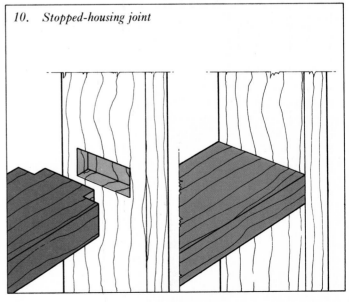

10. *Stopped-housing joint*

11. Tongue-and-groove joint

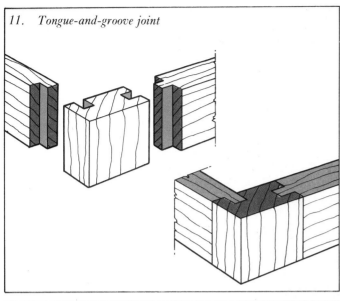

11. Tongued-and-grooved joints are most often found along the edge of ready-made boarding. But a right-angled version of this joint is also found, for example, at the corners of boxes.

12. The lapped joint has a rebate cut in one side to hide most of the end grain. This type of joint is quite often found in inexpensive cabinet work, because it is very easy to make with power tools.

13. The mortise-and-tenon joint is a very strong joint used to form T-shapes in frames. The mortise is the slot on the left; the tenon is the tongue on the right.

14. The through mortise-and-tenon joint is stronger than the simple type just described. It is sometimes locked with small hardwood wedges driven in beside, or into, saw cuts in the tenon.

15. The haunched mortise-and-tenon is used at the top of a frame. The top of the tenon is cut away so that the mortise can be closed at both ends, and so retain its strength.

12. Lapped joint

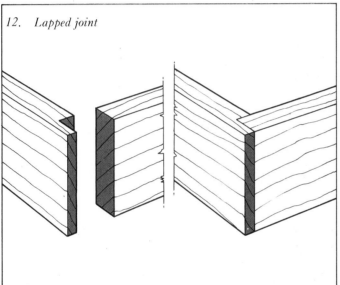

14. Through mortise-and-tenon joint

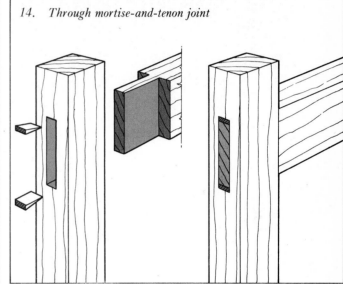

13. Mortise-and-tenon joint

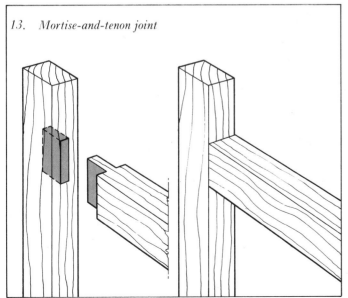

15. Haunched mortise-and-tenon joint

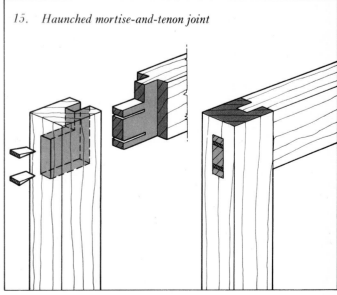

16. The bare-faced tenon is offset, with a 'shoulder' on one side only. It is used for joining pieces of different thicknesses.

17. Twin tenons are used in very thick timber. They give the joint extra rigidity and do not weaken the wood as much as usual. These are ideal for the construction of large items, such as sheds.

18. Forked tenons add rigidity to a deep, narrow joint. The angled edge of the tenon is sometimes found in a haunched mortise-and-tenon joint.

19. Stub tenons are generally used on even deeper joints, but they are weaker and less rigid than the forked tenons just described.

20. The bridle joint is most often used where a long horizontal piece of timber has to be fitted into the tops of several vertical pieces. This joint is best used for interior work as the end grain is exposed.

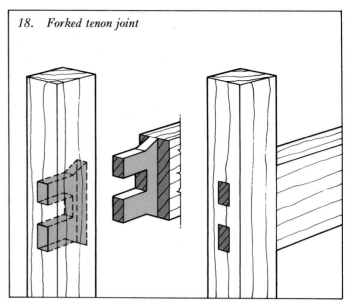

18. Forked tenon joint

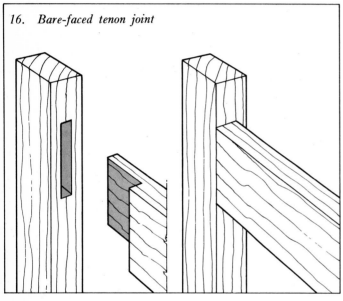

16. Bare-faced tenon joint

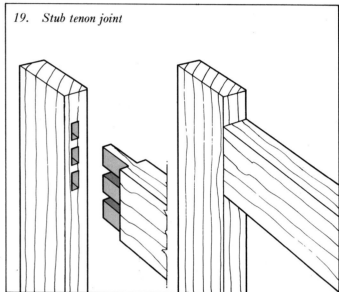

19. Stub tenon joint

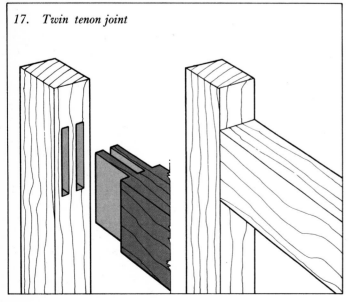

17. Twin tenon joint

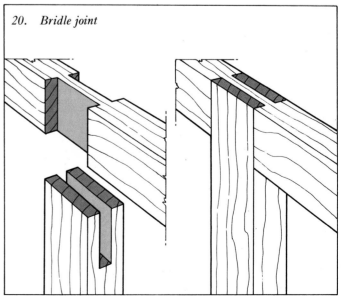

20. Bridle joint

21. Box joint

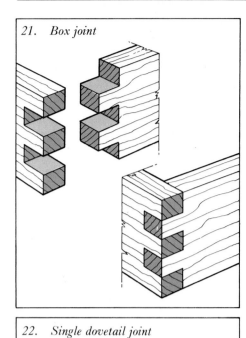

21. The box joint is quite strong and has a decorative appearance.

22. The single dovetail, like all dovetails, is extremely strong.

23. The through dovetail is used at the corners of drawers where strength and good appearance are required.

24. The lapped dovetail is nearly as strong, and also has one plain face.

25. The mitred secret dovetail is also used in very high-quality work.

26. The lapped secret dovetail is easier to make than a mitred secret dovetail.

27. The cogged joint is very strong and rigid.

28. The scarfed joint is used for joining frame members end to end.

26. Lapped secret dovetail joint

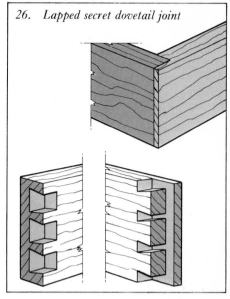

22. Single dovetail joint

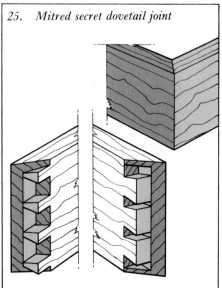

24. Lapped dovetail joint

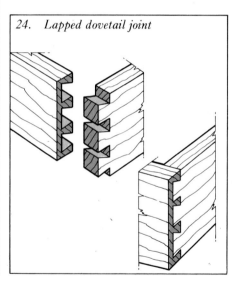

27. Cogged joint

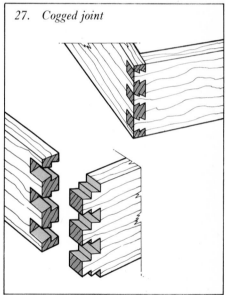

23. Through dovetail joint

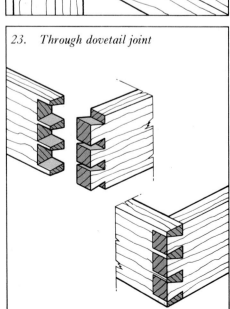

25. Mitred secret dovetail joint

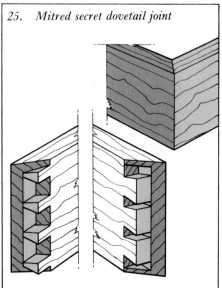

28. Scarfed joint

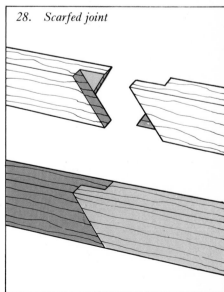

Workmate

The Black and Decker dual height Workmate in the higher workbench position.

For anyone who enjoys carpentry and wants to organise his work space most efficiently, a Workmate will almost certainly prove an invaluable addition to his equipment.

The Workmate is not just a portable workbench, it is also a giant vice and a sawhorse. It folds flat for easy storage, and can be hung on hooks on the wall. Its other great advantage is that instead of having to take the work to your bench, you can take the Workmate to the location where you want to do the work – be it workshop, garage, any room in the house, or even outside in the garden. Yet, despite its portability, any model of the Workmate is strong enough to take loads of up to $\frac{1}{4}$ ton (254kg).

The basic construction is a framework, either of aluminium or pressed steel, with two long, flat vice jaws which enable it to be used as either a working surface, or a vice. Independently operated handles at each end enable it to hold wedge-shaped objects, a considerable advantage over a conventional vice. A series of holes is drilled into each of the vice jaws to take vice pegs. The latter not only extend the maximum width of the object which the Workmate will hold securely, but also enable it to grip irregular shaped objects firmly, even something as awkwardly shaped as a guitar! Horizontal V-grooves along the inner edges of the vice jaws permit tubular objects to be securely gripped. The more expensive models have a dual height facility. A set of folding legs, when folded away, give the lower height, which is more appropriate to use as a sawhorse. When these are erected, they raise the height of the whole structure to a more comfortable height for bench use.

Apart from its versatility in being capable of holding large objects – such as a door – or irregular shapes, another great advantage is that, unlike many conventional fixed benches, you can walk round it to work on your project from any angle.

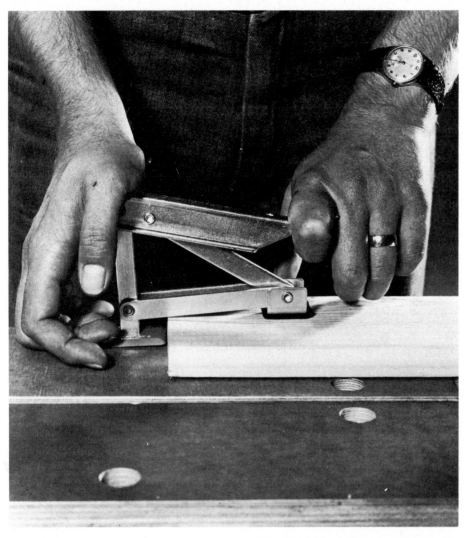

Attachments

To add to the versatility of the Workmate,
a range of attachments is available. The
Gripmate is a device for clamping work
down to the working surface of the bench,
similar in function to a G-cramp. It consists of a vertical shaft, which is seated in
a plastic liner, and can be located in any
of the vice peg holes. A horizontal arm is
lowered to the necessary level to grip the
workpiece securely to the bench top, and
a lever action then clamps it firmly in
place. A rubber pad at the point of
contact prevents damage to the work.

Universal Extender Arms also locate in
the vice peg holes. Available in sets of
four, they are specially designed to hold
large sheets of wood securely. Made of
cast aluminium, each bar is approximately
18in (457mm) long, but with the wide
range of adjustments possible, a Workmate so equipped will accept large sheets
of material up to 6ft × 3ft (2m × 1m), and
such difficult articles as picture frames,
doors and window frames.

The Tool Tray clips onto the outside
edge of one of the vice jaws and is a
useful place to put small tools, nails,
screws and pencils, etc.

Another attachment mounting onto the
edge of a vice jaw is the Saw Table, which
accepts any Black & Decker 5in (126cm)
circular saw, or saw attachment designed
for the home user. It is mounted onto the
Workmate using the screws and fixing
brackets supplied, and has all the usual
saw-bench facilities of a rip-fence and
mitre guide, which can be used and
adapted as described in the section on
Circular Saws.

Metal Vice-Claddings are only available
for use on de-luxe dual height Workmates.
Made of aluminium, they fit simply over
the vice jaws when working with metal
to give surface protection from oil,
grease and accidental abrasions. They
have horizontal and vertical V-grooves
for holding tubes and pipework, and
their metal construction allows light
gauge sheet metal bending.

Power Tools

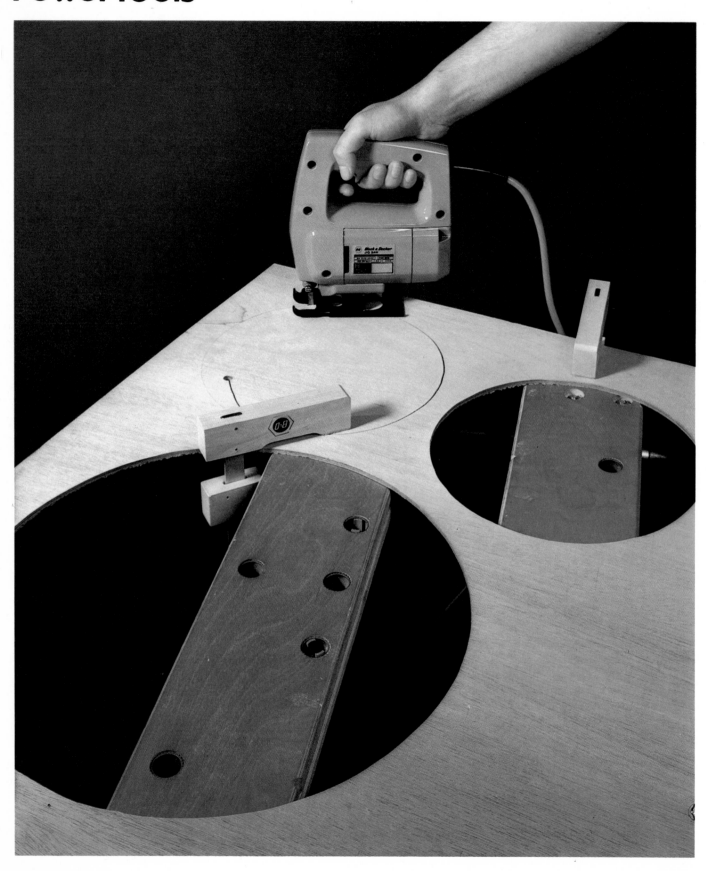

DO

KNOW YOUR POWER TOOL—read instruction leaflets carefully.

KEEP THE WORK AREA CLEAN—untidy work surfaces and benches invite accidents.

WEAR PROPER CLOTHING—do not wear loose clothing, aprons or unbuttoned cuffs, or jewellery which could get caught in moving parts. Rubber footwear is recommended for outdoor work.

WEAR SAFETY GLASSES—with most power tools.

USE THE SAFETY GUARD PROVIDED—keep it in place, and in good working order.

SECURE WORK—clamp down work, or use a vice. It leaves both hands free to operate the tool, and ensures that work cannot be snatched from your grasp.

KEEP TOOLS PROPERLY MAINTAINED—Keep blades and drill bits sharp at all times for optimum safety and performance. Ensure that tools are regularly cleaned and serviced.

DISCONNECT TOOLS WHEN NOT IN USE—so that they cannot be switched on accidentally. Check this especially when fitting attachments and making adjustments.

REMOVE ADJUSTING KEYS AND WRENCHES—make a habit of checking that all such adjusting tools are removed before switching on your power tools.

STORE POWER TOOLS SECURELY—when not in use, store your power tool in a dry, lockable place—away from children.

DO NOT

USE YOUR POWER TOOL IN DANGEROUS ENVIRONMENTS—in wet, damp or combustible atmospheres. Keep the work area well lit.

LET CHILDREN STAND TOO CLOSE—all onlookers should be kept a safe distance from the work area.

FORCE YOUR POWER TOOL—it will perform better and more safely at the rate for which it was designed.

ABUSE CABLES—never carry power tools by the cable, or tug it to disconnect the plug from the socket. Keep the cable clear of sharp edges, oil and heat.

OVER-REACH—keep a good balance and proper footing at all times.

START THE TOOL ACCIDENTALLY—never carry a plugged-in tool with your finger on the switch.

THE DRILL

Power drills can be used for many other purposes than just boring holes. A large number of accessories can be fitted to the basic drill unit, enabling it to do almost anything than can be done by a specialized power tool.

Basically, a power drill is a compact electric motor fitted with a projecting shaft at one end on which is mounted a chuck, a revolving clamp that grips and drives drill bits or other attachments. The motor unit is held in the hand by a pistol grip and the motor is started by pressing a trigger at the top of the grip. For safety reasons, the motor stops if pressure is released on the trigger. But most drills have a locking pin that can be engaged to hold the trigger in the 'on' position.

Electric power is supplied to the drill by a cable that enters the machine through the bottom of the handle. On all modern drills, a complex system of insulation, known as double insulation is built in to keep the user from getting an electric shock. It is symbolized thus
In addition to extra user-safety, it is not necessary to earth such tools.

Should any power tool become hot, through heavy or prolonged use, the quickest way to cool the motor is to hold it safely away from yourself and the work, and run it at full speed in free air. This allows for the fan to provide maximum ventilation.

Many drills can be adjusted to run at different speeds. The normal type is a drill with a two-speed geared reduction, to run at up to 1,000 rpm and 2,500-3,000 rpm. These two speeds are suitable for most household jobs, and a machine with a two-speed gearbox is the best buy for the keen amateur. Some drills are available with two speeds achieved electronically, through a diode switch. This is certainly a low-cost method, but the speed range is narrower, typically 1,700 rpm and 2,500-3,000 rpm, and there is a substantial power loss at the lower speed.

Variable-speed drills, where the speed can be infinitely varied by an electronic device, are also available. This control can either be built into the trigger, working by finger pressure, or through a feedback system, an electronic chip which enables a speed to be 'dialled' and then maintains it constantly, whatever the applied load.

When choosing a drill you should

consider whether or not you want one which incorporates rotary hammer action —although this action has no practical use in carpentry. These are most useful when drilling into brick, concrete or masonry. At the flick of a selector switch, the rotary hammer action can be engaged for easy drilling into such materials. As the drill bit rotates, it also hammers up and down, to break up hard aggregate in its path. Disengage the hammer selector for normal rotary drilling and attachment driving. This feature adds to the cost of the drill, but is well worth it for the additional scope it offers around the home.

Power drills come in various sizes, which are graded by the capacity of their chucks, that is by the largest drill bit that can be fitted into the chuck. Common sizes are $\frac{1}{4}$in (6mm), $\frac{5}{16}$in (8mm), $\frac{3}{8}$in (10mm) and $\frac{1}{2}$in (13mm). These refer to

their drilling capacities in mild steel. In most cases, using a narrow-shanked bit, they will drill holes at least double these diameters in wood. The larger machines have more powerful motors. A medium-sized machine should be adequate for all ordinary jobs. The $\frac{3}{8}$in and $\frac{1}{2}$in sizes fall into this category and are the most suitable for the household carpenter.

An indispensable accessory that every drill user will need is an extension cable. This enables him to use the tool in places remote from a power source. Cables are available in standard lengths from 25ft (8m) to 300ft (100m), or you can make up your own. The longer the cable, the thicker it needs to be to prevent power loss. Heavier machines also need thicker cables. In some countries you must also have an isolating transformer if using a power tool out-of-doors. The supplier of the drill will advise you.

Drill bits and fittings

Many types of drill are sold for cutting different sizes and shapes of hole in different materials. The most common sort are twist bits, used for drilling all sizes of holes in metal and holes in wood up to $\frac{1}{4}$in (6mm) in diameter. The smallest common size of twist bit is $\frac{1}{16}$in (1.6mm) and sizes increase in steps of $\frac{1}{64}$in (0.4mm) up from this.

Larger holes in wood are drilled with Jennings bits, which have a wide spiral to remove the surplus wood, and a centre spur or spike to keep the cut accurate when it is being started. Forstner bits are used in a drill press. They cut neat, flat-bottomed holes, but they have to be withdrawn and cleaned out during the drilling. Dowel bits are like twist bits with a wood-drill-shaped point for extra accuracy.

Very large holes are drilled with flat bits [up to $1\frac{1}{4}$in (32mm)] or hole saws [up to 3in (76mm)]. The flat bit has a flat, spade-like cutter with a central spur to hold it in place. The hole saw (also called a trepanning bit) has a revolving toothed ring attached to a central twist bit. The ring removes wood like a revolving pastry cutter. Different sizes of ring are available.

Other types of bit include countersink bits, for countersinking screw holes, and drill countersinkers or 'screw sinks', which are specially shaped to drill and countersink (or counterbore) a hole for a particular size of screw.

A plug cutter is often used in conjunction with a screw sink to conceal screw heads in wood. The screw sink is used to counterbore a screw hole (to recess the screw head some way into the wood) and then a plug, like a short length of dowel, is cut from a matching piece of timber, glued into the recess over the screw head, and planed flat to give an almost invisible result.

For drilling hard masonry, special masonry bits are available. They look like twist bits, but have cutting tips made of a special hard alloy. If using a drill with rotary hammer action, then masonry percussion bits are required. These have specially hardened shoulders at the tip, to withstand the shock as the drill vibrates. It has recently become possible to buy bits designed for both methods.

Glass and tiles are drilled with a spear point drill, which also has a hardened tip.

Drill bits for power drills have rounded shanks to fit into the chuck. For this

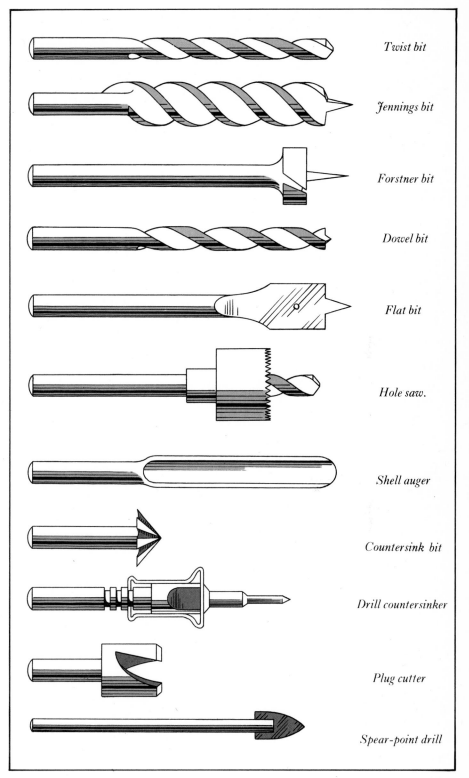

Twist bit

Jennings bit

Forstner bit

Dowel bit

Flat bit

Hole saw.

Shell auger

Countersink bit

Drill countersinker

Plug cutter

Spear-point drill

reason it could be dangerous to use hand-tool bits. These have squared shanks which could slip and fly out of the drill chuck which is rounded in shape.

Twist bits possess heads no wider than the shanks and are made in two types of steel, carbon and high-speed. High-speed steel (H.S.S.) is best for general use. It has a much longer life than carbon steel which blunts very quickly.

Some drill bits have a thickness of plastic wrapped round the shank of the drill to provide depth indication. This can be moved up and down. You can make a home-made depth stop by sticking adhesive tape around the bit.

Above: The electric drill bit sharpener has a special grinding wheel designed to sharpen drill bits at the correct angle. The bit drops into the appropriate hole in the top and is rotated gently between the thumb and forefinger while the machine is operating. Tungsten carbide-tipped bits should not be used.

The bit sharpener

Sharp and accurate drill bits will produce better quality work, without undue time losses or frustration. And the bits blunt surprisingly quickly. You can restore the edge on a grinder or use special drill-bit sharpeners now on the market.

You can change the position of the bit inside the sharpener by an adjusting knob. In this way you can control the cutting of the first two angles. When using the sharpener the following procedure should be followed. Set the adjusting knob on the front in the vertical position and insert the drill into the smallest hole of the top plate into which

it will fit. If you insert it into a larger hole the bit will become misshapen. The point of the bit should be in the centre, otherwise the bit will drill over-sized holes which will result in badly finished work and possibly waste a valuable piece of timber.

You can control the point position by the pressure you apply to the bit during sharpening. Turn the knob in a clockwise direction to increase the angle of cutting and in counter-clockwise direction to decrease the cutting relief.

Drill bits should be sharpened only when they are dry. When sharpening do not use water or any other liquid as a coolant. Sharpening makes the bit hot so do not touch it with your fingertips immediately after you have extracted it from the machine. Only H.S.S. or carbon steel bits can be sharpened in the machine. Masonry, percussion and other bits with specially hard tips, or of a different tip-shape should not be put into the machine or they will be ruined.

Drill stands

There are two types of drill stand: the vertical and the horizontal. With the vertical stand you can drill accurately at an exact angle of 90° to the work surface. The horizontal stand is used mainly for driving rotary sanders, abrasive discs, polishing buffs and bonnets, grinding wheels, and wire brushes. By adding a sanding table to the horizontal stand you can shape, sand and grind objects.

The vertical drill stand consists of a base with slots for bolting to a work bench or Workmate, a collar and clamping bolt for the upright pillar and the drill carriage. The carriage is raised or lowered by a locking knob and you can adjust for depth of hole and the travel of the drill on the pillar by adjusting the height of the collar which clamps the pillar. A spring returns the carriage to the raised position.

When using the drill on the stand it is important to keep the cable out of the way by winding it round the handle of the cradle of the drill. Lightly oil the pillar fairly frequently to prevent rust and also to enable the carriage to slide more freely.

Drill stand vices

This unit enables you to do accurate work on the base of the stand. Clamp the timber to be drilled in the vice and then move the vice so that the centre line of the hole to be drilled is exactly underneath the centre point of the drill bit.

Tighten the vice by securing the bolts with a small spanner. Make sure it is tightly clamped.

Right-angle changer

A right-angle speed changer converts the drill so that you can drill at angles or in awkward places. To use it with the drill you will need special adaptors. You can halve or double the speed of the drill, depending on which way round the changer is fitted into the spindle of the drill.

You can also fit a grinding attachment to the chuck of the changer. But these should not be used at high speeds. Carefully follow the instructions of the manufacturer.

The speed changer enables you to drill at an angle of 90° to the drive line. The letters 'S' for slow and 'F' for fast are stamped on the flat face of the hexagonal drive adaptors at the ends of the accessory. When the drill is connected to S and the chuck fitted to F, the chuck rotates at twice the rated drill speed. When these two positions are reversed the speed is halved. Fast speeds are used for drilling small holes and for high-speed sanding.

The changer can swing through 360° merely by rotating it by hand. The shape of the changer also allows access to drilling thick wood such as floor joists where the overall length of the drill bit and the length of the attachment may cause difficulties. Place the tip of the drill bit a little above the point to be drilled and align the bit as near to perpendicular to the work surface as possible before you start drilling.

Left: The use of a drill stand vice ensures that the work does not move when using a vertical stand.

Bottom left: A vertical drill stand makes for greater precision, particularly where a series of holes is required.

Bottom right: A horizontal drill stand increases the versatility of your drill by holding it firmly when using such accessories as grinding or buffing wheels and polishing bonnets.

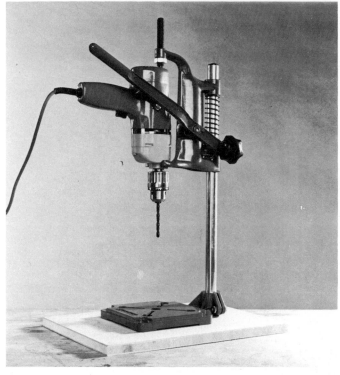

Drilling techniques

Drilling techniques

The great imperative when drilling is always to be careful that you are drilling at right angles to the work surface. Use a drill stand, or a try square, sighting the bit against the square.

To position dowel holes accurately, mark out the centre of the hole on one of the two pieces of timber to be joined. Insert pins into the marks. Nip the heads of the pins until only about $\frac{1}{4}$in (5mm) of shank is protruding. Then position and press the second piece of timber down onto the first. Separate the pieces and remove the pins. You can then drill the dowel holes through the pin marks.

Large pieces can be held firmly by hand, but always hold smaller pieces in a vice or clamp onto the bench or Workmate, otherwise the drill may suddenly snatch the piece out of your hand.

With a drill stand you can considerably widen the scope of your woodwork operations. Mortise cutting, for example, is easy. After marking out the mortise you can drill out most of the waste to a finely controlled depth, finishing the resulting

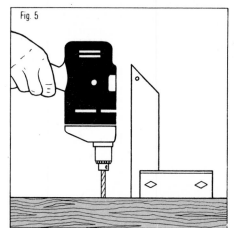

Fig. 5

slot with a chisel.

When inserting the bit make sure it sinks fully into the chuck before tightening with the key. Get into the habit of checking that the chuck is firmly locked.

When drilling thin timber, put a backing piece beneath the work to protect the under-surface. This will also prevent the timber from spinning or breaking.

To drill a really neat hole, set the depth gauge to three-quarters the thickness of the wood; then reverse the wood on the stand and drill from the other side.

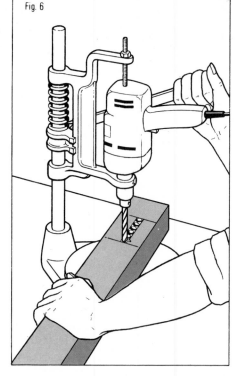

Fig. 6

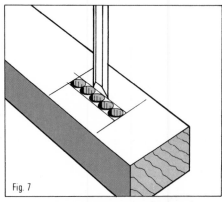

Fig. 7

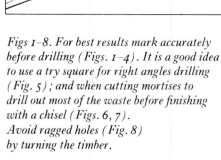

Fig. 8

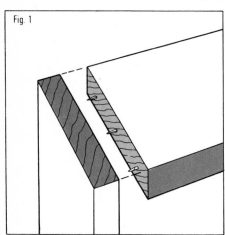

Fig. 1

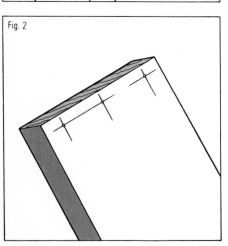

Fig. 2

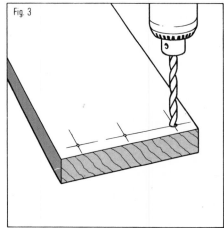

Fig. 3

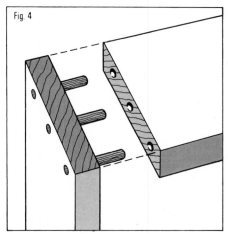

Fig. 4

Figs 1–8. For best results mark accurately before drilling (Figs. 1–4). It is a good idea to use a try square for right angles drilling (Fig. 5); and when cutting mortises to drill out most of the waste before finishing with a chisel (Figs. 6, 7).
Avoid ragged holes (Fig. 8) by turning the timber.

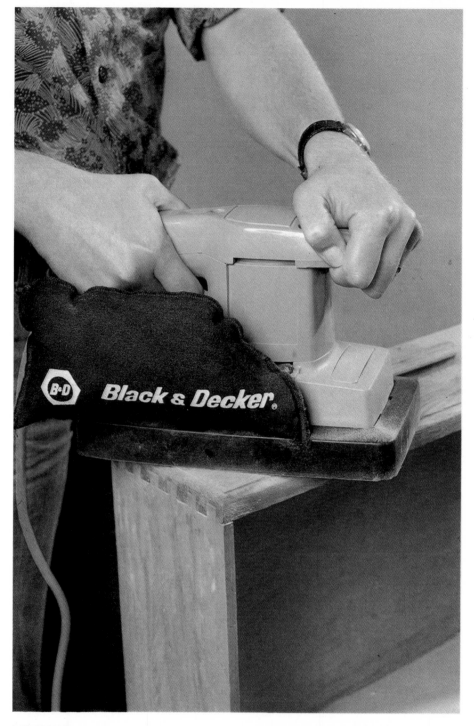

Left: An orbital sander with a dust extractor facility.

smoother the resulting finish. The abrasives used with power tools are available in varying grades, extra coarse, coarse, medium and fine, and are graded according to the size and number of particles for a given area, or 'grit'.

A material such as aluminium oxide is commonly used on sanding sheets for use with power tools, as it is hard wearing and has a longer life than some other materials. The grains are relatively widely spaced to allow the dust to escape, thus preventing clogging, which can drastically reduce the effectiveness of the sander. Ordinary glasspaper is not suitable for use with power tools.

Orbital sanders

The orbital, or finishing sander, can be used to give a perfect finish to any surface. It has a large, flat sanding pad, or platen, covered by an abrasive sheet, and is available in two sizes, $\frac{1}{3}$ sheet which is approximately 9in x $3\frac{5}{8}$in (229mm x 92mm); and $\frac{1}{2}$ sheet which is 11in x $4\frac{1}{2}$in (279mm x 114mm). The sheet size is a reference to the traditional size in which sandpaper is sold, in sheets measuring 11in x 9in (279mm x 229mm). The abrasive sheet is clamped at each end of the platen by a spring-clip or roller at each end. The latter keeps the sanding sheet taut over the length of the pad, which is usually made of felt, or a soft rubber compound.

This type of sander is available as a self-powered unit, or as a drill attachment. With the self-powered, or integral unit, the platen is connected to the motor, housed in a body with handles at front and rear, and has an on/off switch, usually with some form of lock-on device to ensure constant running. The platen, with its covering abrasive sheet, performs a small orbit, perhaps $\frac{3}{8}$in (10mm) in diameter, over the surface of the work at very high speed. This orbital abrasive motion can impart an extremely smooth finish, but is not really suitable for stock removal.

The advantage of the self-powered tool over the drill attachment is that it is always ready for use. However, drill attachments are cheaper, and if you do not anticipate too frequent use, an attachment may well prove adequate. To fit it to the drill, the chuck should be removed and replaced by an eccentric

SANDERS

There are several types of sander available, either as attachments to an electric drill, or self-powered, with their own integral motor. All employ abrasives to remove material, and the choice of which type to use depends on the task and the material. Some sanders are more suitable for stock removal, whereas others are at their best for producing a really smooth finish, prior to painting, or some other form of surface treatment.

Abrasives technology has made great advances in recent years, but the principles remain exactly the same. A tough backing sheet is coated with adhesive, and then surfaced with particles of an abrasive material. It is the action of rubbing this against the surface of the work which removes the excess material and provides a smooth finish. The finish obtained depends on the number and size of the particles or granules; the finer and more closely spaced the abrasive particles, the

Sanders

Right: Orbital sanders are available in ½- and ⅓-sheet sizes. This particular model can be fitted with a dust extractor. These power tools are suitable for use on timber, plaster, most metal surfaces and paintwork. To achieve a fine finish, work through the grades of sandpaper.

drive cam, which fits a socket inside the body of the attachment, connected to the platen, to provide the orbital motion.

The technique for using orbital sanders is the same in the case of the attachment and the self-powered tool. In both cases, hold the unit in both hands, switch on, and apply the tool to the work surface. Move the unit back and forth until a really smooth finish is achieved. The weight of the tool alone should be sufficient.

Disc sanders

A disc sander consists of a 5in (127mm) flexible rubber pad with an abrasive disc fastened to it by means of a central, recessed screw. The whole assembly fits into a drill, either with the chuck gripping the central shank of the pad, or by screwing directly into the drill spindle once the chuck is removed. Abrasive metal discs are available, which substitute for the rubber pad and sandpaper. These have the advantage of longer life, but are not as flexible, and their applications are more limited.

The disc sander is eminently suitable for stock removal, where quantities of unwanted material need to be removed. Rather than applying the disc flat to the work surface, it should be tilted, so that only half its surface area is in contact. Work with light sweeping strokes across the work surface, again beginning with a coarse grade of paper, and working

through to a fine grade.

If the disc is laid flat against the work surface, not only is there a danger that the central screw could mark the work, but the disc will produce circular scratches called swirl marks, which may be deep and difficult to remove. Even with the disc used at the correct angle, slight swirl marks are unavoidable.

A special type of disc called the 'Swirlaway' reduces these marks to a minimum. It is made of metal, but to counter its inherent rigidity its mounting shaft may be bent at a slight angle while it is in use.

Drum sanders

Drum sanders are available in a wide range of widths and sizes. They can be used on concave, convex and flat surfaces, even across the grain.

The tool consists of a revolving drum made of stiff foam rubber, with an abrasive belt fastened around it. The central shaft, or arbor, of the drum fits into the drill chuck, and when the cylinder spins, it is moved against the surface of the timber. Usually, when one abrasive belt is worn out, it can be ripped off to reveal another beneath it. This type of sander produces no swirl marks, but should only be used for sanding small areas or narrow strips of wood. On large, flat surfaces it tends to produce uneven results.

POWER SAWING

The circular saw is a fast and accurate power tool. It can cut, quickly and without strain, a wide range of materials. Using the correct blade, or cutting disc, you can cut metals, as hard as mild steel, as well as asbestos, slate and even marble, bricks and mortar, in addition to timber.

Two types of circular saw are available. The hand-held portable saw consists of a circular blade, which can vary in diameter between 5in (127mm) and 9in (229mm). This is vertically mounted on a shaft connected to the motor. A horizontal shoe, or sole-plate, held flat against the work surface, maintains the cutting angle, while a fixed blade guard protects the user from the teeth of the blade. Beneath the shoe, a retractable blade guard, mounted on a pivot, rotates to expose the teeth of the blade to make the cut. This type of saw is available either as a self-powered tool, or a drill attachment.

There is also a table or bench-mounted saw, where the blade projects upwards through a flat table top. A saw table attachment, to which a hand-held circular saw may be clamped, converts the conventional tool to a bench saw. The advantage of this arrangement is that it leaves both hands free to feed in the wood.

The disadvantage of a circular saw attachment powered by a drill, is that there is a danger of overloading the motor by tackling too large a piece of timber. If you intend to do work involving the use of a circular saw on a regular basis, it is worth investing in a self-powered tool designed for the job.

The hand-held circular saw

Saw attachments should only be used on medium or large sized drills, and then only for work which is not likely to overstrain the motor. The 5in (127mm) blade gives a depth of cut of 1½in (38mm) and the 6in (152mm) blade one of 1⅝in (41mm) when set up normally on the machine.

If the motor shows signs of slowing down or jamming, stop work immediately

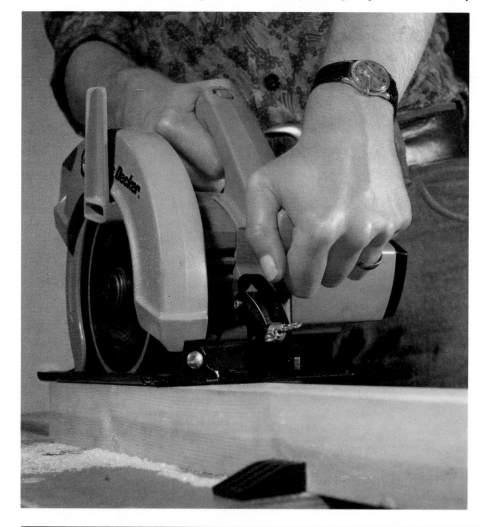

Left: A circular saw being used to rip a length of softwood. Always make sure that the blades are sharp; otherwise, these machines are liable to stall.

or you may burn it out on the spot. It is essential that the blade be removed from the cut before the motor is stopped, otherwise a greater strain would be placed on it upon restarting. It is essential that an electric motor be kept running at near full speed to keep it from being damaged. Do not press the saw forward too hard, and always allow the motor to attain full speed before the blade touches the wood.

You need a straight edge and some practise to bring in the blade at exactly the point where you want to cut. Sighting straight down the blade will make it easier. Saw cuts can be kept straight by nailing a batten to the wood you are cutting, and running the saw along it. Or you can use the adjustable rip fence on the saw, which guides it parallel to the edge of the wood.

There are several types of saw blade: the rip blade, with coarse teeth, for cutting along the grain; the fine toothed crosscut blade; the planer blade, which gives an extra-neat result, and the more usual type, the combination blade, which cuts at any angle to the grain. There is a flooring blade for the occasional cutting where unseen nails might be present, usually in floorboards; and there are coated blades, which reduce friction and prolong blade life, as well as tungsten-carbide tipped blades for hard woods and laminated materials. Other types of abrasive disc are available for cutting metals, masonry and ceramics.

It is essential to remove all nails and screws from the timber. Failure to do this could result in the teeth of the blade catching against the nail, which could stall or jam the saw, or even worse, dangerously jerk it from the user's grasp. To prevent the blade catching on anything underneath the wood, and to reduce the strain on the motor, set the depth gauge of the blade to only slightly more than the thickness of the wood you are cutting. A circular saw blade cuts on the upstroke, so setting the blade as shallow as possible gives a neater result by flattening the angle at which it cuts.

If the blade of the saw wanders off the cutting line, don't try to twist the saw to straighten the line; this will jam the blade in the cut. Take the saw out of the cut, go back a few inches and cut along that section again.

The attachment
The attachment is designed to fit the power drill with the chuck removed. There is a fixed upper blade guard and pivoted lower guard which pulls back in use and is spring-loaded to return to cover the blade when released from the work. The shoe can be adjusted for depth and for sawing at an angle.

All saws and attachments have an adjusting screw to control the lowering of the shoe or base plate of the main frame. Normally, this is to a maximum of 1¼in (32mm).

The saw blade should be fitted so that the manufacturer's name faces outwards and is visible through the blade guard. The blades have a hole so that you can keep the motor mechanism from turning while changing the blade by inserting a screwdriver when tightening the centre locking nut with a spanner. Insert the screwdriver through the hole of the blade and housing, then loosen the blade-retaining bolt with a spanner and remove the blade. Never attempt to fit a blade or make any adjustments with the drill plugged into a power point.

Before starting work, ensure that the self-adjusting curved blade guard is working properly. It should cover every part of the blade, even those parts which are not in contact with the work. Do not buy a saw attachment which does not have a blade guard.

After making a few trial cuts on a waste piece of timber, to ensure that you will cut to the width required, tighten down the fence-retaining screw firmly to prevent vibration working it loose.

A hand-held saw works by the teeth cutting upwards from below the timber. This motion pushes the wood against the bottom of the shoe. The cutting action of the bench saw works in the opposite way, with the teeth cutting downwards against the timber, supported by the saw table.

When cutting large pieces or sheets of timber, the width may be too great to use the rip fence on the saw. In this event, you can pin or clamp battens on the sheet to use as a guide; press the shoe of the saw laterally against them.

If the sheet is large, try using the Workmate with extension arms.

THE BANDSAW
The bandsaw is a machine designed for cutting curved shapes primarily in wood; however, special blades can be obtained for cutting plastics and metals. It can also be used for straight cutting. A number of bandsaws are available either as bench or floor models and also as attachments to wood-turning lathes or as an integral part of a combination machine. They all have the same basic components. The type and size selected will largely depend upon individual requirements.

The bandsaw consists of a continuous length of narrow flexible blade which can be mounted on either two or three bandwheels, one of which is driven by an electric motor. The bandwheels have

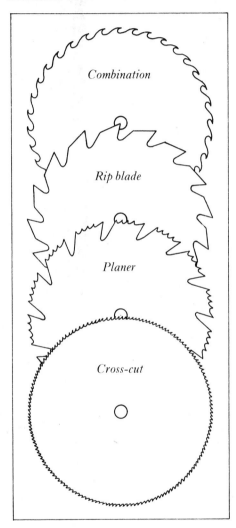

Combination

Rip blade

Planer

Cross-cut

tyred peripheries—these tyres are an integral part of the wheel and are slightly convex. This convexity allows the blade to run centrally on the wheel and counters the tendency for the blade to run off. In order to keep the blade running vertically through the saw table and to support the blade when cutting, upper and lower guide assemblies are provided —the upper being vertically adjustable to allow for varying thicknesses of timber. Both guides should be adjusted so that they will almost touch the blade, a piece

of notepaper between the blade and guide will provide sufficient clearance. The upper guide assembly will also have a thrust roller placed at the rear of the blade to prevent the saw blade being pushed away from the work. The adjustment should allow the blade to run just clear of the roller when not cutting, again a thin sheet of card can be used as a feeler to check this. The blade must run under tension and to enable tensioning to be carried out, the upper bandwheel is adjusted vertically by a tensioning knob on top of the bandsaw case. To enable the saw to run accurately on the crown of the bandwheels, a side knob, which is locked after setting by a locknut, can be used to set the verticality of the band-

wheel. Correct tension can be ascertained by checking the blade at a point between the upper and lower guards, i.e. just above the table—it should have a maximum of tension. The experienced user will instinctively be able to tell that the blade is in correct tension by the high note which rings out when the blade is plucked.

The saw table may contain a slot in which a mitre guide can slide. This guide is used when cutting mitres and angles and also when cutting off battens. Most bandsaw tables can be tilted for angled cutting.

Before commencing to cut a particular job it is as well to make several cuts in a waste piece to ensure even and accurate

cutting. Mark a straight line on a piece of timber, set the upper guide to just allow the passage of the timber. Switch on the machine and cut along the line; no great pushing effort should be required. If the saw doesn't cut accurately, incorrect setting of the guides, incorrect tension or bad sharpening and setting of the blade may be the cause. Cross cutting is easier than cutting with the grain; always begin a curved cut at a point on the cross grain section. Never back track—if the blade should get to the position where no further cutting can take place, stop the machine and withdraw the timber.

When ordering a band, remember to state the length of the band, its width and the material you intend to use it on.

The bench saw

Circular saws of this type have powerful motors—at least $\frac{1}{2}$hp—and large blades ranging from 6in (152mm) to 12in (305mm) in diameter. The blade turns much faster than that on the drill attachment, which not only speeds up the cutting rate but also gives a cleaner result.

However, both integral bench saw and drill-driven saw table are used in exactly the same way, and if you have a drill-powered saw, you can use these operating instructions provided that you do not overtax the motor's limited power.

A bench saw consists of a flat table top through which the saw blade projects. Wood is slid over the table towards the blade, which is adjustable for depth and angle of cut and protected by a slide-away guard that reduces the risk of cutting your fingers, although this is still a tool that must be used with care.

Saw table

If you wish to have the many advantages of a bench saw without the expense of buying one you can buy a saw table attachment, and convert your hand-held saw into a bench saw.

Fit the saw blade between the two washers provided, making sure that it will revolve anti-clockwise, indicated by a printed arrow on the blade.

Fit the blade guard next and make sure that it springs forward to cover the stationary blade.

Then fit the saw to the table itself, checking with a try square that the blade is at 90° angle. Use a calibrated square so that you can also measure the required depth of cut.

Set the guide fence parallel to the blade. Measure the distance by using a piece of timber of the width required.

The rip fence

The rip fence guide enables you to cut timber accurately either across the grain (crosscutting) or along the grain (rip cutting). The width of the fence is adjusted by measuring with a rule. Measure from inside the stock to the outside of the teeth, pointing towards the drill.

The rip fence has a T-angled section which runs along the straight edge of the timber and prevents the saw from veering off course. The fence can be fitted on either side of the power saw, but gives a greater cutting width when fitted on the left-hand side, almost double that when fitted on the right. But if you have any problems of width you can overcome these by turning the timber round and working from the other direction.

A rip fence is also supplied with table or bench saws. A bench mitre guide enables you to cut the face of the timber at any angle. The front of the guide has a protractor which allows you to set the angle of the cut. Improved control of the rip fence can be achieved by screwing a piece of battening on the inside face of the fence, through two holes in the bar of the fence. Do not extend the batten beyond the centre of the saw blade in case it should jam if you run slightly off line.

Mitre guides

The mitre guide is invaluable for enabling you to cut across a board of timber at any angle. Again, the mitre guide can be extended by screwing a piece of battening through its pre-drilled holes. This will ensure that the cut is an accurate one. Make sure to clamp the timber you are working on to the batten when you want to saw it. This will ensure that the blade does not bind or run off.

Sawing at an angle

You can achieve any angle by adjusting the shoe so that it is at an angle to the saw. A protractor scale, now standard on most power saws and saw attachments, enables the base plate to be pivoted and set at the desired angle in 5° steps.

This angle is set by loosening the locking knob and adjusting the base plate until one saw blade tooth juts out below the timber to be cut. Firmly tighten the knob. Allow for a slightly deeper cut to compensate for the angle. When making a 45° cut, for example, the saw should protrude through the sole plate by the thickness of the timber, plus an extra 6mm or so.

Set the saw depth slightly less than the depth of the required groove when cutting a groove with a power saw. Make two passes for the outer edges followed by a series of intervening parallel cuts, leaving a thin wall of wood between each. When the sawing has been completed, finish off with firmer chisel.

Cutting large pieces

When cutting long lengths of timber you may find that the section you have cut traps and binds the blade. This can be easily remedied by wedging a small piece of wood in the cut, or by the use of a riving knife.

Pocket cutting

A pocket cut is a slot cut in the face of a piece of timber. There is some danger when you start to cut that the saw will grab the timber so you should exercise caution. It is best to use an integral saw if possible, as opposed to an attachment, which has a less powerful motor.

Set the saw to just below the thickness of the wood. Rest the back edge of the shoe on the surface and turn the lower guard to open position. Release the guard and tilt the saw forward. The blade should be just clear of the wood surface. Press the trigger and carefully lower the saw.

Sawing small pieces of wood

It is dangerous to feed small pieces of wood into the blade with your hands, because your fingers get uncomfortably close to the blade and the slightest slip may cause a serious accident. Wood is very likely to slip on a bench saw because the tremendous torque of the blade tends to wrench it aside if you are not holding it firmly. This is a problem especially when using the crosscut guide at an angle.

Small pieces of timber should be pushed towards the blade with a push stick, a piece of timber with a V-shape cut out of the end so that it can hold the piece of wood firmly. It does not matter if the push stick gets cut because you can make another one in seconds. Fingers are not so easily replaced.

Mitring and firring

Mitring, or cutting wood at a 45° angle to make a mitred joint, can be done quickly and accurately. To cut a mitre across the face of a piece of wood, as in making a picture frame, set the protractor on the crosscut guide accurately to 45°. Then lay the wood against the guide and slide the guide and wood together down the table into the saw blade.

As a general rule, when crosscutting the timber should be held with both hands on one side of the blade and the offcut allowed to fall away freely. If you push from both sides, the pressure tends to close up the cut around the blade, causing it to jam and buck dangerously. If you must hold both sides, apply pressure upward slightly with your hands to hold the cut open.

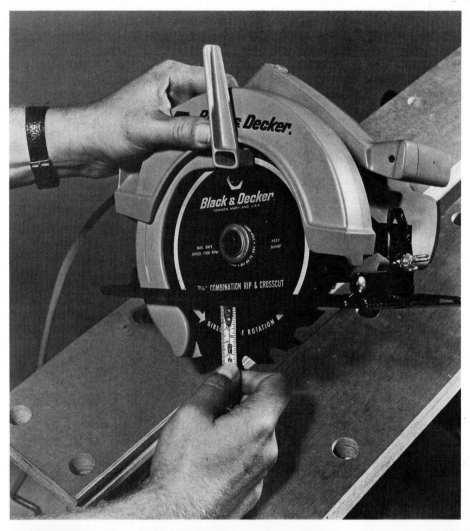

Left: Setting the depth of cut with a steel rule.

Bottom left: Using a push stick for safety when working with small pieces of wood on a saw table.

Bottom right: The mitre guide enables accurate cuts across timber at any angle.

To cut a bevel or mitre along the edge of a piece of timber again set the protractor to a 45° angle. On some bench saws the table tilts instead of the blade. Slide the wood and crosscut guide towards the blade in the normal way but grip the wood extra firmly.

Firring is cutting a very shallow taper on a long length of wood so that it is a few inches narrower at one end than the other. It is used, for example, in cutting rafters for flat roofs to create a slight slope for drainage.

Firring is best done by making an adjustable jig out of two moderately long battens. Set them face to face and fasten them together by a hinge at one end and a slotted metal strip fastened with wingnuts on the other. By moving the free ends a distance apart and locking them at this distance with the strip and wingnuts, the jig can be set at any shallow angle.

In use, the jig is slid along the fence together with the wood to be cut. This method is particularly convenient when a large number of identical pieces have to be cut.

Housing joints

Housings and other grooves can be cut simply and accurately by setting the saw blade to the required depth of cut and setting the sides of the groove first, using the fence to keep them straight. Then slide the fence away and remove the wood between the cuts by repeatedly passing it over the saw blade. Mark the extent of the groove on top of the wood or you may cut past the edges. Except with very narrow grooves or housings, this method is faster than chiselling the whole thing by hand, although for a stopped housing

you will have to cut the last inch or two by hand since the curved blade cannot reach the inside corner of the housing. It is also more accurate because the depth of cut is constant all over the groove. When cutting tenons wood can be removed in the same way.

Rebates

There are two ways of cutting rebates on a bench saw. One way is to cut along one side of the rebate, using the fence to ensure accuracy, and then turn the wood through 90° and cut the other side.

This involves two operations for each rebate. A faster way is to mount the blade on 'wobble washers', a pair of angled washers that make the blade wobble from side to side as it revolves. As a result, the blade cuts a wide groove instead of a neat line. The width of the groove is restricted by the size of the slot in the saw table, because if the blade 'wobbled' too far it would cut the table. But you can always make several passes to cut a wide rebate.

When you have set the blade on its washers, fasten a piece of old battening to the fence to protect it and move it until the blade just brushes the battening at the apex of its wobble. Now any piece of wood that is slid along the battening will have a rebate cut out of it the same width as the wobble of the blade. Or even narrower if you adjust the blade to cut farther into the temporary battening fence. The depth of cut can still be adjusted in the normal way.

Great care should be taken when using wobble washers because the oscillation of the blade makes it even more dangerous than an ordinary circular saw blade. At all costs, keep your fingers well away

from it and use a push stick to move the wood you are cutting.

Kerfing

Kerfing is a special technique that enables a piece of solid wood to be bent in a curve. Rows of parallel cuts are made across the wood on the inside of the curve through half to three-quarters of the wood's thickness, and all the way along the part that is to be curved. The wood can then be bent and it helps if you wet or steam it as well. Use a crosscut or planer blade to make the cuts. A combination blade is too coarse and will give a messy result.

Kerfing reduces the strength of wood considerably, and should not be used for load-bearing frames. It is really only suitable for outside curves, with the saw cuts on the narrower radius. The wood could be bent the other way but the surface would probably wrinkle unattractively. When used correctly kerfing produces a neat curve that is impossible to make by any other method.

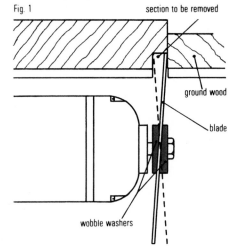

Fig. 1
section to be removed
ground wood
blade
wobble washers

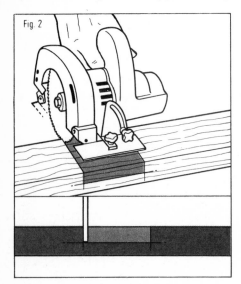

Fig. 2

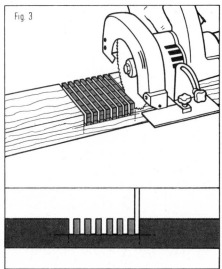

Fig. 3

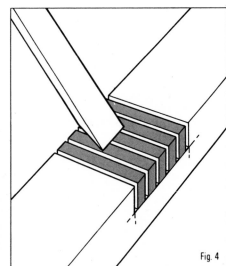

Fig. 4

Tenon joints

To cut a tenon on a bench saw, first crosscut the timber to length and make sure that the ends are square. There are two ways of making a tenon. In some circumstances the first is less satisfactory.

The first method uses horizontal cuts. First adjust the depth of cut and use a batten as a bench guide. Make the first cut on the shoulder of the tenon. Then make a series of crosscuts along the length of the marked tenon and complete. Lap joints can also be made in this way.

The second method is the more obvious. Make a vertical and horizontal cut for each shoulder. When making the vertical cut use a push stick with your right hand to slide the tenon towards the blade.

The rip fence will need two settings so that you will save time by completing all the vertical cuts before completing the horizontal cuts. The corresponding mortise can be made by the method described in the section on the power drill.

Fig. 1 (opposite). A circular saw fitted with a 'wobble washer' enables you to cut slots in timber.

Figs. 2–4. Cutting a housed joint using a circular saw. Fig. 2 shows the first cut being made on the far right-hand side of the section to be removed. A further series of cuts is made on the left-hand extremity. The remaining stock can be removed with a chisel.

Fig. 1 (below). A tenon being cut using a bench-mounted saw. The timber should be crosscut to length first, ensuring that the ends are square.

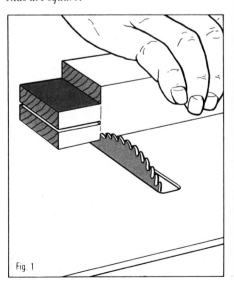

Fig. 1

Left: Long straight cuts parallel to one edge of the timber are best made using a rip fence. Here, the rip fence is set by measuring from the edge of the timber to the position of the intended cut.

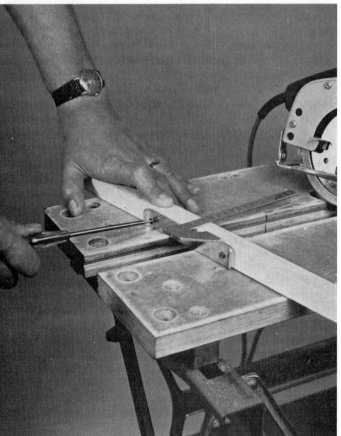

Below left: For greatest control when using the rip fence, its length can be extended by screwing a batten in place.

A jig saw is at its best when cutting curves and intricate shapes. Let the saw cut at its own speed and do not force it. Otherwise you may 'burn' the edge of the work.

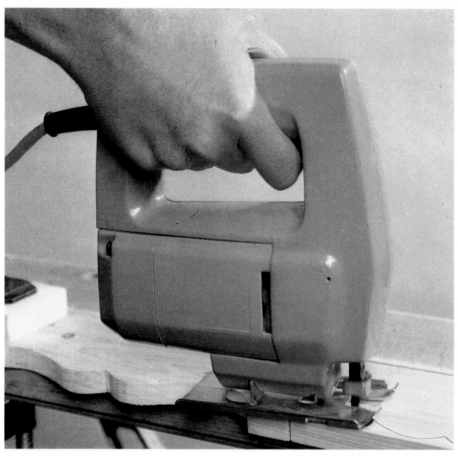

The jig saw

A power driven jig saw can be used in the same way as a coping saw, that is for cutting curves and complex shapes, as well as general cutting and trimming. It has a small, narrow blade, similar to a short hack saw blade, and cuts with an up and down reciprocating motion. Various types of blade are available for cutting wood, plastic and sheet metal. But they will not cut thick timber sections. They can manage $2\frac{3}{4}$in (69mm) thick softwood or hardwood half as thick.

Jig saws should not be pressed forward too hard or the highly tempered blade may snap. But they should be held firmly down onto the material you are cutting to resist the downstroke of the blade.

The blade is narrow enough to cut $\frac{1}{2}$in (13mm) radius curves but will not turn a right-angled corner. It can, however, be started in the middle of a piece of wood by tilting the machine forward on its nose and gradually lowering the blade into the wood until it is upright. This is known as pocket cutting.

Jig saws are available both as power tool attachments and as integral tools. There are integral units available with two speeds, or with variable speed, and this enables much greater control to be achieved when cutting tight curves and intricate detail.

If you should drop the jig saw, never attempt to catch it. This may sound obvious but it is your instinctive reaction to grab.

Cutting

Some jig saws have a built-in blower to prevent wood dust from obscuring the marked line you are sawing along. Air is directed from the drill to behind the saw blade through a plastic tube.

Always clamp large panels of wood to prevent the usual pinching and jamming of the blade. If there is any vibration stop and check the wood supports before proceeding. To start a cut, rest the base plate on the surface of the wood and slowly move the blade towards the edge of the timber.

Pocket cutting

To start a cut in the middle of the timber, tilt the saw forward and allow it to make its own starting hole. This works less well on thicker wood and it may be necessary to drill a hole before inserting the blade.

General cuts

A rounded cut can be cut in one careful operation but several passes are needed for oblongs and squares. The first side should be cut to its fullest extent before bringing the blade back down the cut and curving it gently away from the cut to carve out the second side. The piece left in the corner can be cut out later. Keep the motor running throughout this procedure. Cut the remaining sides in the same way.

A keyhole size opening can be cut by moving the blade backwards and forwards making slight stabs at the wood.

The jig can also be used to cut straight lines although a circular saw is preferable. Keep the line accurate by using a batten.

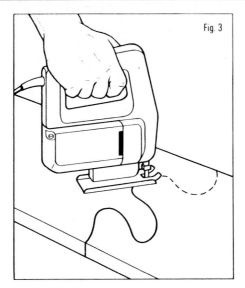

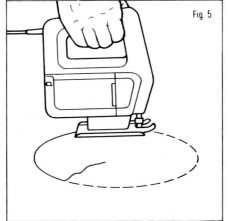

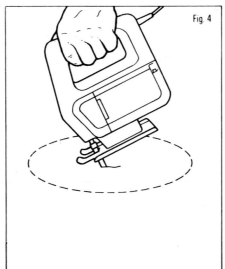

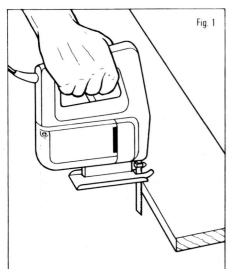

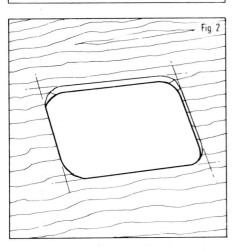

Fig. 1. A jig saw is very useful for general sawing and trimming jobs.

Fig. 2. It is particularly useful where a section has to be removed from the middle of a surrounding surface area.

Fig. 3. Keep the saw vertical when cutting a curved shape.

Figs. 4, 5. To remove a circle section. make a pocket cut into the centre; cut to the edge and then around the perimeter.

Right, above: A power plane is used in the same way as a conventional plane, but with much faster results.

Right, below: A router is one of the most versatile tools in the home workshop.

THE POWER PLANE

One of the most useful of the workshop machines, the power plane, can be used not only for planing wood straight, flat and smooth, but also for rebating, tenoning and chamfering. Planers are available in two distinct forms: either as a table planer, with the wood fed into the blade in a similar way to using a saw table; or as a tool looking rather like an ordinary hand plane, and used in the same way, but with a motor. In both cases, cutting is achieved by means of a rapidly rotating metal drum, into which are mounted the blades, with the cutting edges set just above the level of the drum surface. The drum is adjustable to vary the amount of wood removed at each pass.

The planing machine is usually referred to as the jointer, because of its use in jointing (straightening) wood surfaces. It can also be used to make some types of moulding, and to plane to a specified thickness.

Cutters may be honed in the machine by resting an oilstone on the rear table or the rear of the base plate, suitably protected by thin cardboard, and rubbing it slightly across each blade. The blade must be held in its highest position and the cutter block locked with a small wooden wedge. Always ensure that the machine is switched off and unplugged before attempting to sharpen. When badly blunted, and possibly nicked, the blades will have to be removed and reground, a job best left to an expert.

Using the planer

Follow the same rules when using either type of plane as when using a hand plane. Examine the timber for loose knots and nails or screws, and always plane with the grain. Generally take thin cuts, particularly where the timber appears to be coarse and cross-grained. Do not attempt to feed in too fast, as this results in a wavy finish. Should the timber need to be planed on all four edges, always plane the end grain first, as any slight teasing at the corners will be removed when planing the long grain. When planing end grain only, begin cutting from one end, then reverse the wood to complete the cut.

When using a table plane, wherever possible use a push stick, and keep the cutter guard in position, leaving sufficient clearance to push the wood underneath. To plane boards thicker than the planer, several cuts will need to be made. When planing a curved edge, remove the 'lump' first. When cutting a short taper, use a support stick for the timber and pull the work over the cutters. To cut a long taper, use a push stick.

THE PORTABLE ROUTER

The portable router is undoubtedly one of the most versatile machines available to the home worker, but unfortunately much of its versatility remains unexplored.

Grooving, rebating, moulding of all kinds, curved cutting including disc cutting, housing, dovetailing, tongueing, mortise-and-tenoning, carving and a host of other processes are possible.

The basic machine consists of a motor, complete with a collet chuck which can be fitted with a very wide range of cutters made either of high speed steel or tungsten carbide tipped for cutting man-made boards. The machine fits into a body or housing to which is fitted a means of adjusting the depth of cut and also a method of locking the setting once it has been made. A straight and circular fence can be fitted to the body and to the fence can also be attached a device for cutting circles. The fence is drilled to allow a wooden fence to be secured either for greater depth or to lengthen the fence for greater security when cutting. A dovetailing attachment together with special dovetail cutters permits the jointing of wide boards in cabinet construction.

Using the router

The method of securing the cutters and depth adjustment varies according to the type of machine; the user would therefore be advised to read carefully the manufacturer's instructions before use.

Unlike any of the other machines discussed the speed of the routers is extremely high, often up to 26,000rpm. At these speeds, with cutters in good condition, the quality of finish both with and across the grain is extremely good. When using moulding cutters it should be noted that some of these cutters have pins or pilots placed centrally below the cutter. The pilot runs on the edge of the timber and thus limits the cut to the exact contour of the router bit. Care must be taken in use. Should the machine be traversed too quickly, the motor will be overloaded. Conversely, too slow a rate of feed will result in the timber being burnt and possible drawing of the temper of the tool. If cutting to the full thickness of the timber, when using pilot type cutters, it

will be necessary to attach an additional piece of wood underneath the piece being cut, to provide a running edge for the pilot. The machine must always be moved from left to right when cutting, with the timber held securely. Always wait for the machine cutter to come to rest before returning the router to the bench.

The handyman who wishes to increase the versatility of the router may care to construct a work table in metal or wood, complete with an adjustable fence. This will prove to be most versatile when long lengths of timber have to be cut. Great care must be taken to keep the hands well away from the router bit when using the machine in this way.

THE BENCH GRINDER

One of the most useful tools in any workshop is the bench grinder. It enables all edge tools to be resharpened in an instant —and sharp tools make for easy work. If you have a grinder attachment for a power drill, you will have to set it up every time you want to sharpen something—which is often. In practice, this means that you will not sharpen things often enough. So a bench grinder is a good investment.

A bench grinder is an essential piece of workshop equipment for keeping cutting edges sharp. Most are supplied with wheels of differing grades.

Another advantage of an integral bench grinder is that it has two revolving shafts—one on each end of the motor. Chisel and plane blades are sharpened in two operations; grinding, to get the blade the right shape, and honing, to put an edge on it. Different grinding wheels are needed for each operation, so having both of them on the same machine speeds up work considerably.

Sharpening is done against the front curved edge of the grinding wheel, and not against the flat circular face. The wheel revolves so that the front edge moves downwards. This keeps sparks and fragments of metal or abrasive from being thrown upwards into the eyes. It is, however, essential that a guard be fitted above the wheel of the machine or that the operator wears goggles. Adjustable tool rests are provided in front of each wheel to hold blades steady while they are sharpened.

Cutting wheels come in various grades.

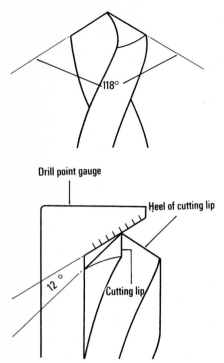

Drill point gauge

Heel of cutting lip

118°

12°

Cutting lip

Above: Maintaining the correct angles is essential for accurate sharpening of drill bits.

For most jobs, a medium wheel for grinding and a very fine one for honing should be all you need. Special extra-tough wheels are made for honing the hardened tips of masonry drills.

The wheels, are fastened to their shafts by nuts screwing down on to the threaded end of the shafts. The wheel on the left has a left-hand thread to stop it from coming undone in use. The wheel on the right has a normal right-hand thread.

Sharpening chisel and plane blades

Chisel and plane blades, though completely different in shape and use, are sharpened in exactly the same way. In both types of blade, the preliminary grinding to shape of the edge of the blade should give the ground surface an angle of 25° to the flat face of the blade. Then it should be honed at the slightly greater angle of 30°. The 5° difference saves you from having to hone the whole ground surface. Only the tip is honed.

To sharpen a blade, first lay it on the tool rest of the grinder with the point touching the stationary wheel, and measure the angle where the point touches. Move the blade until the angle is 25°, and memorize the position of the blade. Now take the blade away, start the wheels and lay the blade lightly against the coarse wheel. High speed and light pressure are the secret of good grinding. Move a wide blade from side to side across the wheel, so that its whole edge is ground evenly.

Grind one side only until the blade is properly shaped, when the length of the ground surface should be 2½ times the thickness of the blade. Every few seconds of grinding, remove the blade from the wheel and dip it in cold water to stop it from overheating. An overheated blade 'loses its temper' and turns blue. If this happens, grind off the blue part.

The freshly ground surface will be slightly hollow in shape because of the curve of the wheel, but that doesn't matter. The next stage is to hone it.

Find the correct angle of the blade against the stationary wheel as you did before, except that it should be 30° and not 25°. Then start the grinder and lay the sloping side of the blade against the fine wheel—but only for a few seconds. The wheel will turn the edge of the blade over, producing a fine 'burr' on the other side. Cool the blade and lay the flat side *flat* on the wheel (i.e. not at 30°) for a few seconds to turn the burr the other way. Then turn the chisel round again and give the other side a few seconds at 30°. This will turn the burr again.

Continue doing each side alternately, using very light pressure and reducing the honing period each time. Eventually, the burr will break off, leaving a razor edge.

Blades can be honed several times before they lose their shape and have to be reground.

Sharpening twist drills

Twist drills and high speed drills can also be sharpened on a fine grinding wheel. The angles have to be watched carefully, but otherwise the job is not difficult. Do not cool twist drills in water, because the extra-hard steel might crack. It is essential not to overheat them.

There are three important angles that must be maintained on a twist drill. The angle of the cutting edge to the shaft should always be 30°. The angle of the sloping shoulder of the cutting edge to the horizontal varies with the size of the drill. For small drills (from $\frac{3}{32}$in to $\frac{3}{16}$in or 2.4mm to 4.8mm) it should be between 20° and 26°. For medium drills (up to $\frac{3}{8}$in or 9.5mm) it should be between 10° and 15°. For large drills (up to $\frac{5}{8}$in or 15.8mm) it should be between 9° and 13°. As a check on these two angles, if you have got them right, the angle of the front of the cutting edge to the chisel point of the drill will always be 130°.

The correct way to sharpen a twist drill is to hold it near the point between the thumb and forefinger of the left hand, gripping it flexibly so that it can be rotated gently between finger and thumb. Rest the left hand comfortably on the tool rest, and use the right hand to poke it through the improvised pivot you have made with your left hand until the cutting edge touches the wheel.

The front of the cutting edge should touch the wheel first, at such an angle that its whole length is in contact with the wheel. As soon as it touches, push the shank of the drill down with your right hand so that the cutting edge rises, simultaneously twisting the bit a quarter of a turn clockwise. This movement is necessary to achieve the correct curve and angle on each cutting edge. You can practice on an old twist bit until you get it right. Once learned, it is never forgotten.

Sharpen both cutting edges of the drill equally so that the point is in the middle. When it is, check the angle of the cutting edge to the chisel part of the drill. This angle should be 130°. If not, keep on until it is.

Special wood bits should not be sharpened on a grinding wheel, but with a small flat needle file with medium fine teeth. Aim only to preserve the original angle of the cutting edges; these bits are so large that sharpening them is a simple job.

THE LATHE

A lathe adds a whole new dimension to your carpentry skills. For the first time, you move beyond square, plain shapes, and are able to make round objects of any contour and with as much (or as little) decoration as you like.

Wood-turning lathes are available in a range of sizes, from small ones powered by electric drills to huge professional models that can make sections for newel posts that are several feet long. A drill-powered lathe can produce good work provided you don't try to make anything too large.

All lathes are designed in much the same way. The main frame, to which all other parts are attached, is called the *bed*.

· The size of the lathe bed controls the maximum length of wood that can be fitted into the lathe. On the smallest drill-powered lathes, it is about 2ft 6in (762mm) long.

The *headstock* is a strong support mounted at the left-hand end of the lathe bed. In integral lathes it houses a revolving cylindrical *mandrel*. This is threaded on the outside and has a hole down the middle so that fitments to hold the workpiece can be attached to it in two ways as described below. In drill-powered lathes the headstock is simply a clamp for the drill and the mandrel is screwed directly to the shaft of the drill.

At the other end of the lathe bed is another support, the *tailstock*, which is

used for the turning of long objects such as lamp stands. The tailstock can be slid along the lathe bed to suit the length of the work piece and can be fixed in any position. In *spindle work*, the workpiece is clamped between headstock and tailstock and spins on a *dead centre*, a flat plate with a blunt central spike, fixed to the tailstock.

In *face plate* work—the turning of wide, flat objects such as bowls—the tailstock is not used and the object is fastened to the headstock only. This is why the mandrel provides two methods of

Below left: The angle at which the cutting tool is held is critical to the final result.

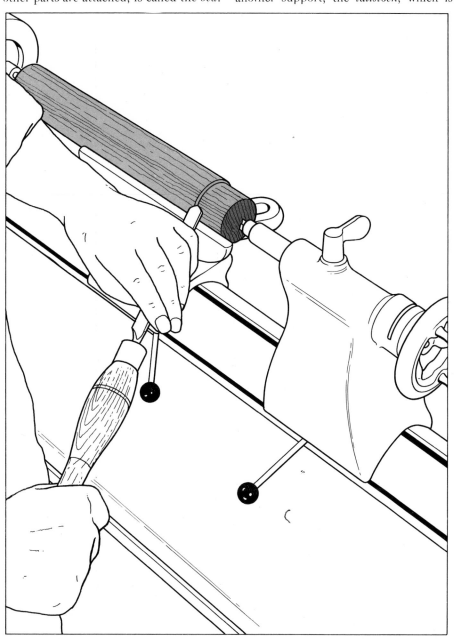

attachment. Spindle work is fixed on a *morse tapered driving fork* inserted into the hole in the mandrel. Face plate work is fixed firmly with large wood screws to a flat face plate, and the face plate is in turn screwed on to the threaded end of the mandrel.

On the near side of the lathe bed there is a *tool rest*. Against which the tools used for shaping the wood are held, and slid along, this rest, which can be adjusted in all directions to suit any type of work.

Lathe tools

Special tools are made for lathework. There are three main kinds; gouges, chisels and scrapers. At first sight, they may look like ordinary bench chisels, but there are important differences and bench tools should never be used for lathe work.

Lathe tools have very robust blades and extra-long handles which are usually made of beech or ash and have strong brass ferrules.

All lathe tools are supplied ready ground to shape, but you have to sharpen them yourself. This must be done in a special way for each type, as described below.

Gouges are used for roughing, or cutting wood roughly to shape. A gouge blade is U-shaped at an angle of 40° around the outside of the U. It can be ground in two shapes: straight across, which makes the gouge suitable for cutting flat, open surfaces; and with the corners ground further back than the centre, which makes the gouge right for cutting inside curves such as the insides of bowls.

Gouges come in sizes from ¼in (6mm) to 1in (25mm) wide. The wider sizes are used for roughing straight lengths and the narrower ones for sharp inside curves. Also, the ¼in (6mm) gouge can be used for boring, such as is done in the middle of a bowl to mark the depth to which it should be cut (see below).

Chisels are used for finishing work once it has been roughed out with a gouge. They have a straight cutting edge, which may be ground square across or on the skew. The range of widths is the same as for gouges, but unlike gouges (and ordinary bench chisels) they are ground on both sides at an angle of 15°, so they come to an edge at 30°. Skew-edged chisels are commoner, because they are easier to hold in the correct position. Both types, however, are used for the same purpose.

There is also a special type of chisel called a parting tool, which is made in one size only. The blade is like that of a chisel, but its end is ground in a V shape rather like a spear. It is used for cutting a finished piece away from the waste wood left at its end. It is also useful for marking out a block before you start cutting it to shape.

Scrapers are similar to chisels, but are used for fine finishing work. They are ground at the very shallow angle of 10°. One popular and useful type of scraper has a round 'nose', or sharp edge. Another commonly available type has a shallow V-shaped nose which most people re-grind to suit their particular needs.

All lathe tools are normally sold with their handles. If you do happen to buy some in 'blade only' form, make sure that the handles you buy for them are the special extra-large lathe tool handles and not ordinary chisel handles. These ordinary chisel handles are too small either to accept the tang of a lathe tool blade or to hold firmly when working.

Grinding and sharpening

When you buy lathe tools, they are generally ground to shape but not sharpened. The method of sharpening differs from that for ordinary bench gouges and chisels: the sharpening angle is the same as the grinding angle so that, when they are sharpened, an equal thickness of metal is removed from all over the ground edge, and its surface remains perfectly flat. Sharpening in this way takes longer, and needs more care, than the conventional method, but is absolutely necessary if the tools are to be used in the right way.

You will need three abrasive blocks for sharpening your chisels, gouges and scrapers: two flat oilstones and a shaped oilstone slip of a suitable size to fit the inside curve of your gouges. One oilstone should be used for gouges, which wear stones unevenly, and the other kept exclusively for chisels and scrapers, which need a perfectly flat surface. Slips have an egg-shaped cross-section, so one slip will be suitable for all the curves on your various gouges if you choose it of the correct size.

Gouges should be sharpened at an angle of exactly 40°. Hold the gouge with one hand at each end and apply the point bevel side down to the stone with its bevelled edge exactly parallel to the surface of the stone—you can feel the angle by raising and lowering the handle until the bevel lies flat on the stone.

Run the gouge backwards and forwards over the stone and rock it from side to side at the same time, so that all of the curved surface of the bevel touches the stone on each pass. Since you are sharpening the blade only on one side, a burr will appear on the upper, visible side of the edge. If this burr appears all round the curve it will show that you are moving the blade in the right way.

As soon as the burr has appeared all round the edge stop sharpening and rest the blade, still bevel side down, on the tool rest of the lathe or some solid surface. Then lay the oilstone slip flat in the groove of the gouge and slide it carefully over the edge to remove the burr—this should happen quite quickly.

Chisels should be sharpened on both sides at 15°. Apply the chisel to your perfectly flat oilstone with its bevel resting flat on the stone as before. Then move it backwards and forwards (but not, of course, rocking it) until a burr appears as before. Turn the chisel over and sharpen the other side in the same way. Remove the burr very carefully on the flat surface of the stone.

Scrapers are sharpened in the same way but on one side only and at 10° instead of 15°. Remove the burr by laying the unground side of the scraper flat on the stone.

Preparing the wood

A piece of wood that is to be spindle-turned should be about 2in (50mm) longer than the finished article to allow for the waste at either end to be cut off when turning is finished.

Wood that is to be turned is normally square in cross-section. It is time-consuming and messy—and can be dangerous—to cut the corner off entirely on the lathe, so it has to be trimmed roughly to a circular cross-section before you begin.

Find the exact centre of the wood at each end by marking the diagonals from corner to corner. Then draw the largest circle on this centre that will fit on to the end of the wood and plane the corners off the wood all along its length to make it roughly octagonal in cross-section. Take care not to cut below the line of the circle at any point.

Use a tenon saw or a chisel to prepare one end of the timber to receive the driving fork making sure that the slot is a tight fit and perfectly central. Prepare the other end for the dead centre of the tailstock by denting the centre mark with a centre punch, and apply a little oil or grease to the mark to make the wood revolve freely.

The wood is now ready for clamping between the headstock and tailstock. This is done simply by tapping the driving fork well home on to its slots, screwing it on the headstock, sliding the tailstock firmly up to the other end and locking it in position. Adjust the tool rest as close as possible to the wood, and turn the wood around once by hand to make sure that it does not catch. The rest should be set just above the centre line of the lathe.

Wood for face-plate turning should be just over 1in (25mm) thicker than the finished work. Plane one face perfectly flat, draw the diagonals and the circle as before, and saw off the corners of the block nearly down to the line of the circle. Lay the face plate exactly over the centre of the block, mark and pre-drill screw holes in the block through the holes in the face plate, and fasten the plate firmly to the block with stout 1in (25mm) screws.

Screw the block and plate on to the mandrel and set the tool rest as close as possible to the face of the work, but just below the centre line.

Safety precautions

Never wear loose clothing when working on a lathe; anything that gets caught will be rapidly wound into the machinery, taking you with it. The ideal clothing is a buttoned-up overall, but it should not have any holes in it; these can be particularly dangerous.

Just in case something does happen, make sure that the 'off' switch of your lathe is placed so that you can reach it in a hurry and without looking. Don't allow anybody to stand near you when turning wood.

Before you start work, always make sure that the workpiece is firmly fixed to the lathe, the lathe is firmly clamped down and all its parts are secure. These last two points are particularly important in the case of a drill-driven lathe which you have to assemble every time you use it.

Lathe speeds

The ideal speed for a particular turning job depends both on the operation being performed and on the diameter of the workpiece. The wider a workpiece is, the faster is its speed (in inches per second) at the outside edge for a given lathe speed (in revolutions per minute). So for most ordinary operations (other than end boring, finishing and final parting off) the smaller the piece the faster it should turn. A list of ideal speeds is given in the list below.

If you are using a drill-driven lathe, you are most unlikely to be able to vary its speed to this extent. Most two-speed drills can be set to 900rpm and 2,400rpm.

The solution to this problem is to buy a variable speed controller for your drill, but there is an important point to observe in choosing one. Some speed controllers reduce the drill speed simply by cutting the voltage and power, and these will prevent the drill from turning at all when heavy work is being done at a low speed. The type to buy is a thyristorized speed controller, which reduces speed but maintains almost full power under load.

Another point to watch is that the speed control must be of the correct wattage for your drill.

Turning techniques

When removing wood with a gouge or chisel, the tool is held point upwards on the tool rest with its bevel towards the workpiece and flat against it. The handle of the tool is then raised slightly to bring the cutting edge into contact with the work. This is why the edge has to be sharpened at the same angle at which it is ground. If there were a double slope the handle would have to be raised a long way to make the edge touch the work, and it would then be likely to catch and fly out of your hand.

The tool must never be pressed against the work or it may catch, or vibrate and chip the wood. But it has to be held firmly, or it will be thrown down by the force of the lathe. For this reason, it must be held with both hands, one as near the point as possible and the other taking a firm grip on the opposite end of the handle. The tool should be supported against the tool rest before it is slid up to come in contact with the wood.

Note that the full width of the cutting edge is never used but only the section of the edge that is nearest the tool rest. The tool should be applied to the workpiece at one end (or side for end plate turning) and moved smoothly across to the other

side (or the centre) in a continuous movement. If you stop, it will create a ridge that will be difficult to remove.

Finding the correct angle and movement requires careful practice, so you should try the techniques out on worthless scrap timber until you get them right.

In spindle turning, the length of the finished object should first be marked on to the prepared timber with the parting-off chisel. This tool should be laid flat on the tool rest and brought into contact with the workpiece to mark it with a neat V-shaped groove.

After the timber has been marked, it should be roughly cut to shape with a gouge; in some cases the parting chisel can be used. The gouge can be held flat on the rest and the centre of the cutting edge used to cut, or tilted at an angle and slid across the work point first, depending on the contour of the part you are cutting. Be very careful that the far, upper edge of the cutting surface does not catch on the wood through incorrect angling.

Once the work is roughly cut to shape it should be smoothed. The correct tool for this is a chisel. Whether you use a straight or skew-edged chisel is entirely a matter of preference.

When you switch from gouge to chisel, lower the tool rest to below the centre line of the workpiece and again move it as near to the wood as possible. You must stop the lathe to do this. Then restart the lathe and lay the chisel on the tool rest with the skew of its edge (if any) tilted towards the centre line of the workpiece, and the edge itself angled at about 45° to the centre line. Raise the handle until the end of the edge nearer the tool rest comes into contact with the wood, then move it across smoothly as before.

Final smoothing is done with the scraper, which is used in a different way from

the other tools. The tool rest remains slightly below the centre line and the scraper is laid on it horizontally and bevel side down, so that it meets the work below the centre line at about 60°. It should be used with great care and the overhang between the tool rest and the workpiece should be kept to an absolute minimum to keep the tool from vibrating.

End plate turning is done in a slightly different way. The sides of the gouges used should be ground well back to make them round-nosed, or they will catch. You will be cutting into a vertical surface instead of one that slopes away from you, so the tools will be held much nearer the vertical.

A tool should be applied to the wood, as usual, but it should not be angled to start the cut. Instead, it should just be pushed gently towards the wood, which will start the cut less violently.

When you are working across the face of a block, you will find that when you get to the middle, the rotation of the block tends to twist the tool around. Even if you hold it firmly to resist this, it will still not cut properly. There is a special technique to overcome this difficulty.

First use the parting tool to draw a circle $\frac{1}{8}$in (3mm) from the centre of the block. Then mark the intended depth on the blade of a $\frac{1}{4}$in (6mm) round-nosed gouge by sticking on a piece of adhesive tape. Start a cut with the gouge about $\frac{1}{2}$in (13mm) from the centre and cut towards the centre in the conventional way. When the trailing edge, which is doing the cutting, reaches the marked circle, swing the handle of the gouge around smoothly so that it is at 90° to the face of the wood. You can then use the gouge as a drill to cut a $\frac{1}{4}$in hole into the wood until the tape is level with the surface.

Diameter of work	Nature of work	Drill-powered lathe speed (in rpm)*
under $\frac{3}{4}$in (19mm)	roughing and general turning	2600-2800
$\frac{3}{4}$in (19mm) - 7in (180mm)	,,	1400
7in (180mm) - 12in (300mm)	,,	900
all sizes	sanding, burnishing	2600 - 2800
all sizes	end boring, lathe drilling, parting off	280 - 300

*Using a speed adjuster.

SPRAY PAINTING

Spray painting is a technique which, if used correctly, can save you a lot of time and trouble in decorating a house or painting furniture. It is suitable for both inside and outside work. On wood it gives a finished, even feel to the furniture you have made.

The type of paint you are planning to use is important. Emulsion paint is the most suitable type for spraying. Gloss paint, although it sprays well in the hands of a professional, is very hard to apply without getting drips and runs all over the surface.

The state of the weather will affect painting outdoors. Obviously, you must choose a spell of dry weather. No exterior painting, by any method, can be done if it keeps raining or if it is windy, as you will waste the paint.

Apart from this difficulty, exterior spray painting is easier than interior spray work. There is less to mask, for one thing. Lawns, flower beds and paving at the bottom of the wall can simply be covered with a tarpaulin or weighted down sheet of polythene. Hard surfaces such as paving can be masked with a thin layer of earth, which is brushed off afterwards.

There are no special tricks about preparing timber for spraying. Exactly the same techniques are used as for any other kind of painting. Holes and cracks in the wood should be filled, and if necessary the surface should be primed. The primer can be sprayed on if necessary, but mask the room and read the section on cleaning out the spray gun before you attempt this.

Masking and protection

Sprayed paint gets everywhere. Anything that you do not wish to be sprayed must be masked thoroughly before you begin—and 'thoroughly' is the operative word. It is no good just hanging a sheet of newspaper in front of an object because the fine mist of paint will easily float round the back of the paper. It must be properly wrapped in newspaper and the edges of the paper stuck down all the way round with masking tape.

Proper masking takes quite a long time and uses a lot of paper and tape. Fortunately, masking tape is not expensive—but do not try to save money by buying cheap tape. Inferior grades of tape stick too well and pull the paint off the things they are stuck to. 'Low-tack' masking

Below left: An airless spray gun will give a really professional finish to a painted surface, but the nozzle setting requires care as the machine will tend to 'spit'.

Spray painting

tape will save you a lot of trouble. Buy two widths: ¾in (19mm) for holding down newspaper, and 2in (51mm) for covering small objects such as door handles and pipes.

Interior and exterior woodwork, drainpipes and other objects that are going to be gloss painted later in the course of redecorating do not need careful masking, and may need none at all. They will get covered in emulsion paint, but this does not normally matter. Natural stonework should be masked with great care, because it is very hard to get paint off it. Indoors particular care should be taken to protect the floor, especially if there is a fitted carpet.

Furniture that cannot be taken out of the room should be stacked in the middle and well covered with dust sheets. A quick way is to use polythene sheets stapled or tacked lightly to the floor. Make sure there are no gaps that paint mist can float through.

When painting indoors, take care to provide proper ventilation. Mask windows in the open position. You should also protect your lungs by buying a surgical mask and plenty of replaceable pads for it, because the paint clogs pads up quickly. Do not laugh at this precaution; it is really necessary. Paint can give you all kinds of diseases from a mild colic to silicosis.

Any clothes you wear for spray painting

will certainly be ruined. This applies to garments that would not be touched by ordinary painting, such as socks. Remember to take off your wristwatch and any rings or bracelets you may be wearing.

The equipment

Whatever you are using it for, spraying equipment should operate at a pressure of at least 40lb/sq in (2.8kg/sq cm). The kind of low-pressure spray gun that attaches to the end of a cylinder vacuum cleaner does not work at all well, so even if you have one, don't use it.

There are two nozzles for the spray gun: one 'fishtail' nozzle, which gives a wide spray for covering large areas, and one plain nozzle for more restricted spaces.

Spraying techniques

All types of paint must be diluted with the appropriate thinner to make them suitable for spraying. Emulsion paint should be thinned with water; gloss paint with turpentine substitute. Note that the latter is very inflammable, so DO NOT SMOKE when spraying with it, and turn off all electric lights when spraying any type of paint.

Thixotropic emulsion paint cannot be diluted and is unsuitable for spraying anyway.

The exact amount of water or thinner to add to any type of paint can only be

found by experience, or by the use of a viscosity measure. Too little makes the paint too thick, so that the nozzle clogs in a few seconds. Too much makes the paint so thin that it does not cover the surface properly. As a rough guide, emulsion paint should be thinned with half as much water as paint; gloss paint about 50/50 with turps substitute. Experiment on a spare piece of timber until you get it right. Even when the paint is the right consistency, the spray nozzle will probably clog occasionally. It should be cleaned out with a very fine wire such as a Primus stove pricker or one strand of an electric flex.

Spray with wide horizontal strokes of the gun, holding it 12 to 18in, (305 to 457mm) away from the surface. Move the gun back and forth parallel to the surface, rather than sweeping it in an arc. Spray on only a thin coat or the paint will run; you will have to put at least three coats on any surface, but spraying is so quick that you will not waste much time doing this. Gloss paint is particularly likely to run if sprayed too thick.

Every time you stop spraying, even for a few minutes, dismantle the gun and clean it thoroughly with the appropriate solvent (the same as you use for diluting the paint). This is important; once the paint dries, you will have a terrible time getting it off.

Projects

Hall stand

If you have ever rummaged for your overcoat among a pile of coats hanging on a solitary hook in the hallway, or stumbled over carelessly left shoes, then this hall stand would be ideal for you. It is very easy to make and has plenty of space for all the family's outdoor coats, as well as room to store shoes and umbrellas. The lower part of the stand can be used as a telephone table, or simply a stand for a flower pot.

All the major parts of the hall stand are cut from one sheet of 8ft x 4ft (2440mm x 1220mm) ½in (13mm) birch plywood. You will need a small extra sheet of plywood for piece F—which is 30½in (775mm) x 14½in (368mm) (Fig. 3). The only other timber you need is 1in x 1in (25mm x 25mm) PAR (planed all round) or 1in (25mm) triangular moulding. The clothes rail of the hall stand can be made from 1in (25mm) timber dowel, but a length of round tubular steel will carry the weight of the coats better.

The construction of the hall stand, with its butted joints, is straightforward. The only difficult job is accurate cutting of the pieces from the sheet of plywood. A power jig saw is an essential tool for this project.

Marking out the panels

Accurate marking out of the plywood sheet is essential, or the finished construction will not be square. To mark out the sheet you will need a tee square, a large set square, and a hard pencil. You will also need a steel tape measure and a straightedge, or a 3ft (1m) rule.

First, make sure that the plywood sheet is perfectly square, by measuring the diagonals. If it is not, you will have to plane it square with a long smoothing plane. Then you can mark out the sheet, taking all dimensions from the marking out diagram (Fig. 1). Mark out the board in a series of straight lines, marking the right-angles from the edges of the sheet using the tee-square. Check that the lines are parallel with the edges of the sheet. Note that ¼in (6mm) has been allowed for the width of the saw-cuts.

All the curves shown in Fig. 1 have a radius of 4in (102mm). The best way of marking these is to make a cardboard template of the curve. Draw a circle with a 4in (102mm) radius on a piece of card-board, and then square a horizontal and a vertical line through the centre point. Cut out the circle.

At the points where the curve is to be drawn (Fig. 1), measure a distance of 4in (102mm) from the corner along the two lines that form the right-angle. Lay the cardboard template on a sheet of plywood with the ends of the squared lines touching the marked points. Then draw round the template to form the curve in the corner.

Cutting out the components

You will need a power jig saw to cut out the panels for the hall stand. You must cut accurately, and follow the order of cutting shown in Fig. 2. To help make the straight cuts you can pin a timber straightedge to the plywood, along the marked lines. This will guide the blade of the jig saw. When you come to the end of the first cuts, and start to make the second cuts, curve the saw out into the waste area of the plywood (Fig. 2). These corners can be trimmed square with a tenon saw later.

When you have cut the panels for the two large sides of the hall stand, clean them up. Trim off any waste plywood. Then lay the two panels together one on top of the other, and clamp them with a few G cramps. Plane the straight edges square with a smoothing plane and shape the curves neatly with a spokeshave or a wood-rasp and glasspaper.

Then unclamp the boards and mark the inside faces. The shaped inside edge of the two large sides should be rounded slightly—this looks better than square edges. Do not do this on any of the straight outer edges of these sides, though, as the other components of the hall stand are butt jointed to these.

The other panels for the hall stand can now be cut from the plywood sheet. Refer to Fig. 1 and Fig. 3 for the dimensions. Trim the panels square, ensuring that the 15½in dimension is exactly the same on all panels.

There is an alternative method of construction if you are not sure whether you can cut two identical panels for the large sides. This method uses two sheets of plywood which are clamped together and cut, after the shape of the large side has been drawn on to one of the sheets.

Hall stand

This, of course, wastes more timber than the procedure described above. Another method, which involves altering the dimensions of the unit, is to cut one 8ft × 4ft (2440mm × 1220mm) plywood sheet in half across its width into two 4ft (1220mm) panels and cut out the outline of the sides, with scaled down dimensions, with the two panels clamped together. This will give you a hall stand about 3ft 10in (1169mm) high—ideal for children's overcoats.

Assembling the unit
All the joints used in the construction are butted and pinned with extra fixing provided by 1in × 1in (25mm × 25mm) strips of timber. If you have square sectioned timber available for these fixing strips, you should cut it to a triangular section with a bench saw. Alternatively, buy triangular shaped moulding. You will have to mitre the ends of the timber at joints so do not cut the pieces of fixing strip yet—'direct measure' and cut them to length just before you pin them in place.

Lay one large side of the unit on a flat surface inside face up and glue and pin the fixing strip to it around the outer edges with 1in (25mm) panel pins, in the position shown in Fig. 3. Mitre the ends of the strip where necessary. The outer edge of the strip should be flush with the edge of the large side, except at the back of the canopy where piece F fits. Here the moulding must be inset ½in (13mm).

When you do this job on the other large side, make sure you pin the fixing strip to the inside surface to make the sides a 'pair'. Lay the second side down on the flat surface with its long edge butting that of the first side and with its inside face up. Then pin the moulding in place on the second side.

The next step is to pin the other panels to the two large sides. This job can be a little awkward because the large sides are unwieldy so you may need some help. Pin and glue piece A forming the front of the table, or lower section. The table top is fixed next. Piece D can then be glued and pinned into place with pieces E and F to follow. Piece C is glued and pinned to complete the main structure.

The umbrella stand
The next stage is to make and fix the umbrella stand. This is a simple box construction, glued inside the two large sides.

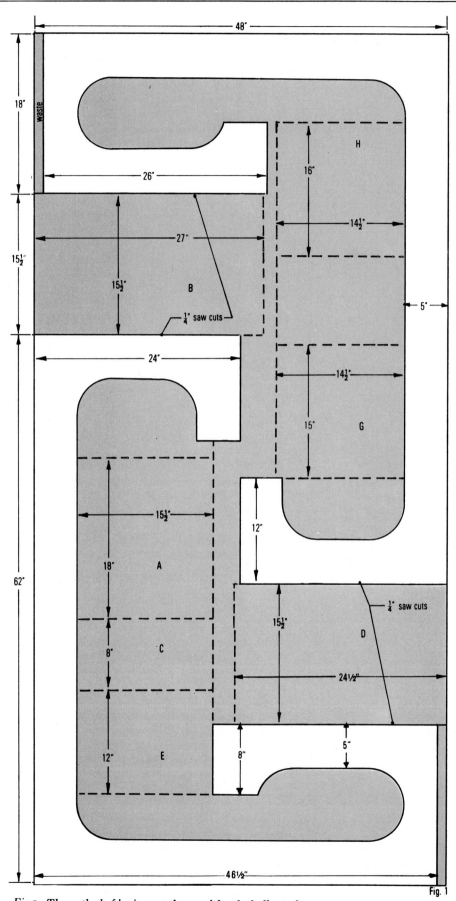

Fig 1. The method of laying out the panel for the hall stand.

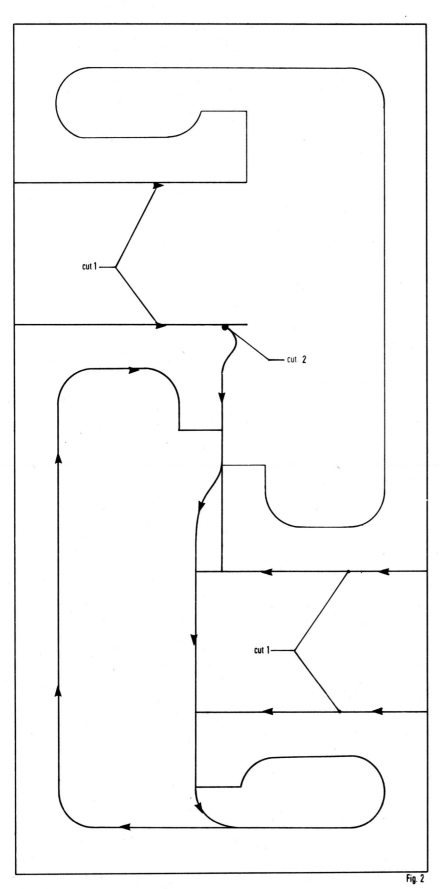

Fig. 2

Fig 2. The sequence of cutting the panel for the hall stand.

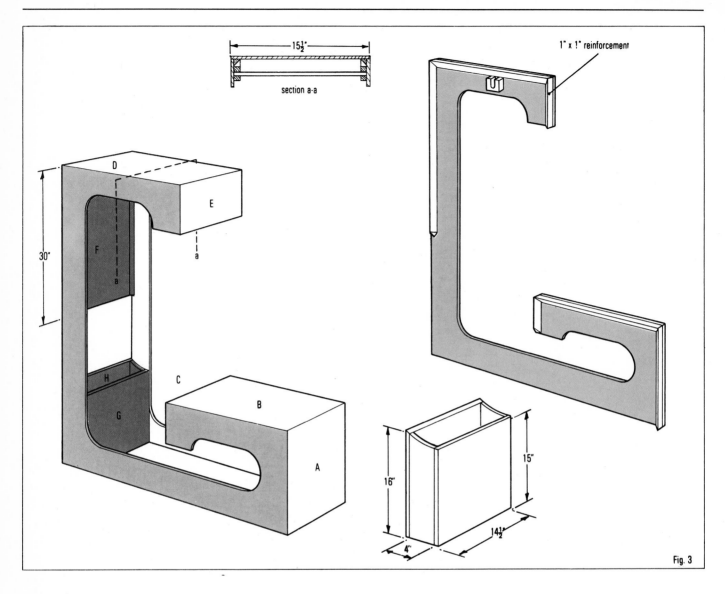

15½"

section a-a

1" x 1" reinforcement

D

E

a

30"

F

a

H

C

G

B

A

16"

15"

14½"

4"

Fig. 3

Fig 3. The construction of the hall stand is not complicated. The main construction details are shown here. The most important point to remember is that the battens at the rear of the side units must be set in ½in (13mm) from the edge so that piece F can fit between the sides.

Cut the sides for the box out of waste wood 16in x 4in (406mm x 102mm). You can mark the curve on the top of the narrow sides of the box using the cardboard template made earlier. Cut the curve with a jig saw with the two narrow sides held together in a vice. Smooth the curved top of the sides and then glue and pin the front and back panels G and H to them. The whole assembly can then be glued and pinned into place inside the hall stand as shown in Fig. 3.

The coat rail

The coat rail for the canopy section of the hall stand is 14½in (368mm) long. It can be made from 1in (25mm) hardwood dowel or 1in tubular steel rod. This can be fixed at the ends with small blocks of plywood with a 1in wide U shape cut into them. These blocks can be made from off-cuts from the plywood sheet, and

glued and pinned in place. Alternatively you can choose one of the proprietary wardrobe rail fixings available. One of the simplest consists of a small chrome or brass disc with a screw hole drilled off-centre and a raised rim around half the circumference. These are screwed in place through the hole and the rail lifted in place to rest on the rim. Whatever fixing you choose, it should be fixed in place about halfway along the canopy sides, and about 2in (50mm) up from the curved bottom edge of these pieces.

Finishing

Rub down the edges of the hall stand with glasspaper and trim up any irregularities with a finely set smoothing plane. Fill any gaps at the joints with wood filler. Then paint the unit in the colour of your choice using the full painting sequence of primer, undercoat and finishing coat.

Telephone table

Telephone table

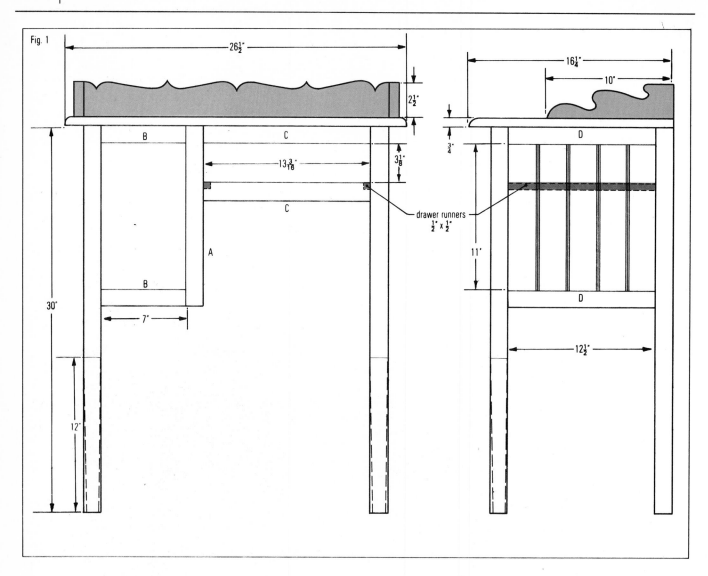

Fig. 1

A properly designed table provides a permanent, safe place for your telephone, and a home for all those directories. In this way it will help make your home a neater, more attractive place. And making a phone call becomes much easier when the telephone rests firmly on a surface which has room for a note-pad too.

This table has been built to a traditional design, and the baroque scroll round the rear and sides of the top lends a rather exotic touch that would enliven a modern hallway. If you prefer a more simple style, just omit the scroll or alter the outline to a more modern pattern of your choice.

Under the table top, one half comprises a directory storage cabinet, and the other half provides a drawer and a recess to enable a small stool to be housed—out of the way ready for those long conversations!

Construction

The joints for the legs, uprights and rails are all glued mortise and tenon. The mortise and tenon is a relatively simple joint, but if you prefer, you could use a dowelled joint.

Use ½in (13mm) ply for the sides. This is laid across the inside of the rails and must then be carefully glued and pinned.

The top is cut and trimmed to size from a single piece of timber measuring 26½in x 16¼in x ¾in (673mm x 413mm x 19mm).

A jig saw will be required to cut the curved baroque pattern on the scroll. This is quite easy to mark if you make a cardboard template but considerable care is needed in the cutting if you do not want to end up trying to remove irregularities in the curves with a spokeshave. The corners of the drawers are rebated.

Whenever possible purchase timber planed all round (PAR), or plane and sand down all pieces before you commence construction; otherwise it will be difficult to obtain a good finish to this unit when it is complete.

Materials

If the table is to be left in a natural finish and varnished, then a suitably attractive wood, or combination of wood, will be needed.

Pine would be a good choice, since it is both attractive and easy to obtain.

Tapering the legs

Cut all four legs to the finished length. On one end of each piece make a mark to indicate the tops of the legs.

Place one of the legs on a table and mark off a line 18in (457mm) from the top of the leg. Continue the line round all four sides.

On the end grain of the bottom of the leg mark ¼in (6mm) all round to form a square as shown in Fig. 2. This can be done with a marking gauge. Place the leg horizontal in a wood vice, with sufficient timber standing clear of the vice to enable you to plane the leg.

With a bench-plane set to fine, carefully plane down to the mark beginning at the bottom of the leg, and gradually work back up to the start of the taper.

Plane the taper down to one side of the square marked on the end and repeat on the remaining three sides, and on the remaining three legs.

The side frames

Set out the mortises by laying two legs down on a flat surface about 14in (356 mm) apart. Put the two rails, D, in position between them with one rail flush with the top of the legs and the other 12in (305mm) from the top of the leg to the top of the rail. Next, mark the positions of the mortises using the tenons as templates.

Square the lines across the legs and cut the mortises by first drilling out the hole with a suitably sized bit. Then square up the opening with a chisel. Repeat the operation with the legs for the other end of the table. Fit the tenons dry and mark them so that you can put them together again in the same order.

When everything fits properly, glue and fit all joints, place the frames one on top of the other and hold the joints in place with two sash cramps while the adhesive sets.

Finish off by fitting the ply side panels between the D rails of each frame. The ends of the side panels are cut to fit flush with the top of the upper D rail, and flush with the bottom of the lower one. They are fixed with glue and panel pins.

The centre frame

Using the procedure described above, construct the centre frame which comprises of the uprights (A), the remaining two D rails and the T&G boarding.

To ensure that it will match the end frames, lay one of them on a flat surface and put the rails and uprights for the centre frame on top of it and mark them using the frame underneath as a guide.

The directory cabinet

The next stage is to build the directory cabinet on to the end frame.

Stand the end and centre frames on

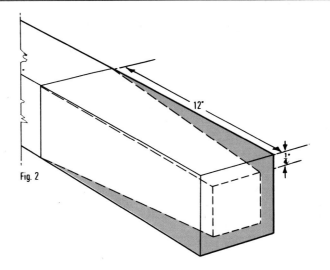

Fig. 2

Fig 1. Front and side elevations of the telephone table showing overall dimensions.

Fig 2. Detail of the legs showing the dimensions of the tapers.

Fig 3. Details of the cross member joints.

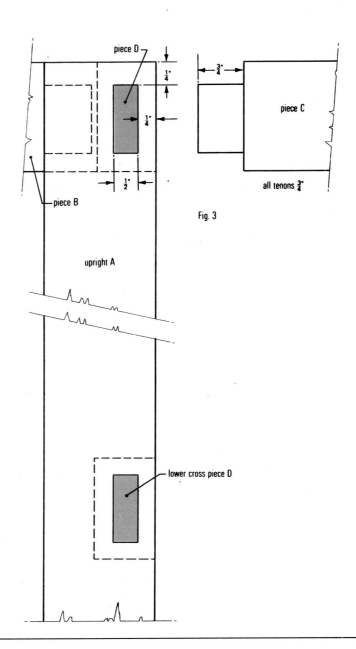

piece D

piece B

upright A

lower cross piece D

piece C

all tenons ¾"

Fig. 3

Telephone table

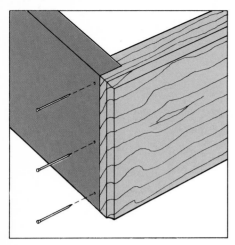

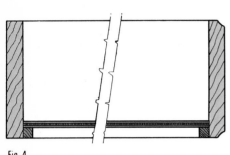

Fig. 4

their back edges on a flat surface about 7in (178mm) apart. They should be in the same positions as shown in Fig. 1, but resting on what will eventually be the back of the table. Mark and cut the 4 rails B, then cut tenon joints in both ends of each rail as shown in Fig. 3.

Following the same procedure as that just described, use the tenons as templates to mark out the mortises in the end legs and the centre upright. They will be in the same position as those already cut so the lines can be simply squared around the legs. When the joints have been cut, glue and cramp them until the glue sets.

Finishing the frame
When the glue has set, use the same technique to mark and cut the joints for the C rails. Then glue and cramp the centre, and the remaining end frame, together to complete the framework.

The cupboard bottom is cut out of $\frac{1}{4}$in (6mm) ply and fixed with glue and pins to the tops of the front and back C rails. For extra support a strip of wood can be glued and pinned to each side of the framework below the ply bottom.

Measure the drawer runners and cut them to length. Pin and glue them to the centre frame, and the end frame, flush with the top of the C rails.

Fitting the top
Stand the frame upright, on its legs. Place the uncut table top in position.

Cut and trim it where necessary.

Take the top off and, with a bench plane set to fine, round off three top edges so that each has a bevelled surface.

Drill screw holes round the top frame members, place the table top back in position and drive the screws home from underneath.

Fitting the back
There will be two openings left in the rear of the frame—the cabinet and drawer spaces. Mark a line $\frac{1}{2}$in (13mm) from the inner edges of openings and cut a rebate step or recess $\frac{1}{4}$in (6mm) deep round each opening. This is best done with a router but it can be done with a chisel and a rebate plane. Clear the corners out with a sharp chisel. Note that the bottom of the directory case forms the rebate at this edge.

Cut the plywood backs to fit into these recesses, and pin and glue them in place.

The drawer
The drawer is constructed as shown in Fig. 4 using a router to cut the rebates. The front panel is chamfered $\frac{1}{4}$in (6mm) deep around the edges and 1in (25mm) onto the face of the drawer. Mark the timber with pencil lines, and, using a smoothing plane set very fine, gently plane down to the chamfer lines. Glue the drawer together then glue and pin $\frac{1}{4}$in (6mm) square strips to the inside, flush with the bottom, to support the base. Fit the drawer into the table. Guides made of thin strips of timber can be glued to the runners if required.

Cutting the scrolls
These are an optional part of the structure. Mark out an outline with tracing paper, then transfer the outline to the $2\frac{1}{2}$in x $\frac{3}{4}$in (64mm x 19mm) timber. Use a jig saw for cutting along the outline, smoothing down any rough edges with a spokeshave.

The scroll is held in position with screws through the underside of the table top, or it could be glued with a good woodworking adhesive. Using the latter method, there will be no holes to fill should you ever tire of the scroll and wish to get rid of it. All that remains now is to decide on the finish and add an attractive handle to the drawer.

Whether you choose to varnish or paint the unit is entirely up to you; you will, however, soon be wondering how on earth you ever managed without it.

Cutting list
Solid wood	standard	metric
4 legs	$30 \times 1\frac{1}{2} \times 1\frac{1}{2}$	$762 \times 38 \times 38$
2 uprights (A)	$15 \times 1\frac{1}{2} \times 1\frac{1}{2}$	$381 \times 38 \times 38$
4 cross pieces (B)	$8\frac{1}{2} \times 1\frac{1}{2} \times 1$	$216 \times 38 \times 25$
4 cross pieces (C)	$14\frac{11}{16} \times 1\frac{1}{2} \times 1$	$373 \times 38 \times 25$
6 cross pieces (D)	$14 \times 1\frac{1}{2} \times 1$	$356 \times 38 \times 25$
1 table top	$26\frac{1}{2} \times 16\frac{1}{4} \times \frac{3}{4}$	$673 \times 413 \times 19$
2 drawer runners	$13 \times \frac{1}{2} \times \frac{1}{2}$	$330 \times 13 \times 13$
2 drawer base supports	$14\frac{3}{8} \times \frac{1}{4} \times \frac{1}{4}$	$365 \times 6 \times 6$
1 drawer front	$13 \times 3 \times \frac{3}{4}$	$330 \times 76 \times 19$
1 drawer back	$13 \times 3 \times \frac{3}{8}$	$330 \times 76 \times 10$
2 drawer sides	$15 \times 3 \times \frac{3}{8}$	$381 \times 76 \times 10$
1 rear scroll	$26\frac{1}{2} \times 2\frac{1}{2} \times \frac{3}{4}$	$673 \times 64 \times 19$
2 side scrolls	$10 \times 2\frac{1}{2} \times \frac{3}{4}$	$254 \times 64 \times 19$
Plywood		
3 sides	$15 \times 12\frac{1}{2} \times \frac{1}{2}$	$381 \times 318 \times 13$
1 storage box base	$15\frac{1}{4} \times 7 \times \frac{1}{2}$	$387 \times 178 \times 13$
1 storage box rear	$12\frac{1}{2} \times 7\frac{1}{2} \times \frac{1}{4}$	$318 \times 191 \times 6$
1 drawer base	$14\frac{3}{8} \times 12\frac{1}{4} \times \frac{1}{4}$	$365 \times 311 \times 6$

You will also require:
Adhesive. Nails and screws. Paint or varnish. Turpentine or turpentine substitute.

Victorian butler's tray

Above: The Victorian butler's tray is ideal for television suppers. When not in use it can be folded up for convenient storage.

First used in the eighteenth century, butler's trays were used as a sideboard for the butler. Later, in the Victorian and Edwardian eras they acted as dumb waiters in the ritual of afternoon tea. Nowadays they are useful for holding everything from drinks to television snacks—the simple design and fold away construction is readily adaptable to changing times.

The tray

The unit is in two parts: the tray, which has one short side cut away to allow easy access to glasses or plates, and a folding X-shaped stand on which the tray rests.

Victorian butler's tray

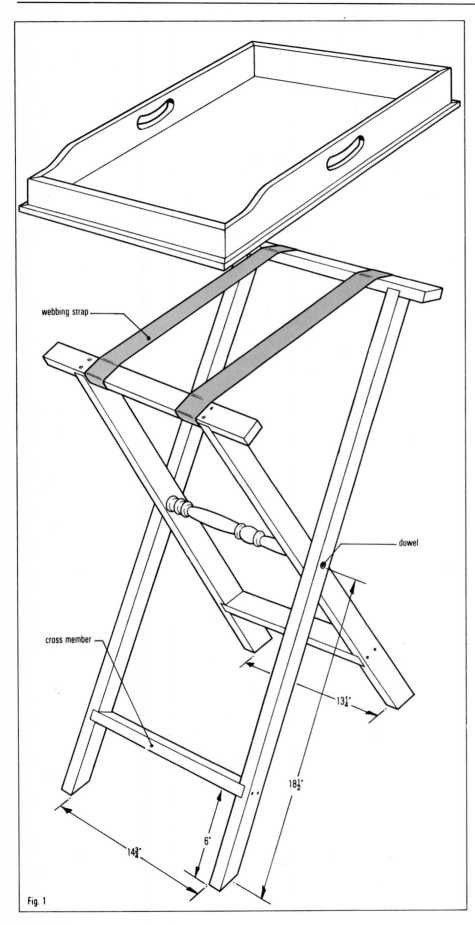

webbing strap

dowel

cross member

$13\frac{1}{4}$"

$18\frac{1}{2}$"

$14\frac{3}{4}$"

6"

Fig. 1

To prevent the tray slipping off the stand, the bottom is covered in felt or baize; and two canvas webbing pieces attached between the tops of the frames hold the frames open.

Choosing wood

Hardwood should be used because it does not stain as much as softwood. Traditionally, mahogany is used but there are attractive alternatives. Good quality utile possesses all the essential qualities and has an attractive finish. In this project the whole frame and the sides and tray edgings are constructed from utile, while the tray base is made from $\frac{1}{2}$in (13mm) plywood veneered with matching mahogany.

Cutting out and preliminaries

Cut out all the pieces to the sizes given in the cutting list. The two long sides are cut down at one end and handles cut in them. Figs. 2 and 3 are templates which give the exact dimensions of these features. Use a jig saw for cutting them but do not attempt to cut exactly to the mark; you will find it easier to leave a small margin which can be sanded down later. You will need to bore a large hole in the handle opening to insert the jig saw blade.

The top edges of the tray sides and the outer edges of the edging strips are radiused with a spokeshave.

Mitre joints are used in the construction of the tray sides. Cut these joints on the ends of the side pieces and edging strips taking care they will butt together exactly.

At this stage, sand all the pieces, and if there are any irregularities on the joints they must be removed.

Assembling the tray

Begin by fixing the edging strips to the base of the tray with glue and veneer pins. The pins should be skew nailed and punched under the surface of the wood, and the holes filled with a filler to match the wood.

The sides of the tray are fitted to the base so that they overlap the edging to base joint by $\frac{1}{8}$in (3mm) all round. Fix by glueing and pinning initially, and to assist in keeping the mitre joints correctly

Fig 1. The butler's tray has a simple construction. The tray rests on the stand and is prevented from slipping by felt on its underside. The style of the centre cross member shown may be changed to straight dowel or square timber.

aligned, clamp blocks of softwood to the internal corners of the tray.

Final fixing is done by screwing 1in (25mm) No. 4 c/s steel woodscrews through the base into the sides. Four screws to each side is sufficient and their heads must be recessed flush with the surface.

Assembling the stand

The stand is made up of two leg frames which are made separately. One leg-frame is narrower than the other so that it will fit closely inside the wider frame. Make the wider frame first.

Housing joints are made at the junctions of the legs and cross-members. Mark two lines ¾in (19mm) apart, 6in (153mm) from the bottom of each leg. Mark, or gauge a depth line ¼in (6mm) down the edge of the leg. Cut down to this line with a tenon saw and then remove the waste with a chisel. Ensure that the bottom of the housing recess is perfectly flat. On one cross-member the housings are made ¾in (19mm) from the ends and on the other, for the smaller frame, the housings are made 1½in (38mm) from the ends.

Assemble the frames with glue and countersink 1¾in (44mm) No. 6 Twinfast steel screws with wood finish plastic caps.

The centre cross member

If you possess a lathe this piece can be turned on the same pattern shown in Fig. 1. Otherwise you can fit a 1½in (38mm) diameter piece of dowel without shaping it.

A ⅜in (10mm) diameter hole is bored 2¼in (58mm) deep into the centre cross member. A corresponding ⅜in (10mm) hole is bored right through the centre point of the inner leg frame and ½in (13mm) deep into the centre point of the inside of the outer frame member. Take two 3½in (89mm) hardwood dowels and drive them through the inner leg frame into the centre cross member. Slip the outer frame over the inner and locate it on the projecting dowels by 'springing' it into position. The frame will now move

Figs 2, 3. Patterns for the side and handle cut-outs.

Fig 4. Section through the tray illustrating the method of construction. Care must be taken when screwing the base to the sides not to hit the pins attaching the edging strip.

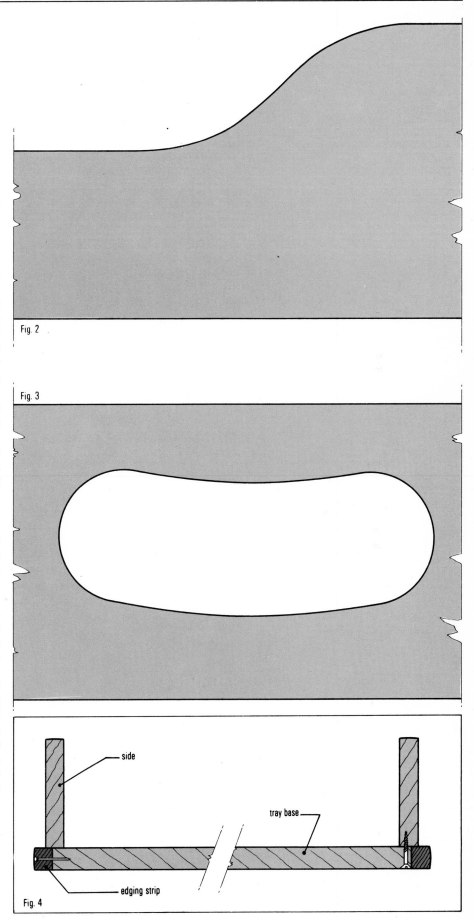

Fig. 2

Fig. 3

Fig. 4

side

tray base

edging strip

round the dowels which allows you to fold the stand when not in use.

Attaching the canvas straps

The stand when open should be fixed so that the angle at the centre between frame members is 60°. This is achieved by fitting canvas webbing strips between the top cross members. Take a 30in (762mm) length of webbing and mark lines 4½in (115mm) from each end. Place the webbing across the two top cross members and open the stand so that 4½in (115mm) of webbing projects at both ends. Tack the webbing in position. The free ends of the strap are wrapped around 2in x 1in (51mm x 26mm) hardboard plates which are then screwed underneath the leg frame top cross members. Repeat the procedure with the other strap and when both are firmly secured remove the tacks.

Levelling the legs

To give greater stability to the stand the legs must be levelled off so that their bases are level with the floor. This involves cutting a section off each leg. The easiest method of measuring and cutting the right amount is as follows.

Place the stand on a perfectly flat surface. If there is any wobble, caused by one leg being shorter than the others, place waste pieces of wood under the short leg until the frame stands level.

Now take a waste block of wood measuring about 4in x 3in x 1in (102mm x 76mm x 25mm). Drill a hole slightly less than the diameter of a pencil through the centre of the 3in (76mm) edge. Push a pencil into this hole so that about 1in (26mm) protrudes, then lay the waste block on the flat surface so that the pencil is parallel to the floor and 1½in (38mm) above it. Carefully draw a line around the bottom of each leg and carefully cut through the legs around these lines.

Finishing and varnishing

Add the piece of baize or felt to the base of the tray and sand all the surfaces for a fine finish. With a soft cloth dampened with turpentine substitute wipe all the surfaces so that the fine dust caused by sanding is picked up.

Using a good quality 2in (50mm) brush, sparingly apply a varnish of clear matt polyurethane and turpentine substitute blended 50/50. When this coat has dried cut down with fine glasspaper, wipe the surface with the cloth again and recoat with the same mixture. Leave this coat to dry then finish with grade '0' steel wool. Clean the surface with neat turpentine substitute, then leave overnight, and apply neat polyurethane as sparingly as possible.

After a few days the unit can be polished with a dry, soft cloth to give it a deep, rich, lasting sheen.

With only a few hours of work you will have built a butler's tray that is a perfect reproduction of a valuable antique. The simple but strong construction ensures that it will give years of useful service.

Cutting list

Solid wood

	standard	metric
2 tray sides	$27 \times 3 \times \frac{1}{2}$	$686 \times 76 \times 13$
1 tray end	$20 \times 3 \times \frac{1}{2}$	$508 \times 76 \times 13$
1 tray end	$20 \times 1\frac{3}{4} \times \frac{1}{2}$	$508 \times 45 \times 13$
2 tray edge strips	$27\frac{3}{4} \times \frac{1}{2} \times \frac{1}{2}$	$705 \times 13 \times 13$
2 tray edge strips	$20\frac{3}{4} \times \frac{1}{2} \times \frac{1}{2}$	$527 \times 13 \times 13$
1 tray base	$26\frac{3}{4} \times 19\frac{3}{4} \times \frac{1}{2}$	$680 \times 502 \times 13$
4 stand legs	$37 \times 1\frac{3}{4} \times \frac{3}{4}$	$940 \times 45 \times 19$
2 stand top cross members	$18 \times 1\frac{3}{4} \times \frac{3}{4}$	$457 \times 45 \times 19$
1 stand lower cross member	$14\frac{1}{4} \times 1\frac{3}{4} \times \frac{3}{4}$	$363 \times 45 \times 19$
1 stand lower cross member	$15\frac{3}{4} \times 1\frac{3}{4} \times \frac{3}{4}$	$490 \times 45 \times 19$
1 turned centre cross member	$13\frac{3}{8} \times 2 \times 2$	$340 \times 51 \times 51$
or round centre cross member	$13\frac{3}{8} \times 1\frac{1}{2}$ dia.	340×38 dia.
2 $\frac{3}{8}$in diameter leg pivot dowels	$3\frac{1}{2}$in length	89mm in length

You will also require:

40 brads. Wood adhesive. 16 1in (25mm) No.6 flathead steel wood screws. 20 1¾in (45mm) No.6 flathead steel screws with furniture plugs. 2 canvas webbing straps 30in x 2in (762mm x 51mm). 1 piece of baize or felt 26¾in x 19¾in (680mm x 502mm). Clear matt polyurethane. Turpentine substitute.

Coffee table

The top of this table fits into the frame but can be reversed to show an alternative cover of your choice.

Construction

The construction outline is shown in Fig. 1. The main point to bear in mind is that the four side rails must be the same length as the long dimensions of the table top: in this case 17¾in (451mm).

The base frame, as shown in Fig. 1, is very easy to make, and consists of four leg members joined by four rails. Two of the rails are fixed so that their top edges are below the tops of the legs at a depth

equal to the thickness of the table top. The remaining rails are fixed at right angles to these, immediately underneath.

The lower rails are screwed into the leg members. The top rails are secured by screwing through the legs, into the end grain of the rails. Screwing or nailing into end grain does not provide a very strong joint, and for this reason the end grain of the top rails is drilled to take No. 8 size fibre screw plugs. The plugs are glued into these holes and, when the adhesive has set, provide a strong fixing location for the screws. A detail of this joint is shown in Fig. 1.

This top is of chipboard covered with a laminated plastic on both faces and on the edges. But you could use blockboard, plywood, or even solid wood if you prefer, with any suitable covering.

Assembling the frame

First, cut the four legs. The length of each leg will be the eventual height of the surface of the table. So if you require a lower, or taller, table, do this by cutting the legs to the desired length.

Next, cut the rails. Use fine glasspaper to smooth down all surfaces, particularly the end grain, because this will be

Coffee table

showing on some parts of the construction.

Now prepare the top. You may have purchased a laminated veneered top already. If it is veneered with a particular wood on the two faces and the edges you may wish to apply different veneer to one of the surfaces. In any case the top should have its final finish before you start to screw the frame together. In this way you can make any small alterations on the rail members at this stage.

Mark out and drill the holes for the screws. The two upper rails have to be drilled in the end grain. Squeeze a little glue into these holes, then press a fibre plug into each one.

Set out the table legs by marking 1in (25mm) from the top of each leg to represent the thickness of the table top.

Make another mark $1\frac{3}{4}$in (44mm) below this to indicate the top rail and another mark $1\frac{3}{4}$in (44mm) further down to indicate the lower rail. Drill two holes through the leg at the top rail marking and use the leg as a jig to mark the corresponding holes in the rails. Glue and

screw these rails to the legs.

Next, drill the lower rails for two screws at each end. Glue and screw these rails into place, keeping the ends of the rails flush with the outside edge of the legs.

Finish the table in the same way as the round table (see page 87).

Cutting list

Solid wood	standard	metric
4 legs	$13 \times 1\frac{3}{4} \times \frac{7}{8}$	$330 \times 45 \times 22$
4 rails	$17\frac{3}{4} \times 1\frac{3}{4} \times \frac{7}{8}$	$455 \times 45 \times 22$
Chipboard or plywood		
Table top	$17\frac{3}{4} \times 17\frac{3}{4} \times 1$	$455 \times 455 \times 25$

You will also require:

Covering material (self-adhesive vinyl, plastic laminate or other veneers), or any other covering you may prefer. 16 $1\frac{1}{2}$in (38mm) No.8 screws with plastic screw caps. Woodworking adhesive. Varnish or paint for the legs and rails. 8 fibre plugs.

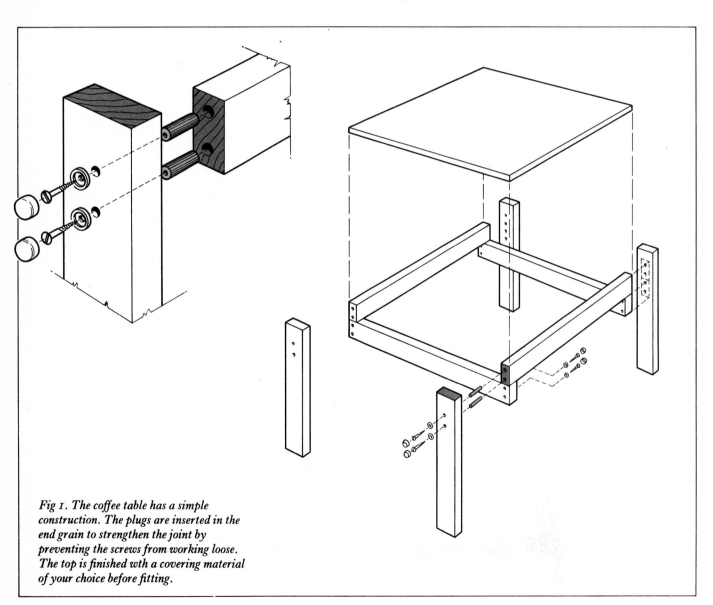

Fig 1. The coffee table has a simple construction. The plugs are inserted in the end grain to strengthen the joint by preventing the screws from working loose. The top is finished with a covering material of your choice before fitting.

Dinette trolley

Dinette trolley

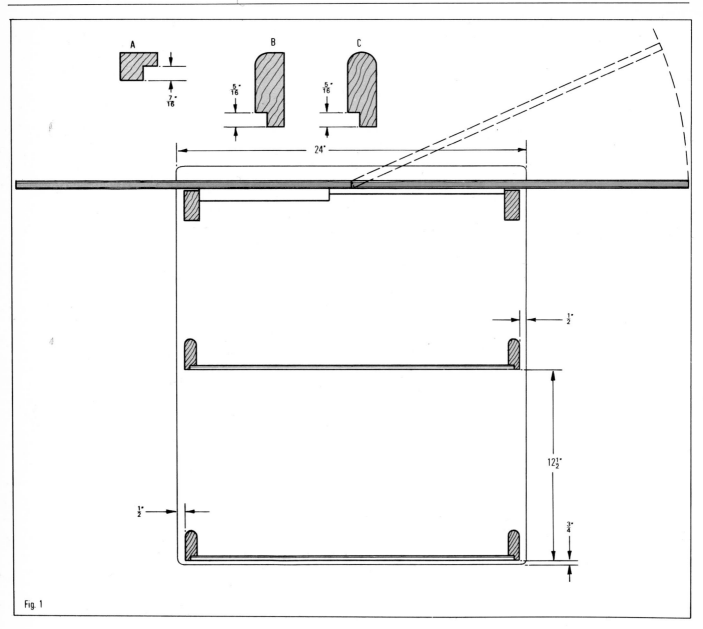

Fig. 1

Figs 1, 2. The construction details of the dinette trolley. The position of the centre cross member is important – if it is too high the table top will be difficult to move.

As living space becomes increasingly more precious, furniture designers have concentrated on producing compact units which combine two or more functions. This dinette trolley certainly fits this design concept. It doubles as a trolley equipped with two easy-to-clean trays for holding food and cutlery, and a folding table top big enough for two to eat at.

Construction of the dinette trolley reflects the straightforward and un-cluttered design; there are no complicated techniques involved, and any properly equipped home carpenter should be able to build the unit without encountering any problems.

Briefly, the trolley is made up of seven parts, consisting of the two sides, two laminated trays, the top cross members and runners, and the laminated table top. The latter is made up of two hinged panels. They are mounted on hardwood runners so that once the table is opened out, it can be centred by sliding it along until both panels project the same distance from the unit. All parts should be assembled in a strict order of working to achieve a professional result.

Preliminaries
When you have checked that you have all the necessary tools and materials, mark out all the pieces to the sizes given in the cutting list.

Do not cut all the pieces out yet; greater accuracy will be achieved by working in stages, checking each piece as it is cut.

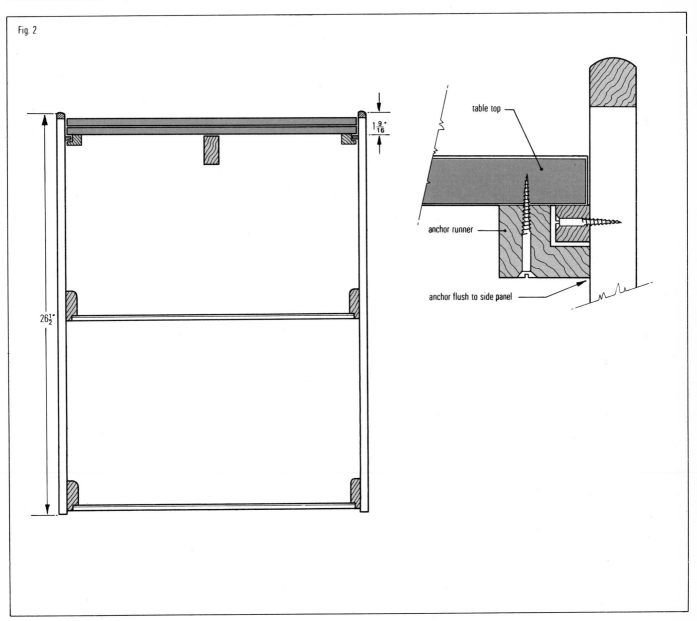

Fig. 2

table top

anchor runner

anchor flush to side panel

$1\frac{9}{16}$

$26\frac{1}{2}$

The trolley sides

These are constructed of $\frac{1}{2}$in (13mm) plywood panels cut to size with a panel saw. Sand all the cut edges with medium then fine glasspaper and check that the edges are flat and smooth enough to take the $\frac{1}{2}$in (13mm) edging strip. Now cut the edging strip to the correct lengths, and mitre both ends of the shorter strips and one end of each of the longer strips. These strips are located on the top and side edges of the panels and are fixed by glueing and pinning. Using a small nail punch, sink the pins well below the surface to allow the surfaces to be radiused with a spokeshave at a later stage.

The tray frames

Cut the sides and ends from $\frac{3}{4}$in (19mm)

softwood. All these pieces need a rebate to house the tray bottoms. The rebates are $\frac{3}{8}$in (10mm) square (see Fig. 1B and C), and run the whole length of each member. Rebating is relatively simple when done with a rebating plane. If working without this tool, you will have to use a handyman's knife and a straight-edge as a guide, taking care not to split the timber.

The tray sides are housed into the ends. These housings are $\frac{3}{4}$in (19mm) wide and $\frac{3}{8}$in (10mm) deep and can be cut out with a tenon saw. When the joints have been cut and tested for fit, assemble the tray frames with glue and $1\frac{1}{4}$in (30mm) screws countersunk below the surface. Now radius the entire top edges of the ends (Fig. 1C) and the

internal half of the top edges of the sides (Fig. 1B).

At this stage, radius the edges of the trolley side panels and round off the corners. Clean up and sand all the assembled parts and fill any holes or cracks with wood filler.

Fitting the frame to the side panels

First cut out the two top main cross members and measure these against the shorter side of the tray frame to ensure that they are the same length. Then cut the top centre member to size.

Refer to the section shown in Fig. 1 to mark the correct location of the trays and top cross members onto the side panels. The bottom edge of the lower tray is located $\frac{3}{4}$in (19mm) from the bottom

Dinette trolley

Fig. 3

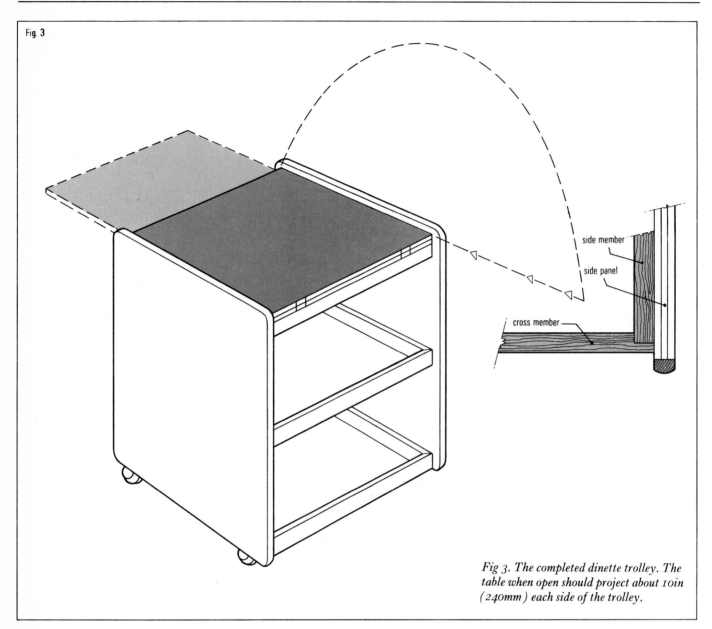

Fig 3. The completed dinette trolley. The table when open should project about 10in (240mm) each side of the trolley.

labels: side member, side panel, cross member

edge of the side panel, the bottom edge of the centre tray is situated 12½in (318 mm) above this point. Each top cross member is positioned 1⅝in (41mm) below the top edge of the side panels.

Take one side panel and fix the tray frames into position, using glue and 1in (25mm) screws inserted through the tray sides into the side panel. The top cross members are secured with glue and 1½in (38mm) panel pins. Then turn the structure over and fix the second panel in position in the same way.

The table top runners
The table top runs on three bearing points, the centre member which has already been cut and two ⅜in (10mm) square hardwood runners which are fixed to the side panels. Cut these hardwood runners to size and fit these and the centre member into position according to the plan shown in Fig. 2. All the runners must stand 1/16in (2mm) proud of the cross members so that the sliding table top at no point comes into contact with them. The hardwood runners are fixed with glue and ¾in (19mm) screws to the side panels; the centre member is glued and pinned between the cross members. At this stage sand the entire structure and fill any holes with wood filler.

The tray bottoms
The bottoms of the trays are made of hardboard covered with a rigid plastic laminate 1/16in (2mm) thick. If you intend putting hot food containers on the trays, choose a laminate that is heat resistant—formica is ideal. Cut out the hardboard tray bottoms to size and test for fit by temporarily locating them in the rebates cut into the bottom of the tray frames.

Now cut the laminate to the same size as the tray bottoms, using a tungsten-tipped straight laminate cutter. Power tools, such as a jig saw, can be used for cutting laminates, but they should never be forced through the material as this will splinter its edges.

Ensure that the rough sides of the hardboard tray bottoms are dry and grease free, then apply a thin but even layer of contact adhesive onto them.

In the same way, apply the adhesive to

the rougher surface of the laminate and wait until the adhesive on both surfaces is nearly dry before pressing the two surfaces together. Clamp the two materials together to give a strong bond.

When the adhesive has set properly, drill No. 4 countersunk screw holes at 5in (125mm) intervals round the tray bottom. The centre of each screw hole is situated $\frac{3}{16}$in (6mm) from each edge to coincide with the centre of the rebate. Do not fix the tray bottoms at this stage.

The table top

This is constructed from two $\frac{1}{2}$in (13mm) panels entirely covered by laminate and hinged together. The size of these panels is given in the cutting list but, due to unavoidable errors in cutting the other pieces, the measurement may have to be modified very slightly. In order to construct a well-fitting table top, first measure the width between the tops of the side panels, then subtract $\frac{1}{4}$in (6mm) from this measurement to give the exact width of the table top. The subtraction represents $\frac{1}{16}$in (2mm) clearance on each side of the table between table and side panel, and the thickness of two laminate edging strips.

Mark out the correct dimensions of the table tops and cut these pieces out. Now mark out and cut the laminate sheets and edging strips, remembering to allow $\frac{1}{8}$in (3mm) extra all round which can be trimmed down later. The best method to employ when cutting the laminate is to lay a straight-edge in place along the line to be cut and, using a handyman's knife or straight laminate cutter, start scoring gently from one end of the sheet. Hold the cutting blade against the straight-edge to keep it straight while it travels the entire length of the pencilled guide line. Do this at least three or four times, increasing the pressure of cut each time, until the dark under-surface of the laminate appears as a clean, unbroken line.

Work steadily and do not rush. If you apply too much pressure at the first few strokes, you might cut into the straight-edge, or your cutting tool could slip, damaging the surface away from the cutting line.

Once the dark score line shows, remove the straight-edge and continue scoring in the deepening cut—the knife will not slip out now—until the whole line is cut through.

When all the laminate has been cut to size, glue the shorter edging strips to the shorter edges of the table and plane these down flush with the table top and sides before adding the long edging strips. Plane these to size, then cover the large surfaces using the technique given previously for the trays. Hinge the two flaps together with brass counter flap hinges having first cut out the required depth and shape in the table tops to allow the hinges to be properly recessed.

Fixing the table to the frame

Lay the folded table top on a flat, clean surface and pack it up $\frac{1}{2}$in (13mm) clear of the surface. Now turn the frame upside down and place it onto the table top, and carefully align it all round to give the correct location. One flap of the table top is secured to the frame by anchors which slide along the two outer hardwood runners. Cut these anchors to the size given in the cutting list and make a $\frac{7}{16}$in (11mm) square rebate in them as shown in Fig. 1A. This rebate loosely houses the hardwood runner and so, when the anchor runner is fixed to one table flap, the whole table top slides easily along the runners.

To fix the anchors correctly when the table top and frame are correctly aligned, lay them on the table flap with the rebate enclosing the runners. Having checked that there is sufficient clearance between the rebates and runners, locate the long edges of the anchors almost flush against the inside faces of the side panels, with their ends butting against one of the top main cross members. Once in position they are screwed to the table with 1in (25mm) screws whose heads should be recessed.

Turn the whole structure the correct way up and test the operation of the table top. The closed flaps should slide to project approximately 10in (254mm) beyond the main structure and the hinged table top should then flap over to project approximately 10in (254mm) on the other side. If there are large discrepancies in these measurements, or if the table top does not slide easily, adjust the runner anchors.

Painting the trolley

It is easier to paint the trolley before fixing the tray bottoms in place and with the table top removed. It is a simple operation to unscrew the anchor runners and the job of painting will be made much simpler. Apply primer and at least one undercoat and finish with a coat of a resistant and easy to clean paint.

When the paint has thoroughly hardened, refix the table top and add the tray bottoms by screwing them into the rebate housings in the tray frames. Fix ball type castors to the base of the trolley by screwing them onto small plywood plates glued to the corners of the lower tray base.

Cutting list

Solid wood	standard	metric
4 softwood tray ends	$22 \times 2 \times \frac{3}{4}$	$559 \times 51 \times 19$
4 softwood tray sides	$22\frac{1}{2} \times 2 \times \frac{3}{4}$	$572 \times 51 \times 19$
2 softwood top main cross members	$20 \times 2 \times 1$	$508 \times 51 \times 25$
1 softwood top centre member	$21\frac{1}{4} \times 2 \times 1$	$540 \times 51 \times 25$
2 hardwood table top runners	$21\frac{1}{4} \times \frac{3}{8} \times \frac{3}{8}$	$540 \times 10 \times 10$
2 hardwood table top runner anchors	$10 \times 1 \times \frac{3}{4}$	$254 \times 25 \times 19$
4 softwood edging strips	$26 \times \frac{1}{2} \times \frac{1}{2}$	$660 \times 13 \times 13$
2 softwood edging strips	$24 \times \frac{1}{2} \times \frac{1}{2}$	$610 \times 13 \times 13$
Plywood		
2 plywood panels	$26 \times 24 \times \frac{1}{2}$	$660 \times 610 \times 13$
2 plywood table flaps	$23 \times 19\frac{7}{8} \times \frac{1}{2}$	$584 \times 504 \times 13$
Hardboard		
2 hardboard tray bottoms	$22\frac{1}{2} \times 19\frac{1}{2} \times \frac{1}{4}$	$572 \times 495 \times 6$
Laminate		
4 sheets plastic laminate	$23\frac{1}{4} \times 20\frac{1}{8} \times \frac{1}{16}$	$590 \times 510 \times 1.5$
2 sheets plastic laminate	$22\frac{1}{2} \times 19\frac{1}{2} \times \frac{1}{16}$	$572 \times 495 \times 1.5$
1 strip plastic laminate	$192 \times \frac{3}{4} \times \frac{1}{16}$	$4877 \times 19 \times 1.5$

You will also require:

2 1in (25mm) hinges, 4 mini ball-type castors. Wood adhesive, contact adhesive. 60 1$\frac{1}{4}$in (32mm) panel pins. 48 1$\frac{1}{4}$in (32mm) wood screws.

Sofa~bed

The design of the couch has been kept as simple as possible and this is reflected in the wide choice of materials available for the construction. Depending on how much you are prepared to spend and the particular finish you desire, you can use hardboard, plywood, softwood or hardwood for the basic frame—or any combination of these materials. For example, you could use laminated hardboard for the sides, back, base and fascia, and softwood for the base supporting frame. In this way you reproduce the design economically, and the finished couch lends itself well to a fine paint finish. Alternatively, you can use solid wood throughout to produce a more solid and sophisticated result. This latter method lends itself to further modification. The sides can be built of single wood panels or can be made up of separate strips of wood joined together, as shown in Fig. 3. It is this kind of construction which is described here, but the basic construction method is the same whatever materials you use.

There are several different ways of making the cushion-supporting base. Perhaps the simplest is to fit a single hardboard panel across the frame. Provided you supply adequate cushioning, the result will be perfectly comfortable. Another but more expensive method, is to fit rubber webbing across the frame.

Shop-bought cushions are expensive and it is unlikely that you will be able to obtain them in a size to fit the couch. By following the instructions given in this project you can easily make up the necessary cushioning yourself.

Making the sides
Having decided on what materials to use, begin by cutting out the side panels, or, if you intend making up the side panels from strips of timber, cut each piece to the size given in the cutting list. Each side consists of four parallel members with a cross-section of $5\frac{1}{4}$in x $1\frac{3}{4}$in (133 mm x 45mm), which are flanked by two vertical members of the same section. Fig. 5 shows how the side and top members are mitred together for greater strength, and also shows the tongued and grooved joints by which the separate pieces are fixed to the sides.

To make these joints, first take each of the vertical side members and, having marked in a line from one corner, at an angle of 45° to the long edge, cut the mitred end. In the same way, mitre the ends of the top horizontal member, but remember that this piece has a tongue cut on it and must, therefore, be cut 1in (25mm) overlength at each end.

Now take the vertical members and, using a plough-plane, make a groove 1in (25mm) deep and $\frac{1}{2}$in (13mm) wide down each mitre and the inside long edge. Clean up these grooves with a chisel and sandpaper. Then take the top horizontal member and, with a rebate plane, cut a tongue on each mitred end 1in (25mm) long and $\frac{1}{2}$in (13mm) wide. Similarly, make tongues on each short edge of the other horizontal members as shown in Fig. 5.

If you have no rebate plane, you can cut the tongues in the ends of the timber like cutting tenons. First saw down the grain to make a central $\frac{1}{2}$in (13mm) tenon, then cut across the grain to form the shoulders of the joint.

With the pieces of both side panels cut to shape, trial assemble and, when you are satisfied that each joint fits perfectly, begin construction by glueing the lower horizontal members into the grooves on the vertical members. Complete the construction by adding the top in the same way. Allow the glue to set, then trim off that part of the mitre-tongue which protrudes beyond the outer edge of the vertical members.

Sides and back assembly
Assembling the side panels to the back is straightforward. However, you must ensure that the butt joints between side and back panels really are secure. Extra strength can be given to the joint between the back and side panels by drilling the edge of the back panel at 4in (102mm) centres to take fibre Rawlplugs. Glue these into position so that you can screw into them.

Fit the sides into position and screw through them, at previously marked locations, using 3in (76mm) wood-screws countersunk below the surface. The surface should be filled with a suitable stopper. For this job you can use a special countersinking bit fitted to your drill.

Sofa-bed

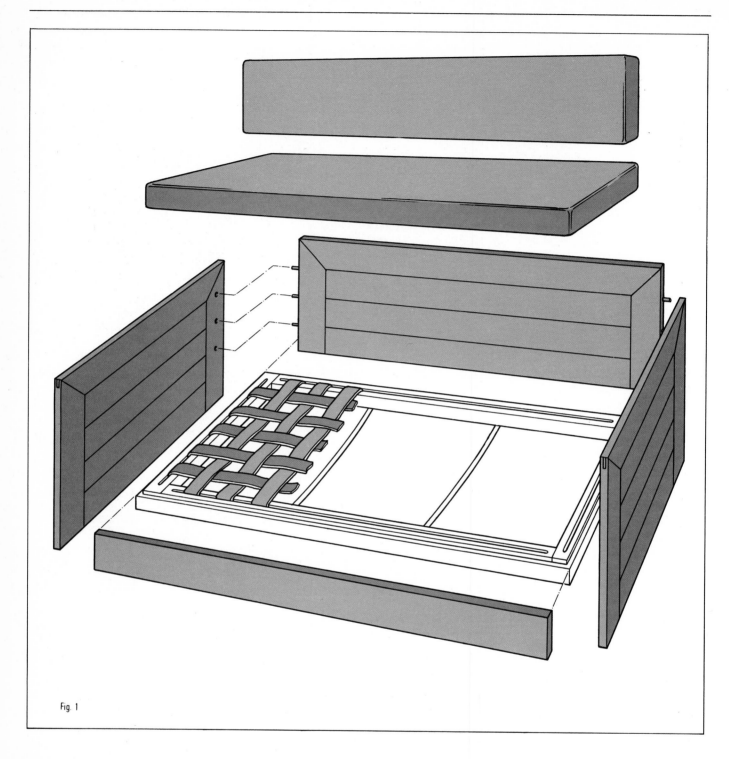

Fig. 1

Fig 1. The exploded diagram of the sofa bed shows the main components.

Figs 2-6. Details of the construction. The conduit is very important as it strengthens the frame. It is these two components which take the stress when the unit is in use.

Making the base frame

The frame which supports the seat is constructed separately, then fitted, pre-assembled, to the back and sides. To make it, begin by cutting out the rails to the sizes given in the cutting list, then mitre all the ends to an angle of 45°. Ensure that each mitred end joint fits closely, then glue and pin the rails together, checking that the structure is square by measuring the diagonals. A fascia panel is fitted across the front rail, but this piece is not added until the base of the seat has been fixed to the frame. It is then glued and screwed to the front rail of the seat and the side frames.

Next, fit the frame inside the side and back panels, with its lower edges located 5¼in (133mm) above the base of the sides and back. Fix the frame with 3in (76mm) woodscrews driven through the frame members at 6in (152mm) intervals.

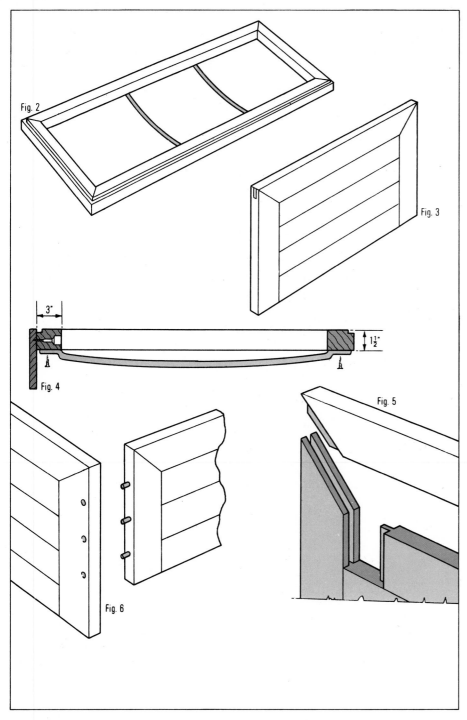

Fig. 2

Fig. 3

3"

1½"

Fig. 4

Fig. 5

Fig. 6

The only disadvantage of plywood as a material for the base of the couch is its rigidity. It will not yield under pressure and consequently you must make cushions extra thick. An alternative, more luxurious base is provided by rubber webbing stretched between the frame. Webbing can be obtained in a continuous roll and there are several methods of fixing it in place. The easiest way is simply to tack or staple it to the top edges of the frame, having first removed any sharp edges on the frame with which the rubber may come in contact. Another method is to fit special clips to the ends of the webbing. These are anchored in a groove cut in the top of the frame. Whatever method you choose to fix the webbing, make sure that it is fitted under the correct tension and will give complete support.

Making the cushions

The sofa bed is finished by making the cushions in a hardwearing fabric. Both the seat and the back cushions use foam rubber as a foundation. This is both inexpensive and easy to cut and the only problem occurs in choosing a foam filling of the correct density. It is this density which determines the resilience of the finished cushion. As the unit will be used for sleeping on, you must take extra care in choosing and making up the foundation.

For best results you require at least three layers of foam for the seat. The top and bottom layers should have a density of about 1.8lb per cubic foot, and sandwiched between these should be a layer with a density of no less than 2.5lb per cubic foot. This arrangement gives ample support while being extremely comfortable. The back cushion or cushions can be cut from a single piece of foam and, because it does not support so much weight, need not have a density exceeding 2lb per cubic foot. Comfort also depends on the thickness of the cushions. The base cushion must be at least 4½in (115mm) thick, the back cushion 3in (76mm).

Cut out the foam to size, using a fine-toothed hacksaw or an electric carving knife. All the foundations should be cut slightly oversize, the reason for this being that when they are covered by fabric of the correct size, they will be slightly compressed, preventing wrinkles forming in the fabric cover and giving it a smooth-looking finish.

Because the couch is long and must bear the weight of more than one person sitting on it, reinforcement must be fixed across the frame to maintain its strength and rigidity. Conduit tubing cut and bent to the shape shown in Fig. 4 is ideal. To make these pieces, cut ¾in (19mm) tubing to the lengths given in the cutting list, flatten the ends with a hammer, drill the ends to receive screws, then screw the tubing across the under-

side of the frame at the locations shown in Fig. 2.

Making the base

As mentioned above, you can make the base from a single sheet of laminated hardboard or plywood—½in (13mm) plywood is the stronger and, therefore the most suitable material. Simply cut the base panel to the correct size and screw in onto the top edges of the frame.

Sofa~bed

*Right: An alternative method of
construction. The dowels for the fascia
panel are allowed to show as a decorative
feature.*

Cutting list

Solid wood	standard	metric
2 top side members	$34\frac{1}{2} \times 5\frac{1}{4} \times 1\frac{3}{4}$	$869 \times 133 \times 45$
8 horizontal side members	$24 \times 5\frac{1}{4} \times 1\frac{3}{4}$	$610 \times 133 \times 45$
4 vertical members	$26\frac{1}{4} \times 5\frac{1}{4} \times 1\frac{3}{4}$	$666 \times 133 \times 45$
3 horizontal back members	$66\frac{1}{2} \times 5\frac{1}{4} \times 1\frac{3}{4}$	$1682 \times 133 \times 45$
1 top back member	$75 \times 5\frac{1}{4} \times 1\frac{3}{4}$	$1905 \times 133 \times 45$
2 vertical back members	$21 \times 5\frac{1}{4} \times 1\frac{3}{4}$	$533 \times 133 \times 45$
2 frame cross rails	$29\frac{1}{2} \times 3 \times 1\frac{1}{2}$	$756 \times 76 \times 38$
2 frame long rails	$75 \times 3 \times 1\frac{1}{2}$	$1905 \times 76 \times 38$
1 fascia panel	$75 \times 6 \times 1$	$1905 \times 152 \times 25$

The size of the couch can be modified to suit individual requirements. For economy,
man-made wood, such as plywood, can be substituted for solid wood.

You will also require:
Plastic webbing or a plywood base. 3 lengths $29\frac{1}{2}$in $\times \frac{3}{4}$in (749mm $\times$ 19mm) tubing. Foam
cushion foundations and fabric covers. Wood glue. 12 fibre plugs. 3in (76mm) wood
screws. Wood filler. Sandpaper. Wood stain and varnish, or paint.

Studio couch & chair

Studio couch & chair

These two units comprise a studio couch and studio chair, built to the same design. The couch 6ft 9in (2056mm) long and the chair 2ft 6½in (763mm) can be built as individual units or as a complete living room suite. The couch is perfectly adequate for sleeping adults while the chair can convert to a small bed suitable for a child.

The unit consists of a basic frame, which is the support structure, and two additional frames for the seat and back rests. When you wish to convert the unit for sleeping, two bolts, which secure the back rest to the rear legs, are withdrawn. This allows the hinged back rest to fall into a horizontal position, supported at the far end by two retractable legs as in Fig. 2.

Although the back rest is fully upholstered, the retaining bolts and legs, situated in the interior of the back rest, are easily reached through an opening.

The type of timber
The timber used in this couch is utile, a hardwood suitable for furniture, flooring, veneers, joinery and construction work. Sapele, a similar African wood, could be used instead. But it is not essential to use either of these. You may prefer something a little lighter, or darker, or with a richer grain, in which case almost any other wood will do providing it is a hardwood.

Tools and materials
In addition to commonly used tools you will require a bit for your power drill, capable of drilling a hole through a coach bolt and nut.

For the studio chair, you will need two 6ft (2m) sash cramps, and if a couch is being made, two extension bars will be needed for the cramps. It is not usually necessary to go to the expense of buying sash cramps, as they can often be hired. Ask your local D.I.Y. store. Refer to the cutting list for the timber required for this project.

Buying the timber
Hardwood for furniture should be purchased from a wood merchant who specializes in hardwoods. You will require 'prepared' timber—which is supplied machined and planed in exact widths, but only approximate lengths. So when you give your order, give the exact measurements for the widths, but add an inch (25mm) to each length illustrated in Figs. 3 to 5 just to be certain.

Before you order the timber, enquire whether your dealer will exchange any that have unsightly blemishes. Most reputable merchants will agree to this.

Marking out
Using the try square and marking knife, mark off the exact length of each piece of wood. As each piece is marked, carefully examine each surface to ensure that the best face on each piece will be placed where it is visible. It is pointless, for instance, having the most attractive surface of an arm rest on the underside, where it will be out of sight.

Mark out the joints. The rails are joined to the legs by mortise and tenon. To avoid weakening the legs, the mortise and tenon of each side rail is 'haunched'. In this way they will not meet the front and rear rail tenons at right angles. The arms are joined at the rear legs by twin mortise and tenon, and at the front legs by open twin mortise and tenon. The joint at each corner of the seat and back carcases is formed by a box or comb joint.

For the plywood panels, which support the cushions, a 'grid' of 3in (75mm) squares is drawn of the surface of each panel. This will provide a network of 'crosses' created by lines meeting at right angles. Each cross is drilled with a brace and ¾in (19mm) bit to form the rows of holes as illustrated.

Cutting the joints
It is best to cut out all the joints before anything is fitted. Note that some of the box joints are mitred at a 45° angle at the corners. These are at the bottom of the front edges of the back rest frame panels and at the top of the back edges of the seat frame panels. These mitres will allow the back rest to be brought up to a seating position (Fig. 5).

Mark the tenons on the rails and cut them out. Then mark the legs using the tenons as a guide. Cut the mortises using a power drill and chisel to remove waste. Most of the waste can be drilled out with a suitable sized bit and the mortise hole can then be squared up with a chisel. Do not forget that the haunch only goes into the leg ½in (13mm).

The open mortises for the chair arms and the combed joints for the seat and back carcases are cut with a tenon saw and then the waste is chopped out with a chisel working from each side of the wood to give a neat finish and avoid splitting the timber faces. When marking out the combed joint shade the waste pieces with a pencil, as it is very easy to start cutting on the wrong line.

Cut out the two blocks which are used to house the centre brace of the seat frame. Do not at this stage drill any holes for the bolts or screws.

Pre-assembly finishing
The final finish of the woodwork is a matter of personal preference. But whatever method you choose, there will be surfaces that are almost impossible to treat once the couch is complete—so they should be finished at this stage.

Assembling the frame
The first parts to assemble are the sides of the main frame. Each comprises a front and rear leg, an arm rest, and a side rail. Each side should be glued and cramped, and left for the adhesive to set. It is advisable to join the side frames one on top of the other so that they are exactly the same.

While the sides are setting, the seat and back rest frames could also be glued provided you have additional sash cramps. If not, you might be able to improvise by 'wedging', as shown in Fig. 6. The unit to be cramped is placed between two battens screwed to the bench, and wood wedges are driven between one batten and the unit to force the cramping action. If you have a really solid bench you could get away with placing one end of the frame against a wall and only using one batten or block.

When the glue has set on the sides of the main frame, the front and rear rails (the 'long' rails if you are making a couch) are glued and fitted to the sides, and cramped. The sash cramp will be adequate for a chair, but you will need extension bars for the cramp if you are making a couch.

When the adhesive has set on the back and seat frames, fit all interior battens. Glue these and screw them at 2in (50mm) intervals.

Glue and screw the blocks for the centre brace (or blocks for both braces for a couch) and then glue the centre brace into the block slots.

At this point you will have to cut recesses at the front of the front panel of the seat frame, just behind the box joint. This is necessary in order to accommodate a double thickness of upholstery. Using the tenon saw, cut to a depth of about ¼in (6mm) just behind each joint. Mark lines across the width of the panel 1½in (38mm) in from the ends of the panel. Chisel down from these lines to the bottom of the ¼in cut. Chisel recesses to house the hinges. Fit and screw the hinges for the junction of the back and seat frames.

Place the seat frame in position. This will enable you to mark and drill the coach bolt holes in the correct positions. Insert the coach bolts, but only screw them up finger-tight.

Raise the back rest up to seating position. Drill the holes for the casement screws. Fit and secure the screws.

The folding legs are now fitted to the inside side panels of the back rest.

Drill the holes in the plywood panels, plane the panels to fit, and glue and screw them to the interior battens of the seat and back rest frames.

The studio couch or chair is now fully assembled except for the upholstery.

Upholstering
For upholstering the couch you will need a 75in × 30in × 6in (1905mm × 762mm × 152mm) foam biscuit for the seat, and a 75in × 24in × 6in (1905mm × 610mm × 152mm) one for the back; to pad the seat and the back, two strips each of 75in × 2½in × 1in (1905mm × 64mm × 25mm) and 75in × 10in × ½in (1905mm × 254mm × 13mm).

For the chair you will need a 24in × 24in × 6in (610mm × 610mm × 152mm) foam biscuit for the back, and a 30in × 24in × 6in (762mm × 610mm × 152mm) one for the seat; for padding, two strips each of 24in × 2½in × 1in (610mm × 64mm × 25mm) and 24in × 10in × ½in (610mm × 254mm × 13mm).

The biscuits should be of medium hard foam and the padding of the hard type of foam.

Other materials you will need are: No. 3 or 4 piping cord; contact adhesive (make certain that is it the kind which will not dissolve foam); decorative upholstery and pins and gimp pins.

Cushion covers
If you are using plain fabric allow a piece of furnishing fabric (minimum 48in [1220mm] wide) equal to twice the length of each foam biscuit, plus 2in (51mm) seam allowance (the box strips can be cut from the leftover fabric of the main pieces).

If using a fabric with a one-way design, you will have to make up the length for the cushion cover by joining widths of fabric so that the pattern will run the right way on both the back rest and the seat cushion, i.e. from top to bottom for the back, and back to front for the seat. To determine the number of widths of fabric you need double the length of each foam biscuit and divide the width of the fabric into it. If it does not divide exactly, take it to the next half width. Multiply this number of widths by the width of the biscuit to give the amount of fabric needed for the top and bottom sections of the cover.

Follow the same method to calculate the amount needed for the box strips on each side of the biscuit, multiplying the total of fabric widths by the cushion's depth plus 1in (25mm) seam allowance.

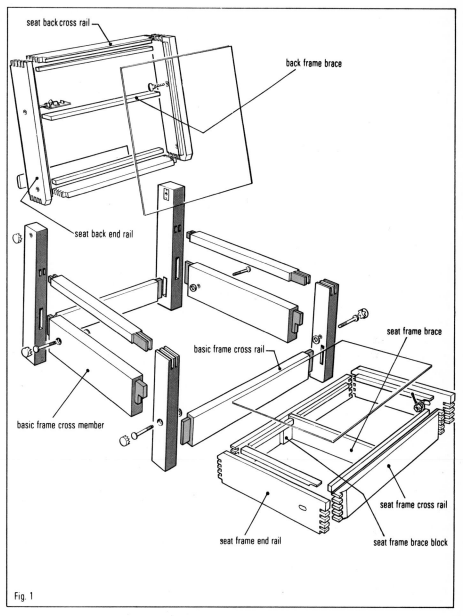

Fig. 1

seat back cross rail

back frame brace

seat back end rail

basic frame cross rail

seat frame brace

basic frame cross member

seat frame end rail

seat frame cross rail

seat frame brace block

Fig 1. The component parts for the couch and chair. The seat centre brace and blocks are omitted from the construction of the chair.

To cover the fascia and back, allow 2yd (1.8m) of 48in (1220mm) wide fabric for the couch and 1yd (91.4cm) for the chair. For the amount of bias-cut casing fabric and piping, measure the perimeter of each biscuit and double it, allowing an extra 6in (152mm) for joining. For the fascia piping, you will need an additional 18in (457mm). (As a guide, 1yd of 48in [91.4cm of 1220mm] fabric will make about 28yd [25.6m] bias strip, 1½in [39mm] wide).

Cutting out and making up

Cut out the fabric for the top and bottom sections of the cover, leaving ½in (13mm) seam allowance, and join the widths for each side if using one-way patterned fabric. Cut the box strips for each side separately, again leaving ½in (13mm) seam allowance on all sides. Join all the box strips together along their short edges with a ½in (13mm) plain seam, tapering the stitching into the corners ½in (13mm) from both ends. Make the casing for the piping and attach it to both sides of the box strip so that the line of stitching is ½in (13mm) from the edges.

With the 'right' sides together, pin one edge of the box strip to the outer edge of the cover top. Clip the casing at the corners—the tapered seam of the strip will give enough 'ease' to go round the corners smoothly, so there will be no need to clip this. Tack and machine stitch, then neaten the raw edges.

Attach the bottom cover to the other edge of the box strip in a similar way, but leave one of the long sides open. Turn the cover the right side out and press it. Insert the foam biscuit and slip stitch the opening together, using a curved needle (these stitches can be unpicked easily for removing the cover for cleaning).

Covering the fascia and back

For the padding, use a contact adhesive to stick on the strips of 1in (25mm) thick foam to the front edge of the seat and the top of the back. Wrap the ½in thick foam round these and the seat or behind the back, and stick them in position.

For the fascia, cut out a strip of fabric the same size as the ½in foam, plus 1in on all sides. Stitch piping to the short sides and then turn under the ¼in (6mm) seam allowance and piping casing, and press. Fix the fabric over the foam, using tacks or decorative-headed upholstery pins. To secure the sides, lift up the piping and tack with gimp pins.

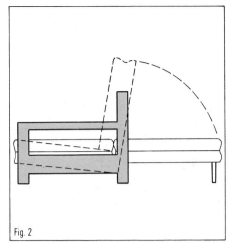

Fig. 2

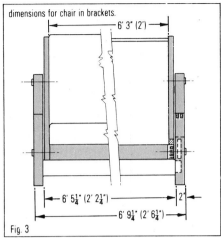

dimensions for chair in brackets.

Fig. 3

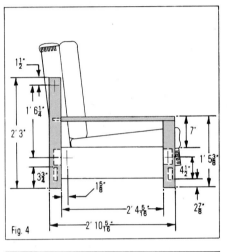

Fig. 4

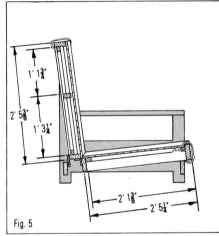

Fig. 5

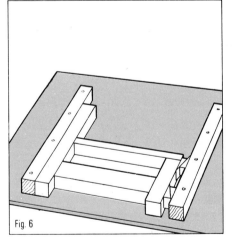

Fig. 6

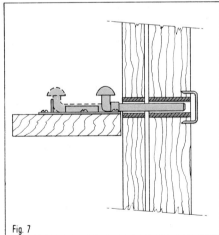

Fig. 7

Figs 2-5. Overall dimensions and main construction details for the studio couch.

Fig 6. Methods of clamping the basic frames while glueing.

Fig 7. The seat back locking mechanisms may be cut from ordinary door bolts.

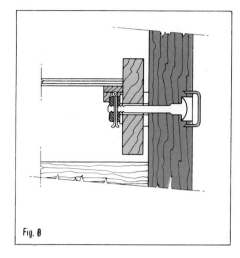

Fig. 8

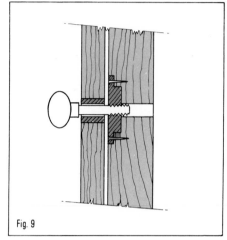

Fig. 9

Fig 8. The pivot for the seat. Note the cotter pin through the nut and bolt to prevent the assembly coming undone.

Fig 9. As an alternative to the door catch, a casement screw can be used. This is the better arrangement giving a more professional finish.

For the back, cut a piece of fabric the same size as the $\frac{1}{2}$in (13mm) foam plus 1in (25mm) all round. Then cut another piece to fit the inset section of the back, plus $\frac{1}{2}$in (13mm) seam allowance. Join these pieces together with a $\frac{1}{2}$in (13mm) seam, leaving the ends open 8 to 10in (203 to 254mm) to provide either for the insertion of zip fasteners, or a placket for hooks and eyes. Turn under the outside edges $\frac{1}{2}$in (13mm) and press down. Tack the fabric over the foam.

Cutting list: Couch

Solid wood	standard	metric
Basic frame		
2 legs	$17\frac{3}{8} \times 3 \times 2$	$442 \times 76 \times 51$
2 legs	$27 \times 3 \times 2$	$686 \times 76 \times 51$
2 arms	$33\frac{5}{16} \times 3 \times 1\frac{3}{4}$	$840 \times 76 \times 45$
2 cross members	$32\frac{13}{16} \times 6\frac{1}{2} \times 2$	$834 \times 165 \times 51$
2 cross rails	$80\frac{1}{4} \times 4 \times 1\frac{1}{4}$	$2038 \times 102 \times 31$
Seat frame		
2 cross rails	$77 \times 4 \times 1$	$1956 \times 102 \times 25$
2 end rails	$29\frac{1}{4} \times 5 \times 1$	$743 \times 127 \times 25$
1 front interior batten	$75 \times 2 \times 1$	$1905 \times 52 \times 25$
1 back interior batten	$75 \times 1 \times 1$	$1905 \times 25 \times 25$
1 end interior batten	$25\frac{1}{4} \times 1 \times 1$	$641 \times 25 \times 25$
1 centre brace	$27\frac{3}{4} \times 3\frac{5}{8} \times 1$	$708 \times 92 \times 25$
4 centre brace blocks	$3\frac{5}{8} \times 3\frac{5}{8} \times 1$	$92 \times 92 \times 25$
Back frame		
2 cross rails	$77 \times 4 \times 1$	$1956 \times 102 \times 25$
2 end rails	$29\frac{3}{8} \times 5 \times 1$	$745 \times 127 \times 25$
1 centre brace	$75 \times 3 \times 1$	$1905 \times 76 \times 25$
2 interior battens	$73 \times 1 \times 1$	$1854 \times 25 \times 25$
1 interior end batten	$27\frac{3}{8} \times 1 \times 1$	$699 \times 25 \times 25$
Plywood		
Seat frame	$75 \times 27\frac{1}{2} \times \frac{3}{8}$	$1905 \times 699 \times 10$
Back frame	$75 \times 27\frac{3}{8} \times \frac{3}{8}$	$1905 \times 698 \times 10$

Cutting list: Chair

Solid wood	standard	metric
Basic frame		
2 legs	$17\frac{3}{8} \times 3 \times 2$	$442 \times 76 \times 51$
2 legs	$27 \times 3 \times 2$	$686 \times 76 \times 51$
2 arms	$33\frac{5}{16} \times 3 \times 1\frac{3}{4}$	$840 \times 76 \times 45$
2 cross members	$32\frac{13}{16} \times 6\frac{1}{2} \times 2$	$834 \times 165 \times 51$
2 cross rails	$29\frac{1}{4} \times 4 \times 1\frac{1}{4}$	$743 \times 102 \times 32$
Seat frame		
2 cross rails	$26 \times 4 \times 1$	$660 \times 102 \times 25$
2 end rails	$29\frac{1}{4} \times 5 \times 1$	$743 \times 127 \times 25$
1 front interior batten	$24 \times 2 \times 1$	$610 \times 51 \times 25$
1 back interior batten	$24 \times 1 \times 1$	$610 \times 25 \times 25$
2 end interior battens	$25\frac{1}{4} \times 1 \times 1$	$641 \times 25 \times 25$
Back frame		
2 cross rails	$26 \times 4 \times 1$	$660 \times 102 \times 25$
2 end rails	$29\frac{3}{8} \times 5 \times 1$	$745 \times 127 \times 25$
1 centre brace	$24 \times 3 \times 1$	$610 \times 76 \times 25$
2 interior battens	$22\frac{3}{8} \times 1 \times 1$	$569 \times 25 \times 25$
2 end interior battens	$27\frac{3}{8} \times 1 \times 1$	$698 \times 25 \times 25$
Plywood		
Seat frame	$27\frac{1}{2} \times 24 \times \frac{3}{8}$	$699 \times 610 \times 10$
Back frame	$27\frac{3}{8} \times 24 \times \frac{3}{8}$	$698 \times 610 \times 10$

You will also require:

For couch and chair – 2 2in (51mm) casement screws or door bolts. 4 coach bolts, nuts and washers $\frac{3}{8}$in $\times$ 4in (10mm $\times$ 102mm). 4 2$\frac{1}{2}$in (64mm) back flaps. Screws. Nails.

Mix~and~match living room suite

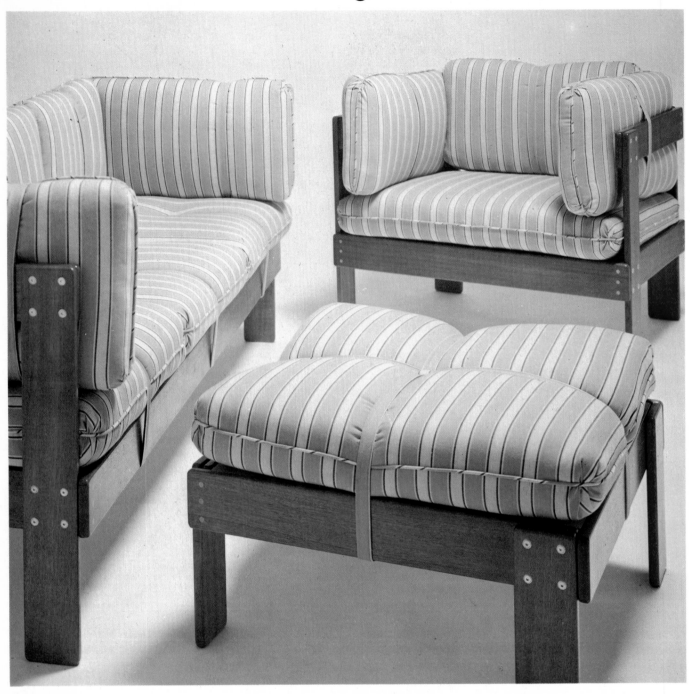

Above: Three of the suite units. The staggered legs enable the stools (but not the chairs) to be placed together along a wall.

These units are constructed mainly of utile. This is a medium priced African wood, similar to mahogany, and is suitable for most joinery projects. You may, however, prefer a lighter or darker wood, or one with a richer grain, in which case most hardwoods will do. If you have no experience in the selection of various woods, talk the matter over with your timber merchant, because the correct wood for a specific job depends not only on appearance but also price, type, and how it will eventually be finished.

Basically, the main frame consists of 4in x 1in (100mm x 25mm) PAR (planed all round) hardwood that has been radiused (all corners rounded off). Radiusing, if not carefully done, can easily result in uneven edges, and for this reason it is advisable to make a radius template, as in

Fig. 1, to obtain the correct curvature.

Where frame members cross by lapping, they are joined with four bolts as shown in Fig. 5. The hole positioning is extremely critical and it is essential that a hole template be made as in Fig. 2. This will ensure that drill holes match perfectly.

Where main frame members butt against one another, they are joined with three dowel rods drilled and fitted in dovetail fashion as in Fig. 3. Here again, the positioning of the holes—in this case to take the dowel rods—is extremely critical and it is essential to use a dowel jig (Fig. 3) if the members are to be joined level and at right angles. If you do not wish to make your own jig you can buy a steel jig specially made to be used with a power drill.

The method of upholstering the suite is detailed at the end of the project.

Fixings

These units are secured or joined with special fixings. The bolts are hexagonal countersunk GKN 2025 and the nuts are BSW pronged 'T' nuts. The screws are Pozidriv No. 8 Twinfast.

Some of these fixings are not available in certain countries, but they are not essential. In most places there are virtually identical alternatives but there is no reason, for instance, why ordinary coach bolts and screws should not be used. (See parts list for sizes.) And where alternative fixings are particularly ugly, covering caps can be fitted over the ends. These are small domes, usually nickelled or chromed, with three prongs which allow you to fasten them to the wood.

Making a radius template

This working aid is used to ensure that the rounded edges of the members are of a uniform curvature. The template is lightly held over the edge that has been rounded, and any irregularities can be seen by viewing along the surface. Note that the template illustrated in Fig. 1 is drilled out with a 1¼in (32mm) bit, which makes the diameter slightly wider than the wood being worked. This is because only the corners are being rounded, and this is achieved with a template curve that is slightly larger than the thickness of the wood. If you wanted to make a template for a completely rounded edge, the drilled hole would have to be the same diameter as the thickness of the wood.

First, obtain a piece of hardboard or

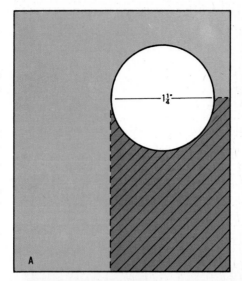

Fig. 1

Figs 1A, 1B. The pattern for the radius template.

Left: Method of using the dowelling jig.

Below left: Detail of leg and rail assembly showing both bolts and dowels.

Mix-and-match living room suite

thin plywood approximately 3in (75mm) square. Make sure that it really is square by checking each edge with the inside of a try square.

With a brace and 1¼in bit, carefully drill a hole in the top half of the square, slightly right of centre, as in Fig. 1A. The actual placing of the hole is not critical, so an approximation will do. Clean out the inside of the hole with fine glasspaper to ensure that there are no jagged edges.

The shaped portion of the square is cut away (Fig. 1A) with a trimming knife or fine toothed tenon saw to produce the template illustrated in Fig. 1B.

A hole template

The holes to take securing bolts must be drilled with precision, and for this reason a template must be made to ensure that the positions of the bolt holes for the legs and rails will match.

To make the template you will require two pieces of hardboard or thin plywood, at least 2in or 50mm longer and wider than a 'long' leg member; sufficient 1in × 1in (25mm × 25mm) battening to fit around three edges as in Fig. 2; panel pins and adhesive.

Lay one piece of hardboard on a flat surface and place one of the long legs on it. Cut and fit three lengths of batten round one long edge and both ends as in Fig. 2. Glue and nail the battening in position. Place the other piece of hardboard over the battening and nail and glue to complete the template body.

You now have an 'envelope' into which long or short leg members, or the end of a rail, will fit. Trim the hardboard flush with the outside edges of the battening.

The next step is to mark out two sets of holes. First ensure that the 'open' side of the template is absolutely flush with the edge of a long leg member placed inside it, so that accurate measurements can be taken.

Mark out the position of the holes as illustrated in Fig. 2, then carefully drill the holes. If you do not wish to repeat the marking process you can lay a sheet of paper over the first set of marks, outline the hole positions, and transfer the paper along to position the next set of holes.

It is absolutely essential that the holes are drilled at right angles to the surface of the hardboard. If possible a vertical drill stand should be used for the job. If this is not possible align the drill bit with a try

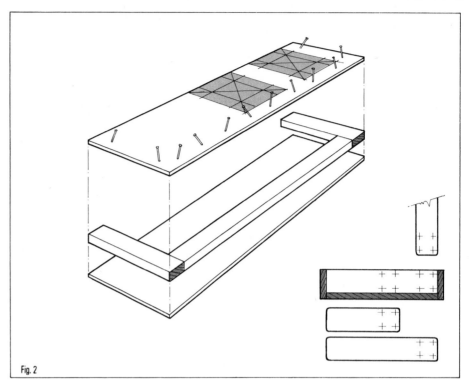

Fig. 2

Fig 2. The drill hole template and its method of use.

square (see Techniques section).

Making a dowelling jig

A dowelling jig must be made to ensure that the dowel rods are accurately and consistently placed. The complete dowel jig assembly is shown in Fig. 3.

The base is constructed from either blockboard or plywood about ¾in (19mm) thick and 30in (762mm) square, and 2in × 1in (50mm × 25mm) battening. It is essential that the support marked 'A' in Fig. 3 is of the same thickness as the leg or rail members of the furniture.

Cut the battens to length and mark out their positions on the base board as detailed in Fig. 3. Glue and pin the battens in position.

The guide block 'B' correctly positions the overlap of the rails 'E', and also guides the drill bit for the dowel holes. This block should be made from hardwood—the harder the better—and is hinged to block 'D' with a 2in (50mm) back-flap hinge. This allows accumulated sawdust to be removed from the jig between drillings. When the jig is being used it should be screwed or cramped to the working surface.

Having completed the bolt hole template and the dowelling jig, you can start on the construction of the furniture. First

decide whether you want to build the 'formal' suite or the 'dovetail' suite the construction outline of which is in Fig. 8.

Place the lengths of timber for assembling one unit of furniture to one side, and examine these for 'matching'. This is done to ensure that all timber surfaces that can easily be seen—such as the outside faces of legs or rails—harmonize with one another. For instance, the leg timbers might come with a prominent grain on one side, and little or no grain on the other, which could present a jumbled visual appearance if fitted at random. Mark the 'inside' of such timbers lightly with a pencil to identify them.

Cutting the timber

Cut all lengths and right-angles accurately to their final dimensions. This is easily achieved by nailing three lengths of batten around the edges of a leg so that it forms a three-sided stop. Next, construct a 'bridge' that will exactly span the leg from side to side; this will require two short pieces of batten, and one piece sufficiently long to span the width of the leg and be nailed securely on to the two shorter battens. The whole assembly can be made in a few minutes. The bridge is held in place by a cramp at the correct distance along the leg, rail or arm, and will enable you to cut several lengths of timber to the same length while guiding the tenon saw blade at right-angles.

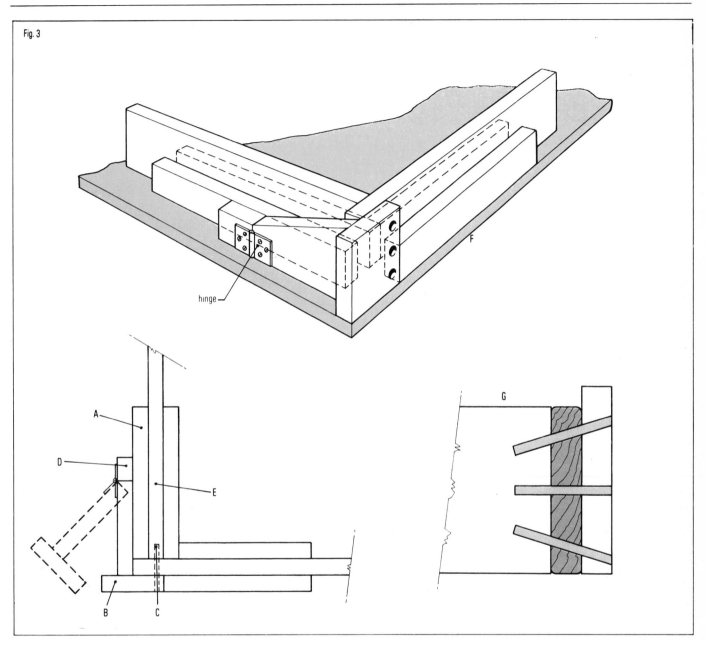

Fig. 3

hinge

A

D

E

B

C

G

F

Below: The construction of the jig is quite simple.

Fig 3. The cross rail dowelling jig. Again, care is required to ensure a good fit.

Using a try square and marking knife, mark one leg, rail (and arm if required), to the correct length. Do this carefully to ensure that you do not make a mistake —you can measure as many times as you like, but you can cut only once!

The cutting should be done with a fine toothed tenon saw with at least 14 points to the inch.

Radiusing

Radiusing consists of rounding the corners of timber to eliminate sharp edges. It is done here to soften the lines of the furniture which, by design, tends to be angular in appearance. The radius, in this case, is carried out to the extent that only the corners are rounded off, not the complete edge.

While it is a simple technique, radiusing requires a certain amount of skill and care if you are to avoid bumpy, undulating edges. If you have not done this before you should either get your timber merchant to supply the timber ready radiused—this will cost more and not all merchants will do it—or practise on some spare pieces of wood until you get the hang of it.

To radius by hand you will need a marking gauge, ½in (13mm) bevel edged chisel, hammer, smoothing plane, block plane, fine toothed flat file, and grade 0

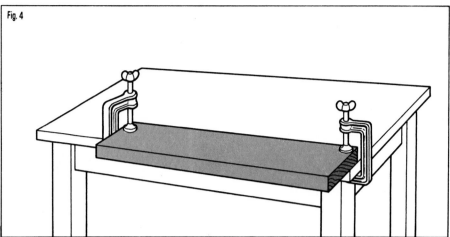

Fig. 4

Above: The corners of each leg and rail must be rounded using a block plane or Surform.

Fig 4. Each component must be clamped to a bench for radiusing.

glasspaper.

Set the marking gauge at $\frac{1}{4}$in (6mm) and run a *light* line at this depth along the edge of each piece of timber, including the ends. Repeat this by drawing another line, in between the first line and the edge, setting the marking gauge at $\frac{5}{32}$in (4mm).

Place one piece of timber in a wood vice so that one long edge is upwards. If you do not have a wood vice, the piece can be cramped to a table top, Fig. 4, but in this case the edge will be placed horizontally, which is slightly more inconvenient as you will have to turn the timber over to radius the other edge.

With the smoothing plane, chamfer the corners of one long edge down to the $\frac{5}{32}$in line. Do not forget to plane with the grain, not against it, and make sure that your strokes are long and even to prevent the radius from being irregularly shaped and bumpy. Repeat this along the corner of the opposite edge. You should now have a piece with flat bevels on both edges.

Now, still using the smoothing plane, round the same corners down to the $\frac{1}{4}$in line. Use a very light, smooth stroke for this because if you plane deeper than the line you will have to end up rounding the edges completely. Alternatively, a router may be used fitted with a special carbide tip.

When you have radiused the long edges of all the timbers, finish off the work with the fine glasspaper.

Next, you will have to radius the ends,

which is slightly more difficult because you are working with end grain, and this is liable to splinter or split much more easily.

Lay the length of timber down on the bench or table top and, with the hammer and chisel, take a triangle of wood off the tip of each end corner down to the first marked line.

With the block plane, chamfer all round the end, down to the first line. As you are working on end grain, do not plane along the line as you did with the side edges because the wood will only splinter. Plane starting from each end towards the middle. Check with the template that the curvature is uniform. If it is, continue with the block plane, chamfering down to the second line all round. After a final check with the template, glasspaper down to a fine finish.

Applying a protective coat

At this stage it is best to apply a protective coating so that any stains or marks that occur as the result of working can easily be wiped off. For economy, dilute the coating. A varnish consisting of clear polyurethane and turpentine or turpentine substitute in the proportions of 1:1 is perfectly adequate. Rub off all pencil marks and finger marks first, and wait for the coating to dry thoroughly before starting work again.

Drilling bolt holes

Mark out the positions of all the bolt holes with something that is easily erased, such as chalk. Now run through a 'trial assembly', to ensure that the bolt holes are in the correct positions. When you are sure that all the pieces have been marked in the correct places, put each piece in

turn in the drill template and mark each drill hole position positively, with an awl or a drill bit, through the template holes.

Drill the holes for the bolts through each marked position. It is essential that the holes are drilled through at exactly right angles and for this you will need a vertical drill stand. It is possible to drill the holes by hand, but great care must be taken to ensure accurate alignment.

Next, counterbore the tee nut and screw cup recesses. The depths to which the recesses are taken will depend on the type of bolt and nut used. And of course the counterbore bit, in each case, should be of a diameter equal to either the nut or cup, whichever is being used.

Dowelling preparation

The dowels are drilled and inserted in dovetail fashion, as in Fig. 3G. Once again, mark the intended dowel hole positions with chalk and 'trial assemble' the unit. It will be even easier this time because you can insert the bolts—tightening them gently by hand—to hold part of the unit together.

Insert each piece of timber in turn in the dowelling jig and drill holes through the *outside* timbers only. Note that the internal holes—which in all cases are drilled in the edge or end grain—are drilled when the unit is being assembled. If you drill both external and internal dowel holes together, it is almost certain that they will not match the bolt holes exactly when assembling, and necessitate some ugly alterations.

The dowelling rods must now be slightly chamfered. This consists of planing a 'flat' along the length of the rods. The chamfer allows air and excess glue to be forced out of the dowel holes when the dowel is being inserted. If this is not done, it will be impossible to insert the dowel to the full depth because of the excess glue.

Cut the dowelling into lengths of 2¾in (70mm). Then, to facilitate the insertion of each dowel, radius or 'round' one end. The method is the same as sharpening a pencil and can be carried out with a trimming knife or block plane.

Assembly

Place a dab of adhesive in all the screw cup holes and insert the screw cups. Insert the four bolts through the two timbers for one of the joints and tighten down with your fingers the pronged tee nuts on the ends of the bolts. Then screw them in fully. Repeat this for all the lapped joints. You will now have several parts of the unit ready, and these have to be butt-jointed with the dowelling.

Position two of these parts so that they are ready for drilling the dowel holes. This is quite simple because they will be at right angles to one another. Now cramp the corner together as shown in Fig. 6; the near end of the clamp, pressing on the surface containing the dowel holes, will be fixed directly over the middle dowel hole. When the assembly has been cramped firmly, place the drill bit in one of the exposed dowel holes and drill through into the second timber. Repeat this on the other hole. You have now drilled the holes for the dowels that actually 'dovetail' towards the middle dowel. Smear some adhesive round the dowels, and put some of it into the dowel holes. Tap the two dowels in position. There will be a small portion of dowel protruding but ignore it at this stage—it will be planed down later.

Having completed the dowelling for the outside holes, you can remove the clamp. Now drill and fit the dowel for the centre hole. This procedure is repeated for all the dowelled joints.

When the glue has set, fix the support battens around the inside of the framework to take the seat base plywood. For the conventional chairs these battens are positioned at an angle on the side rails from ⅜in (9mm) below the front edge to ½in (13mm) above the bottom edge of the

Fig 5A. Exploded view of the chair unit.

Fig 5B. Exploded view of the corner unit of the suite. The seats of these units must be mounted level in contrast to the elevated front edge of the main seat units.

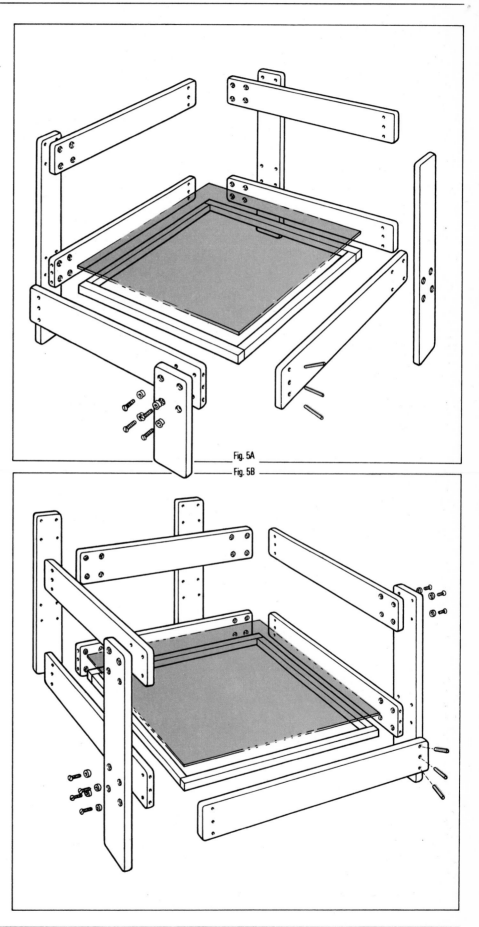

Fig. 5A

Fig. 5B

back rail, as shown in Fig. 9. For the corner chairs the battens are parallel with the rails. Drill and countersink the battens, then glue and screw them into place.

The battens for the table top must be fixed exactly the thickness of the table top below the top of the rails. You can either measure the position, or you can cut the top to size, place it face down on a flat surface and turn the unit frame upside down placing it over the table top; the whole unit will now be upside down, and the top of the table will be level with the top rim of the table frame. You can now measure and fit the battening from the underneath.

Finishing

Plane the protruding dowelling down carefully to prevent marking the timber, and finish off with glasspaper.

Smooth all the remaining surfaces with grade 0 glasspaper and wipe all over with a cloth dampened with turpentine to remove any dust. Then go over the timber with fine steel wool and wipe again with the cloth.

For the final finish use wax and polish, a polyurethane varnish, or paint. Allow varnish or paint to dry thoroughly before fitting domes of silence or similar coverings for the bolt heads.

Upholstery

The final touch is added to your suite with the construction of seat, back and side cushions for upholstery. The style of the suite is such that it blends with most modern fabric patterns.

The cushions for the suite can be made in two ways. If the filling is wrapped round the foam biscuit before covering, you will end up with deep, pliant cushions. This is the type that has been made here. But if the Dacron is omitted and the foam used on its own, the cushions will be firmer, with more pronounced edges—and cheaper to make.

Materials

It is important that the foam biscuit for the cushions is of the correct type. A foam cushion for seating should be firmer, or denser, at the inner core with a softer exterior. The thickness of the foam depends on which type of cushion you are making. If you are adding a Dacron filling, then foam 3in (75mm) thick will be quite adequate; but if you are not using any additional filling, the foam must

Fig 6. The corners of the units must be clamped and the outer dowels inserted first. When these are dry the clamps are removed and the remaining dowel installed.

Fig 7. Detail of the construction of the corners and a plan view of the suite unit illustrating the staggered legs.

Fig 8. Plan view of the completed suite.

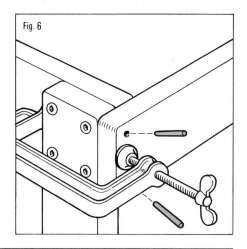

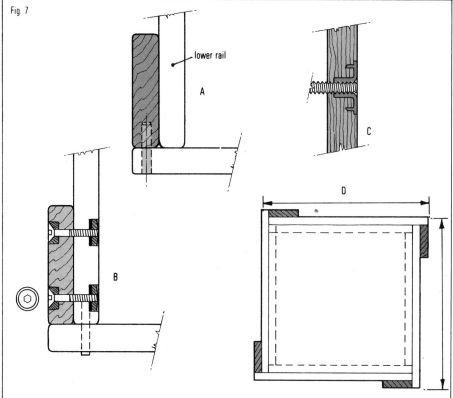

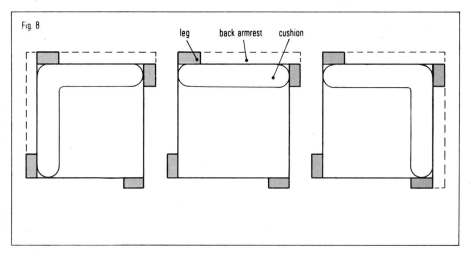

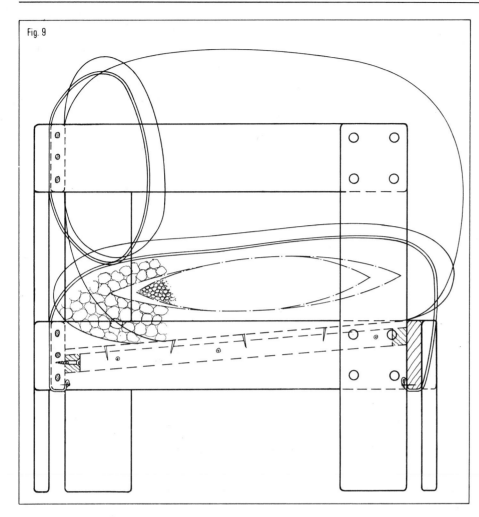

Fig. 9

Fig 9. Side elevation of the chair. Note that the battens supporting the seat must be fixed 1in (25mm) above the bottom of the rails at the back. The method of attaching the seat panel is also shown — the canted nails provide a better purchase on the surrounding batten.

be around 4¼in (108mm) thick.

The Dacron filling is made specifically for upholstery and is sold in sheets, something like a giant roll of cotton wool. It can be obtained from many large stores.

Piping cord will be required for running a piping seam round the joins. Buy size 1½ or 2; you will need 8ft (243.8cm) per cushion plus 10 per cent margin.

The cushions are mainly held in place by straps, which can be made from the same material as the main covering or from any strapping or webbing that you think will match or contrast well.

Buttons are used on some of the upholstery shown here. These can be ornamental or plain buttons chosen for a specific effect; or they can be covered with the main covering material. If you wish the buttons to be covered, buy the bases and cover them yourself, or ask the shop where you purchase the buttons if they can arrange to have this done.

The back rest and side cushions should be fastened to the frames—especially if you are going to omit the straps—to stop them from slipping out of place. There are several methods of doing this, such as carpet snap fasteners, or Velcro tape.

A final covering can be made from any type of fabric, but it is best to use a soft fabric such as velvet or linen if you are covering the foam with Dacron; or a firmer material such as denim if you are not adding the Dacron.

Preparing the foam

If the foam biscuits are to be covered with Dacron filling, then they will only need to be cut into squares or rectangles of a suitable size. But if the Dacron is not being used, the edges of the biscuits should be rounded in order to prevent the appearance from being chunky and angular.

Cutting should be done between two pieces of hardboard overlapping the edge of a table or work bench as shown in Fig. 10. The hardboard must be wide enough to spread any pressure evenly over the foam. Short strips of hardboard will not allow you to hold the foam securely over the whole area, and will tend to make you exert too much pressure at the edge, which will result in concave edges after being cut. This effect is shown in Fig. 11.

If a curved or irregular shape has to be cut, the hardboard should be tied through as in Fig. 12. This will enable you to handle the complete 'sandwich' as a unit instead of three separate pieces which keep drifting out of place.

A felt pen is ideal for marking the surfaces of the foam, and the best tool for cutting it is an electric domestic carving knife. Failing this a hacksaw can be used—with or without the saw frame. If you use a hacksaw frame, ensure that the blade is set at 90 degrees to the frame.

Shaping the edge is easily done by spreading contact ('impact') adhesive along the edges, then folding the ends towards the middle as shown in Fig. 14.

Before you do this, check with your supplier to ensure that the adhesive you use will have no adverse effect on the foam. Some adhesives will dissolve certain foams.

Padding the foam

If the foam is to be covered with filling, to estimate the quantity required, measure the length and width of a cushion and add the thickness of the foam to each measurement. In this case, your 24in x 24in x 3in (610mm x 610mm x 75mm) foam will require filling 27in x 27in (686mm x 686mm) and you will need two such pieces for each cushion. Lay the pieces along each side of the foam with the edges slightly overlapping the edges of the foam and then sew it along the join.

Making the cushion cover

For the length, measure the cushion

Figs 10-14. The method of cutting the foam for the cushions. The cutting should be done between two pieces of hardboard overlapping the edge of a table or work bench.

length along the inside of the frame. To this measurement add 4in (100mm) to allow for the swell of the cushion and an extra 1in (25mm) for the seams. For the depth, measure the depth of the frame and add 4in plus 1in as before. This will give you one panel. You will need two panels for each cushion.

Lay the fabric out on a table. Sometimes this selvedge will cause the edges of the material to wrinkle or pucker, in which case the selvedge should be

carefully cut away. This will enable the material to lie flat.

Make sure that the bottom edge of the material is square at the corners. This is ideally done with a tailor's square, but any similar instrument such as a try square could be used.

Mark out—preferably with a yard-stick—one of the panels, using tailor's chalk. Make sure, if a patterned fabric is being used, that the pattern is the right way up and in the centre of the pieces to

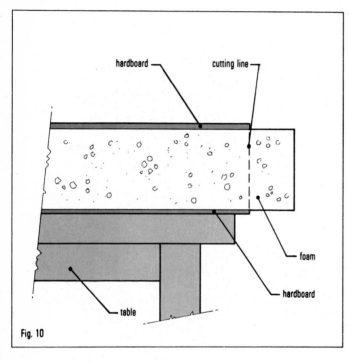

Fig. 10

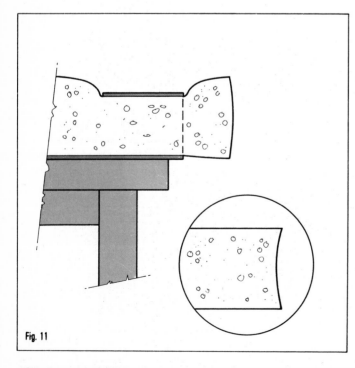

Fig. 11

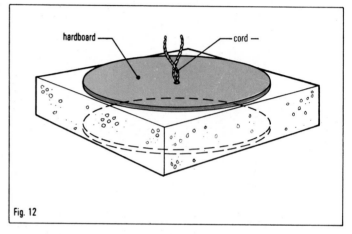

Fig. 12

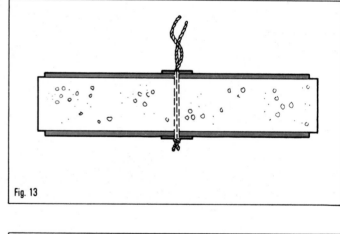

Fig. 13

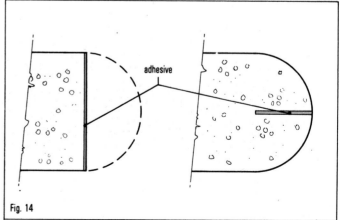

Fig. 14

be cut. Lay one panel on the table. Starting from the top left hand corner, measure 2in or 50mm inwards along the horizontal edge and mark with chalk. Repeat this down the vertical edge. Draw a chalk line between these marks and cut along the line with scissors. This will snip off the corner of the panel. Each corner of both panels must be cut off in the same way.

These corners are now stitched with a running stitch (or a long stitch if using a sewing machine) to form the gathered corners.

Piping will have to be done on a sewing machine. Cut $\frac{1}{4}$in (6mm) strips of material on the bias (diagonally) across the material. Join these pieces end to end using $\frac{1}{2}$in (12mm) seams. Press the seams with an iron.

Fold the piping strips evenly, placing piping cord inside the fold. Sew the cord into the piping strip (using a piping foot or one-sided foot on the machine)

Below: The suite may be finished in either clear or coloured polyurethane. The cushions are attached underneath with snap fasteners.

Mix~and~match living room suite

until you have enough piping to go round all four sides of one of the panels. Sew this piping strip round the edges of one panel, starting at the centre of the back. Join the piping on the right side of the material using $\frac{1}{4}$in (6mm) seams, butting up the cord to make a neat finish.

Place the second panel on top of the piped cushion panel, and starting at one of the back corners, join together with $\frac{1}{2}$in (12mm) seams making sure that gathered corners come together. Leave the back edge open for insertion of the foam.

Straps and fixings

For the strap fastenings, use curtain heading tape for contrast, or make up matching straps by covering the tape with the cushion material. Heading tape can be obtained in various colours and widths. For a 'different' strap, you could even try leather strip.

The straps are joined underneath, or behind, the furniture, using an ordinary buckle, or Velcro tape, or any other fastening that is convenient.

Where the straps cross, as with the seat cushions, fix them to the centre of the cushion with a button threaded though the straps and cushion with nylon tufting twine. Fasten it underneath with another button (Fig. 13).

At any point where the cushion should be more permanently fixed to the frame to stop it moving, carpet snap fasteners can be fixed to the frame and stitched to the fabric. A better alternative is Velcro tape, which can be stitched to the cushion and glued to the frame with a contact adhesive.

Parts List

Part	Description	Quantity	Length	Cut length to allow for waste	Size
CORNER CHAIR					
Legs	⎫	3	$24\frac{7}{8}$ (627mm)	$25\frac{3}{8}$ (645mm)	4 × 1 ⎫
	⎪	1	$11\frac{3}{4}$ (298mm)	$12\frac{1}{4}$ (311mm)	4 × 1 ⎬ (102mm ×
Rails/arms	⎬ hardwood	6	26 (660mm)	$26\frac{1}{2}$ (674mm)	4 × 1 ⎭ 25mm)
Seat supports	⎪	2	$24\frac{3}{4}$ (629mm)	$25\frac{1}{4}$ (642mm)	1 × 1 ⎫ (25mm ×
	⎭	2	$22\frac{7}{8}$ (581mm)	$23\frac{3}{8}$ (594mm)	1 × 1 ⎭ 25mm)
Seat	plywood	1	$24\frac{3}{4}$ sq (629mm sq)	25 sq (635mm sq)	$\frac{3}{8}$ (9mm)
Dowels	hardwood dowelling	18	$2\frac{1}{2}$ (64mm)	$2\frac{3}{4}$ (70mm)	$\frac{3}{8}$ (9mm) diameter
Bolts	GKN 2025	24	$1\frac{1}{2}$ (38mm)		$\frac{1}{4}$ (6mm) BSW
Nuts	BSW pronged 'T' Nuts	24			$\frac{1}{4}$ (6mm) BSW
Screw-cups	M12 countersunk	24			No.12
Screws	Twinfast Pozidriv	12	$1\frac{1}{2}$ (38mm)		No.8
BACKED CHAIR					
Legs	⎫	2	$24\frac{7}{8}$ (627mm)	$25\frac{3}{8}$ (645mm)	4 × 1 ⎫
	⎪	2	$11\frac{3}{4}$ (298mm)	$12\frac{1}{4}$ (311mm)	4 × 1 ⎬ (25mm ×
Rails/arms	⎬ hardwood	5	26 (660mm)	$26\frac{1}{2}$ (674mm)	4 × 1 ⎭ 102mm)
Seat supports	⎪	2	$24\frac{3}{4}$ (629mm)	$25\frac{1}{4}$ (642mm)	1 × 1 ⎫ (25mm ×
	⎭	2	$22\frac{7}{8}$ (581mm)	$22\frac{3}{8}$ (594mm)	1 × 1 ⎭ 25mm)
Seat	plywood	1	$24\frac{3}{4}$ sq (629mm sq)	25 sq (635mm sq)	$\frac{3}{8}$ (9mm)
Dowels	hardwood dowelling	15	$2\frac{1}{2}$ (64mm)	$2\frac{3}{4}$ (70mm)	$\frac{3}{8}$ (9mm) diameter
Bolts	GKN 2025	20	$1\frac{1}{2}$ (38mm)		$\frac{1}{4}$ (6mm) BSW
'T' Nuts	BSW pronged 'T' Nuts	20			$\frac{1}{4}$ (6mm) BSW
Screw-cups	M12 countersunk	20			No.12
Screws	Twinfast Pozidriv	12	$1\frac{1}{2}$ (38mm)		No.8
STOOL/COFFEE TABLE					
Legs	⎫	4	$11\frac{3}{4}$ (298mm)	$12\frac{1}{4}$ (311mm)	4 × 1 ⎫ (102mm ×
Rails	⎬ hardwood	4	26 (660mm)	$26\frac{1}{2}$ (674mm)	4 × 1 ⎭ 25mm)
Seat/top supports	⎭	2	$24\frac{3}{4}$ (629mm)	$25\frac{1}{4}$ (642mm)	1 × 1 ⎫ (25mm ×
		2	$22\frac{7}{8}$ (581mm)	$23\frac{3}{8}$ (594mm)	1 × 1 ⎭ 25mm)
Seat/top	plywood	1	$24\frac{3}{4}$ sq (629mm sq)	25 sq (635mm sq)	$\frac{3}{8}$ (9mm)
Dowels	hardwood dowelling	12	$2\frac{1}{2}$ (64mm)	$2\frac{3}{4}$ (70mm)	$\frac{3}{8}$ (9mm) diameter
Bolts	GKN 2025	16	$1\frac{1}{2}$ (38mm)		$\frac{1}{4}$ (6mm) BSW
Nuts	BSW pronged 'T' Nuts	16			$\frac{1}{4}$ (6mm) BSW
Screw-cups	M12 countersunk	16	$1\frac{1}{2}$ (38mm)		No.12
Screws	Twinfast Pozidriv	12	$1\frac{1}{2}$ (38mm)		No.8

Round table

There are only two simple types of joint used in the construction of this round table. The most complicated part is the top. Even this is not difficult if you use the right tools. You will require three 5ft (1.5m) sash cramps to clamp the five table top timbers together while the glue is setting, and four G cramps for the main frame joints. If you do not own

or cannot borrow sash cramps, you can probably hire them.

Materials
The table top shown here is made from Parana pine, which was chosen for its attractive grain, but there are many other woods you could use. If you wish to paint the finished table you should use a

cheaper wood such as white pine. The dimensions of the parts are given in the cutting list.

The top is screwed to the frame underneath with No. 8 steel screws. The joints should be glued with PVA adhesive, but only if the unit is to be used exclusively indoors. If it will be used in the open, or somewhere where it could get damp, a

Round table

waterproof adhesive such as a urea formaldehyde type should be used.

For cutting out the circular table top, you will need an integral power jig-saw, or a jig saw attachment for your power drill.

Construction details

The support structure—which in this case means all the timbers below the table top—consists of two interlocking frames as shown in Fig. 1C. Each frame has two horizontal members and two vertical members. Each horizontal piece has a cross halving joint cut out of the centre of its narrow edge, flanked by two more halving joints cut out of its wide face (see Fig. 1D). The pairs of horizontal members intersect at the centre cross halving; the additional cut outs are to accept the vertical legs, which are halved at each end to form the joints.

The top is formed by glueing five pieces of timber together to form a square approximately 48in (1.220m) each way, from which the circular top is then cut.

With regard to the top, when ordering these five pieces, ensure that the timber is 'dressed'. Dressed timber is supplied machine-planed, and this is essential if the table top is to have an absolutely level surface and the joined edges are to match. If you try to do this job yourself, you are almost certain to end up with a bumpy table top; furthermore, it is virtually impossible to hand plane the edges so that they will fit exactly to give an absolutely even join.

Making the top

The table top is made from wood 1¾in (45mm) thick and is a circle 48in (1.220m) in diameter when finished. You will not be able to purchase a plank as wide as this, so five 10in (254mm) wide planks should be butted together and glued along their long edges.

First, arrange the planks side by side on a flat surface so that a 48in x 50in (1.220m x 1.25m) (approx) rectangle is formed. With dressed timber, the edges should butt against one another with no unsightly gaps in between, but if there are some high spots on the edges of the planks, carefully plane these down. Be very careful when doing this; set the blade very fine and make only a stroke or two at a time to avoid taking off too much wood. Otherwise, you may have to take off the whole edge to level it off again. If the high spots are only slight, buff them

down with fine glasspaper wrapped round a block of wood. Unless the top is to be painted, arrange these planks so that the grain forms an attractive pattern. Remember, this is the surface that will be constantly in view.

When you have finished fitting the planks together in a 'dry run' mark all the joints in sequence with one pencil line across the first joint and two across the second joint and so on, so that they can be lined up again in the correct order.

Next, glue the planks together, ensuring that all the joint marks line up exactly. Apply the three sash cramps using a small piece of wood at each cramp-shoe to prevent the cramp marking the timber.

Apply the glue and cramp the pieces together. Spread adhesive evenly along the edges of the planks that are to butt, and cramp them together carefully. Place the two first cramps near each end of the planks with their bars running along and touching under the surface of the planks. Place the third cramp near the middle of the planks with its bar running over the top surface of the planks. In this way, the planks are held flat on each side, which prevents them from jack-knifing when the cramps are tightened.

The planks must be completely level to fit together perfectly with what will be the top surface. If one plank is slightly higher than the others, loosen the cramps a little, place a piece of waste wood on the raised plank and bang it with a hammer. This will force the raised plank down without marking the surface.

Re-tighten the cramps and wipe every trace of adhesive from the surface of the planks with a soft damp cloth. If you do not do this thoroughly, any trace of adhesive will show through as a white patch when the wood is eventually varnished.

Allow adequate time for the adhesive to dry, 24 hours is usually enough, but follow the manufacturer's instructions. It is better to be over-cautious than to spoil the job and have to do the work all over again.

The circle of the table top must now be marked out. Do this on the underside of the table top, using a nail, pencil and length of string. Lightly tap a nail about ½in (13mm) into the exact centre of the panel. Tie a length of string to this, let the string out 24in (610mm) and tie the other end round a pencil as near the writing tip as possible. You can now swing the pencil round in a complete

Figs 1A, B, C, D. The construction of the round table basic frame. The construction consists entirely of halving joints as shown in Fig 1F.

Fig 1E. The completed table top.

circle, marking the surface ready for cutting. For cutting the circle out of the glued planks, you will need a power jig saw.

The important part is to ensure that the top is held securely while you are cutting round the line. It must be clamped to a bench or table top with sufficient protruding over the edge to allow you to make a part sweep round the line. Protect the surface with scrap wood blocks. When you have cut the sweep, loosen the cramps and move the top round to a position where you can continue to cut.

When you have cut the circle out, finish the edge with a plane, then glasspaper it down.

Cutting the joints

Check your timber dimensions when setting out the joints because the timber you purchase may not be exactly 2¼in x 1¾in (57mm x 45mm). It will probably be slightly less, so set out all joint recesses by direct marking, using the mating piece of timber for accuracy.

Each horizontal member (or rail) has a cross-halving joint cut at the centre on its narrow edge. This cut-out should be as wide as the thickness of the wood and as deep as half the width.

Next, cut the halving recesses for the legs. These must be the width of the timber, and as deep as half its thickness. One of these is cut on each side of the central cut-out, with a space 2¼in (57mm) between each of the joints as

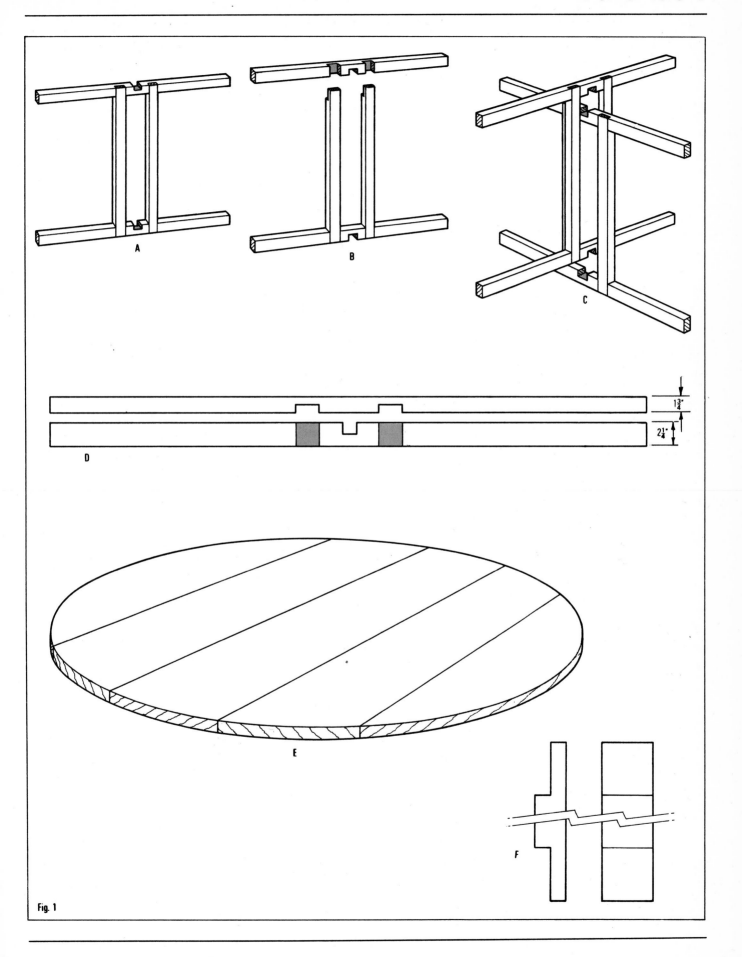

A

B

C

$1\frac{3}{4}"$

$2\frac{1}{4}"$

D

E

F

Fig. 1

shown in Fig. 1D.

Now cut the halving joints in the ends of the legs, following the same direct marking procedure and cutting to the same depth.

Using Fig. 1C as a guide, dry assemble the two frames and interlock them. This will enable you to adjust any of the joints so that the surfaces are absolutely flush. When this has been done, lightly pencil mark the two mating parts of each joint with a number, so that you can re-assemble them in the same order.

Assembling the frames

The construction and fitting sequence for the frames is shown in Fig. 1A-C. Make up the first frame as in A. To do this properly, you need four 'G' cramps, one at each halving joint. Spread adhesive on the surfaces of each halving joint and cramp the joints firmly in position, making sure that the assembly is square by measuring the inside diagonals of the rectangle formed in the centre. Both diagonals should be the same length. If they are not, adjust the frame until they are. Wipe any excess glue from the joints and leave the frame for the adhesive to set.

When the adhesive has set, make up the second frame as shown in Fig. 1B and 1C. First, fit the two legs into the halvings on the bottom rail. When these joints are set, put the assembly in position and glue the cross-halving joint between the two bottom rails. Finally, fit the top rail in place glueing the rail halving and the leg joints at the same time. The base, or leg frame, is now complete.

Fitting the top

The table top is secured to the framework underneath by screws passing through the top horizontal members and into the underside of the top.

Drill countersunk holes at 3in (75mm) intervals from edge to edge through the top horizontal members. The countersunk ends of the holes should be underneath the members. Place the table top on the framework, making sure that it is centred properly—the end of each top member of the leg framework should be the same distance away from the edge of the table top. Mark the position of pilot holes through the holes in the frame using a bradawl. Remove the top, drill the pilot holes, and then replace the top and screw it firmly in position.

Finishing

If you are painting the table remember to use a tough polyurethane paint, particularly on the table top, because it will take a great deal of wear and this is one surface you do not want to look unsightly.

If you have chosen a natural wood finish, you will have to prepare the surface thoroughly so that it does not wear or mark so easily, and at the same time bring out the rich grain of the wood.

Glasspaper all surfaces with grade 0 glasspaper down to a smooth finish using an orbital finishing sander. Then use a soft cloth dampened with turpentine substitute to wipe all surfaces, so as to pick up the fine dust caused by the sander. With a good quality 2in (50mm) brush, sparingly apply a varnish of clear matt polyurethane and turpentine substitute blended 50/50. When dry, rub down again with glasspaper and wipe the surface with the cloth again. Re-coat with the same varnish when it is dry. Smooth it with grade 0 steel wool and apply a final coat of neat polyurethane.

After a few days, the unit can be polished with a soft cloth, and you will be the proud owner of a superb dining table.

Cutting list

Pine

	standard	metric
4 horizontal members	$43 \times 2\frac{1}{4} \times 1\frac{3}{4}$	$1092 \times 57 \times 45$
4 vertical members	$27 \times 2\frac{1}{4} \times 1\frac{3}{4}$	$686 \times 57 \times 45$
5 table top planks	$48 \times 10 \times 1\frac{3}{4}$	$1219 \times 254 \times 45$

You will also require :

16 $3\frac{1}{2}$in (93mm) No.8 flathead wood screws. Adhesive. Varnish and turpentine substitute or paint.

For this project you will need 5ft (1524mm) sash cramps.

The sizes for the members are the finished dimensions and do not include any allowance for waste. The sizes for the table top planks are the dimensions before the pieces have been glued together and the circle cut out.

Table with a rural look

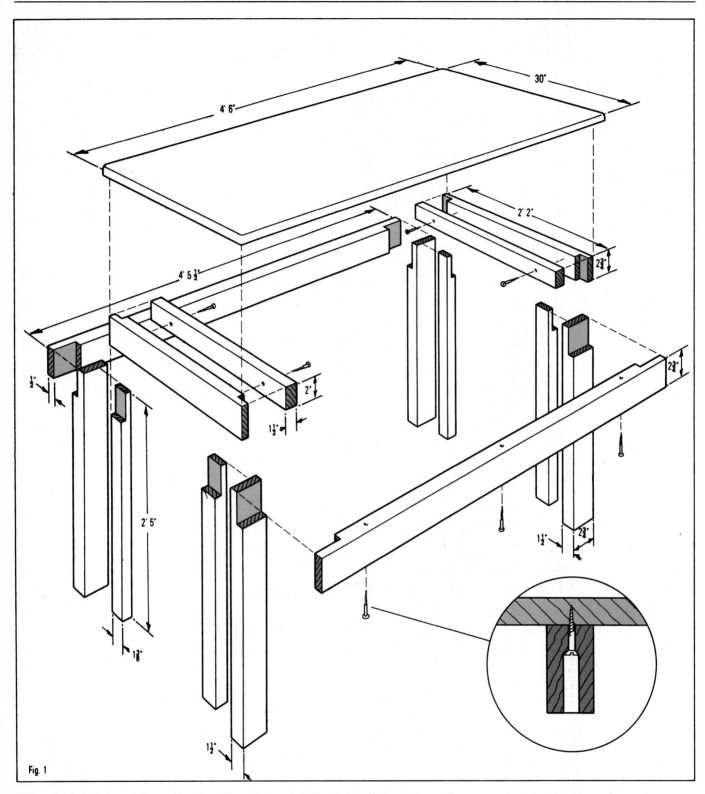

Fig. 1

Fig 1. Exploded view of the rural table. All leg to rail joints are half laps. Each side is constructed as a separate unit and joined at a later stage.

This solidly built furniture will complement any home. The strong grain pattern of the tops gives a hint of old fashioned country charm, blending well with the more modern finish on the legs. The simple construction of the table and benches makes them an attractive proposition to the less experienced wood-

worker. The only jointing involved is the cutting of lap joints.

Materials

The dimensions of the finished components of the table and benches are given in the cutting list. The wood used in the units illustrated is Parana pine, but any softwood with an attractive grain and capable of being sanded to a smooth finish will do.

You will also need some No. 8 steel screws and some glue. If you intend to use the furniture solely indoors, a PVA adhesive, is ideal, but a waterproof glue should be used if the table and benches are likely to be used outdoors.

Construction

The main feature of these units is a compound leg, stronger than the usual type of kitchen table leg but lighter and hence more attractive looking. In these instructions, the larger component is described as the 'outer leg' and the smaller as the 'inner leg'.

The two rails that run parallel to the long sides of the table and bench tops are half-lap jointed to the outer legs. The rails that run parallel to the short sides are half-lap jointed to the inner legs, and this U-shaped construction is fixed in place between the long rails and the outer legs. Fig. 6 shows a cross section of the finished legs.

The rails and legs are screwed to the underside of the benches and table. On the table only, extra support for the top is provided by two bearers which run parallel to the two short rails and are butted against them.

The cross-sections of the wood in the legs and rails of the table are exactly the same as those used for the legs and rails of the benches.

Making the top

The top of the table is made from wood ¾in (19mm) thick and has a finished width of 30in (762mm). You will not be able to buy a single plank of this width so three planks, each 10in (254mm) wide, are butted and glued along their long edges. You will find that 10in (254mm) is not a standard width of planed-all-round (PAR) (sometimes called 'dressed' or gauged) timber; so-called 10in (254mm) board starts out 10in (254mm) wide when rough sawn, but is reduced in the planing process. So you will have to buy wider boards and, for reasons which follow, it might be wise to buy five 12in (305mm) planks—three for the table top and one for each bench top.

The finished width of the bench tops is 11¾in (298mm). You should be able to obtain single planks of this width, but as 12in (305mm) planed-all-round timber is not much larger in fact than 11¾in you

will have little margin for planing. So select your pieces carefully at the timber yard. If you have difficulty you can butt two planks of half this width along their long edges, but this obviously takes longer and does not give so neat a finish.

The first step in making the table top is to cut the planks slightly longer than the finished length—about 1in (25mm) too long. Then lay the planks together with their long edges touching. Since the top is later finished in clear polyurethane, choose the face of each plank which has the most attractive grain and lay them out to make the best pattern as a whole. Do this on a dead-flat surface to make sure that any cupping or bowing in the pieces is in the same direction; otherwise you will have difficulty obtaining a smooth top surface. Then mark the joints lightly with a pencil (Fig. 3) to ensure that the right edges are butted and that you do not accidentally reverse one of the planks.

Now plane exactly square the edges that are to butt. Use a long plane to do this—a short smoothing plane will simply follow the contours of the wood (Fig. 2). Check that the planed edges are perfectly flat and level by drawing a straight-edge along their surfaces.

The next step is to glue the planks together, using either a PVA adhesive or a waterproof glue. To do this you will need three sash cramps and some waste blocks of wood. So that you can quickly join the planks once the adhesive has been applied, pre-set the cramps to the correct length by cramping the planks together dry. Place the waste blocks between the shoes of the cramps and the edges of the planks. This will spread the cramping pressure more evenly and protect the edges of the planks from damage.

Now glue can be applied and the pieces cramped together. To do this, first release the cramps. Spread adhesive evenly on the edges of the planks that are to butt. Cramp them together again. Position one cramp near each end of the planks with their bars running along the under surface of the planks. Place the third cramp near the middle of the planks with its bar running across the top surface of the planks

The planks must fit together perfectly with their surfaces completely level. If one plank is slightly higher than the others, loosen the cramps a little. Place a waste piece of wood on the raised plank and bang it with a hammer. This

Fig. 2

Fig 2. When planing the planks for the top a jack plane will give better results.

will force the raised plank downwards so that its surface is flush with the other planks.

Now re-tighten the cramps. Wipe every trace of adhesive from the faces of the planks, using a soft damp cloth. Any adhesive left on the surface will show as a white patch under the polyurethane finish that is applied later.

Check that there are no irregularities in the planks by running your finger along the joins. Allow adequate time for the adhesive to dry. A day is usually long enough, but follow the manufacturer's instructions. It is better to be over-cautious than spoil the job and have to do the work all over again.

When the adhesive has dried, the top can be cut exactly to length. Square a line near the end of the planks right across the top face. The finished length of the table top is 4ft 6in (1371mm) and the finished length of the bench tops is 3ft 11½in (1207mm). Measure these distances on the relevant pieces from the squared line. Square lines through these new marks.

The next steps are to saw just outside the marked lines, then plane away the waste. You must be careful, however, not to damage the corners of the planks, which is always a danger when planing end grain. There are three ways of doing this.

The first method is to cramp a waste block of wood to the end to which you will be planing. The top of the waste block should be level with the top edges

Table with a rural look

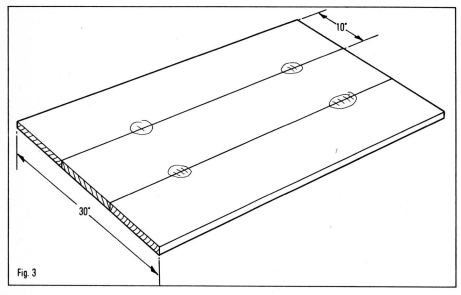

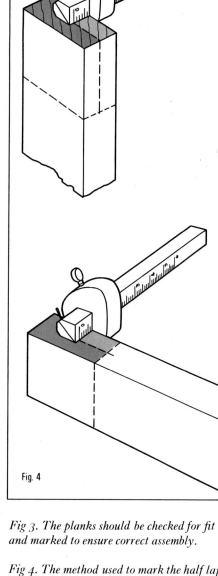

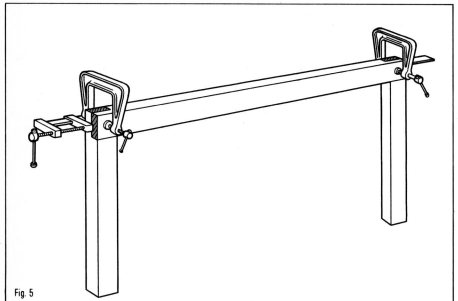

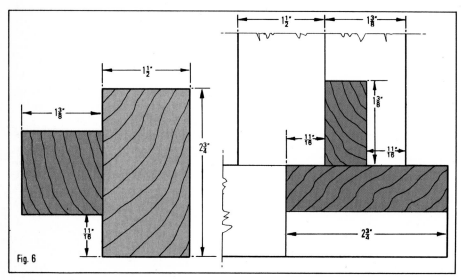

Fig 3. The planks should be checked for fit and marked to ensure correct assembly.

Fig 4. The method used to mark the half lap joints for the legs and cross rails.

Fig 5. The legs and cross rails are clamped together using two G cramps and one sash cramp.

Fig 6. The way in which the legs and cross rails joint together.

of the planks so that any damage that is done when planing will be to the waste block. The second method involves planing from each end of the planks towards their centre. The third method is to chisel away the waste at one corner for up to 1in (25mm) and then plane from the opposite corner. But you must be careful, when chiselling, not to cut away any wood below the squared line.

Using one of these methods, finish the top to the required size with the ends perfectly square.

Jointing the rails and legs
The thickness of the legs and rails of the table is the same as that of the rails and legs of the benches. The method described below of making one half-lap joint, therefore, applies to all of them.

Joint the outer legs and rails first. Cut the rails 1in (25mm) oversize and mark out the positions of the joints on both pieces at the same time. Place the rails together face-side to face-side, then square a line across one end and, from that line, measure the length of the rail and square a line across at the other end of the timber. From these lines set out the width of the legs, using the prepared timber as a pattern. Separate the rails, mark the face sides and square the lines around all sides.

Set a marking gauge to exactly half the thickness of the timber and working from the face-side score a line on the edge of the rail and across the end grain (Fig. 4) to indicate the depth of the halved joint.

Set out the legs in the same way. First, cut them over size and mark the length. Use the rails to set out the width of the joint. Score the depth of the joint with the marking gauge working from the face-side as before. Shade the inside face of the rail joints with a pencil so that you will know this is to be cut out. Then shade or mark with a cross the outside of the leg joint as this will be the waste side.

Cut down the waste side of the line using a tenon saw. Then, score over the pencil joint-line, across the grain, using a handyman's knife and a try-square. Saw down this line to remove the waste. The scored line will give you a neater finish to the shoulders of the joint.

When all the half laps in the long rails have been cut and tried for fit, the rail can be sawn to only $\frac{1}{16}$in (2mm) longer than their finished length at each end. This will be smoothed off later.

The half lap at the top of the legs can now be cut. The method is exactly the same as that for the rails. As each leg is cut, lightly mark with a pencil both the leg and the rail into which it fits, so the components do not get mixed up.

The short rails and inner legs
Now cut the short rails and the inner legs. The rails are the same width and thickness as the long rails—2$\frac{3}{4}$in x 1$\frac{1}{2}$in (70mm x 38mm)—and are a finished length of 2ft 2in (660mm) for the table and 8$\frac{1}{4}$in (209mm) for the bench rails. The inner legs are 1$\frac{3}{8}$in x 1$\frac{1}{2}$in x 2ft 5in (34mm x 38mm x 737mm). These again are jointed together with half-lap joints which are marked out and cut in the manner described with, of course, the necessary adjustment for the different dimensions. Note that the dimension given for the leg length is the finished dimension. At this stage 1in (25mm) waste should be allowed for levelling.

Fixing the legs to the rails
Now the rails and legs can be glued together. Apply adhesive to both faces of the lap joints and push the pieces together. Lightly cramp the two laps at each end together with a G cramp. The G shaped bar should run over the top edge of the rail. Then apply a sash cramp so that the bar of the cramp runs along and parallel to one face of the rail (see Fig. 5). Check with a try square that the angle between the legs and rails are perfectly square and tighten all the cramps. Wipe any excess adhesive from the surfaces of the pieces and allow adequate time for the glue to dry.

When the glue has dried, use a sharp, smoothing plane to remove the small pieces of the lap joints that protrude.

Fixing the frame together
When the legs and rails of the table and benches are of the finished size, the inner legs can be fixed inside the outer legs. The outside face of the inner legs is butted to the inside face of the outer legs. It is essential to work accurately here or the frame will not be square.

First, mark out the correct positions of the inner legs on the insides of the outer legs. The centre of the edge of the inner legs should run along the exact centre of the inside face of the outer legs. In order to find the correct position, first mark a line along the centre of the inside face of the outer legs. Then mark on each side of this line half the thickness of the inner leg $\frac{11}{16}$in (17.5mm). Mark a line through this point parallel with the edge of the legs.

Fix the short rail and leg assembly and the long rail and leg assembly together with adhesive. To ensure that the pieces do not move out of position while the glue is wet, knock panel pins part of the way into the inside face of the outer leg along the two lines that indicate the correct position of the inner legs. Space the pins about 2in (50mm) apart and knock them in at an angle as shown in Fig. 7. This will enable you to remove them more easily when the adhesive has dried.

Now glue the pieces together. Apply adhesive to the face of the inner legs and

Fig 7. Pins are used to align the inside legs.

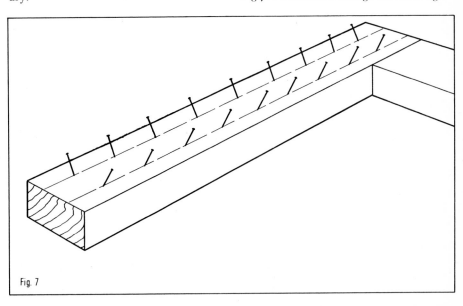

Fig. 7

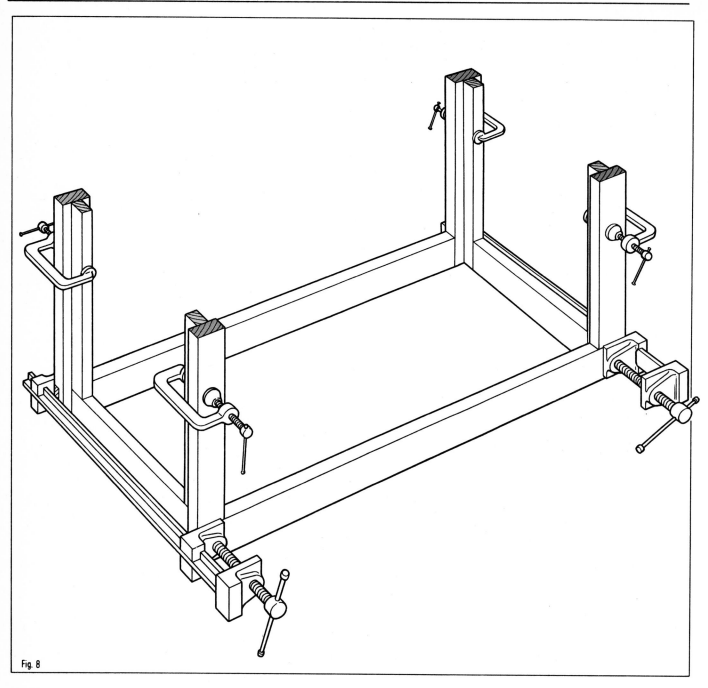

Fig. 8

Fig 8. The finished leg and rail assemblies are glued and clamped together using sash and G cramps.

push the four components of the frame together. Before cramping them, turn the assembly upside down on a perfectly flat surface so that the legs stick up in the air. Use sash cramps along the level of, and parallel to, the rail of the inner leg assembly. Apply only light pressure at first. Then check that the frame is perfectly square and tighten the sash cramps. Use G cramps to cramp the outer legs to the inner legs (Fig. 8). Wipe any excess adhesive from the surfaces of the legs. Allow the adhesive to dry. When the adhesive has dried remove the panel pins. The holes can be filled with wood

filler, but they are not in a conspicuous place.

Finishing the furniture
The frame and legs and the top are finished before the assembly is complete. Sand down all surfaces with glasspaper. Apply a clear polyurethane to the tops of the table and benches. Use several coats, rubbing down the previous coat with steel wool before applying the subsequent coats. The varnish should be applied to both the top surface and the under surface of the tops.

The finish applied to the legs is a matter

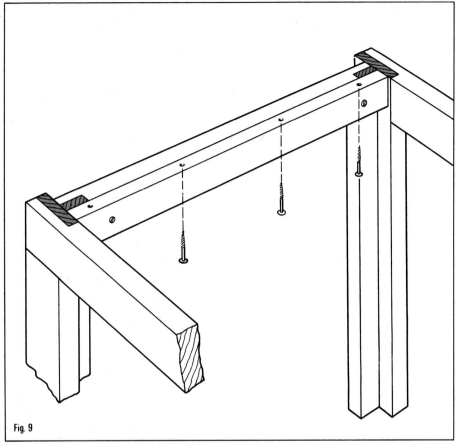

Fig. 9

Fig 9. The table top is screwed to the table via a bearer which fits inside the ends of the table. If the colour of the top is to be different to that of the frame it is advisable to finish both components before screwing together.

Fig 10. Exploded view of the bench. The method of construction is exactly the same as that of the table.

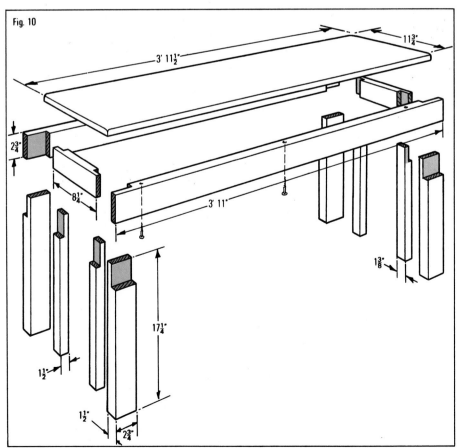

Fig. 10

of taste.

Fixing the frame to the top

The framework of the table and benches is screwed to the tops. They cannot be glued in place first as this will spoil the polyurethane finish—and the two colour finish cannot be applied neatly once the pieces have been fixed.

The frame must be held in its correct position while it is being screwed to the top. This can be done by laying a plank across the bottom edge of the rails and kneeling on it while you fix two screws.

In the case of the benches these first screws can be fixed in the centre of each short rail. For the table, however, the first two screws should be fixed through the long rails, one at each end and diagonally opposite. This is because holes drilled through the bottom edge of the short rails of the table will tend to be conspicuous (this is not, however, the case with the benches). The inner leg assembly of the table is fixed to the top by means of bearers which are screwed to the table top and to the inside face of the short rails.

The frame is fixed to the top with $1\frac{1}{2}$in (38mm) No. 8 countersunk steel screws. The heads of the screws are buried in the rail through a second hole the diameter of the screw head, which should be drilled part of the way into the rail down the first hole. This will do away with the need for unnecessarily long screws and will also eliminate a lot of work.

When drilling through the rails into the top you must be very careful not to cut the holes too deeply. The rails are $2\frac{3}{4}$in (70mm) wide and the tops of both the table and the benches are $\frac{3}{4}$in (19mm) thick. The first drilled holes, therefore, should be about 3in (76mm) deep. To cut these holes to an accurate depth, wrap a piece of coloured sticky tape around the drill this distance from the drill tip. You can then stop drilling as soon as you reach the tape. The same method can be used to drill the countersinking holes, which are the diameter of the screw heads. These should be drilled to a depth of $1\frac{3}{4}$in (44mm).

Mark the positions of the holes on the rails. For the benches use one screw in the centre of each short rail and three along the long rails. Position one centrally and one near each end. For the table use three screws in each long rail, positioned as for the benches. Do not drill any holes in the short rails of the table.

Table top bearers

The next step in the construction of the furniture is to fix bearers to the table top. These measure 2ft$1\frac{3}{4}$in x 2in x $1\frac{1}{2}$in (654mm x 50mm x 38mm) and fixed so that one face butts against the inside face of the short rails of the inner leg assemblies (Fig. 9). Use two 2in (50mm) No. 9 countersunk steel screws to fix the bearers to the short rails. Position the screws about 6in (152mm) from the ends of the bearers and ensure that you do not drill too deeply by using coloured tape around the drill, as previously above. To fix the bearers to the top, use four 2in (50mm) No. 8 countersunk steel screws for each bearer. Position one screw about 2in (50mm) from each end of each bearer and one screw about 7in (180mm) from the first, towards the centre of the bearer.

Cutting the legs to length

This is the final stage in the construction of the table and benches. The legs were originally cut $\frac{1}{2}$in (12mm) too long. You do not have to remove exactly $\frac{1}{2}$in (12mm) provided you cut the right amount of wood from all the legs of each article. It is also likely that at least one of the pieces will wobble when placed on a flat surface.

To cut the legs to an equal length stand the article on a perfectly flat surface. If there is any wobble, caused by one leg being shorter than the other, place waste pieces of wood under the short leg until the piece stands level.

Then take a waste block of wood measuring about 6in x 2in x 1in (152mm x 51mm x 25mm). Drill a hole, slightly less than the diameter of a pencil, through the 1in (25mm) edge. With a mallet knock the pencil through the hole so that about 1in (25mm) of it protrudes. Then lay the waste block on the flat surface so that the pencil is parallel with the floor and its point is touching the leg. Draw a line around the bottom of each leg. Now carefully cut through the legs, around these lines.

Sand the sawn ends smooth with glass-paper, and finally, touch up any damage to the ends of the legs with polyurethane paint or varnish, depending on the finish you have chosen.

Cutting lists

Table

Solid wood	**standard**	**metric**
3 tops	4ft 6in × 10in × $\frac{3}{4}$in	1.37m × 254mm × 19mm
2 long rails	4ft $5\frac{1}{2}$in × $2\frac{3}{4}$in × $1\frac{1}{2}$in	1.36m × 70mm × 38mm
2 short rails	2ft 2in × $2\frac{3}{4}$in × $1\frac{1}{2}$in	660mm × 70mm × 38mm
4 outer legs	2ft 5in × $2\frac{3}{4}$in × $1\frac{1}{2}$in	737mm × 70mm × 38mm
4 inner legs	2ft 5in × $1\frac{1}{2}$in × $1\frac{3}{8}$in	737mm × 38mm × 34mm
2 top bearers	2ft $1\frac{3}{4}$in × 2in × $1\frac{1}{2}$in	654mm × 50mm × 38mm

For each bench

Solid wood		
1 top	3ft $11\frac{1}{2}$in × $11\frac{3}{4}$in × $\frac{3}{4}$in	1.20m × 299mm × 19mm
2 long rails	3ft 11in × $2\frac{3}{4}$in × $1\frac{1}{2}$in	1.19m × 70mm × 38mm
2 short rails	$8\frac{1}{4}$in × $2\frac{3}{4}$in × $1\frac{1}{2}$in	209mm × 70mm × 38mm
4 outer legs	$17\frac{1}{4}$in × $2\frac{3}{4}$in × $1\frac{1}{2}$in	438mm × 70mm × 38mm
4 inner legs	$17\frac{1}{4}$in × $1\frac{1}{2}$in × $1\frac{3}{8}$in	438mm × 38mm × 35mm

These sizes are to the finished dimensions of the table and benches and do not include any allowance for waste.

Dining chairs

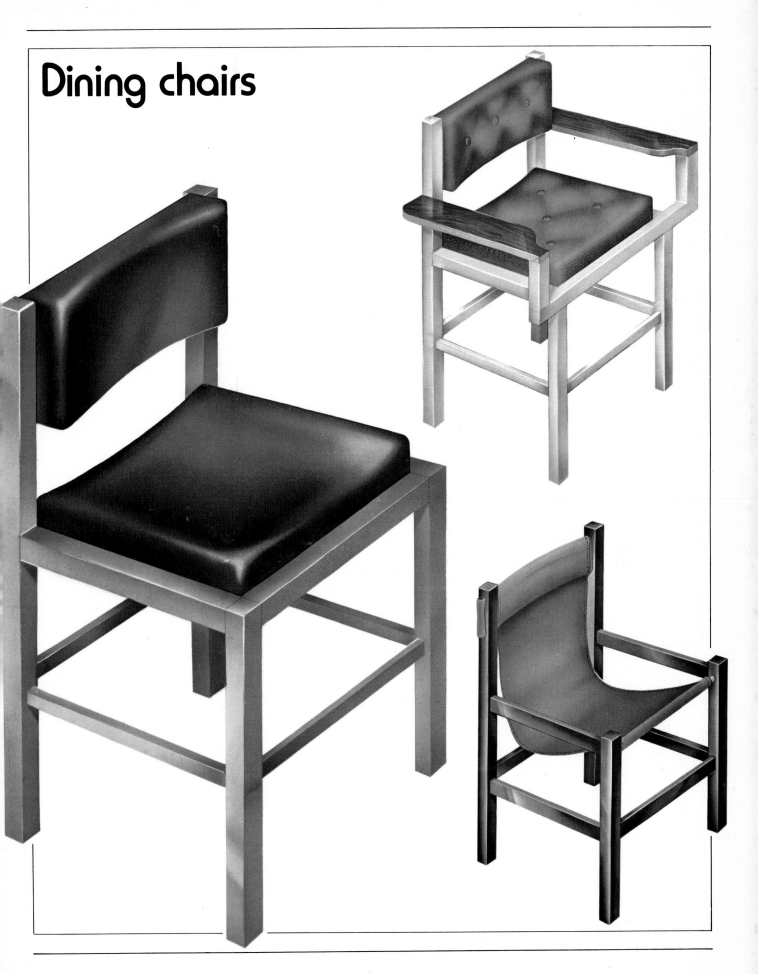

Dining chairs

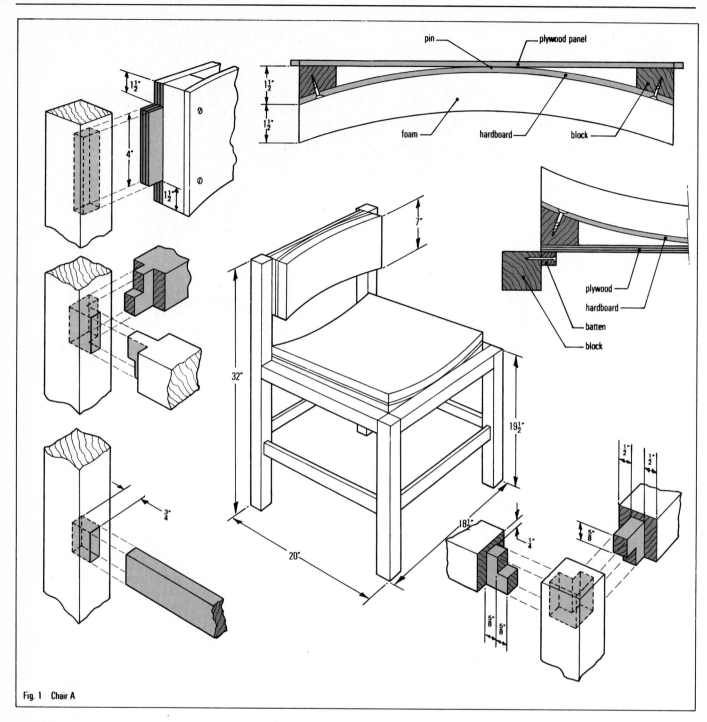

Fig. 1 Chair A

Fig 1. Chair A is suitable for use both in the dining room and kitchen. This illustration shows details of its construction.

Of the four chairs described, the first three are all built around one design. This design has been carefully worked out with four aims in mind. First, to be attractive, second, to be of sturdy construction, third to be simple to construct and last, to be adaptable enough to allow individual modifications.

These aims have been met. All the chairs are constructed using simple, but strong joints and they are devoid of unnecessary frills. In this respect they are ideally suitable for the home carpenter

who wishes to build a matching set of chairs without an overwhelming amount of work and expense. For simplicity, the chairs are called A, B, C and D.

Chair A

Chair A (Fig. 1) is suitable for use both as a dining chair and a kitchen chair. Your choice of wood is wide and can largely be dictated by the intended use of the chair. If, for example, it is to be a dining chair, a hardwood, such as beech, elm, teak or mahogany gives a pleasantly sophisticated appearance. On the other hand, if you intend using the chair in the kitchen, a softwood, such as pine (painted or unfinished) presents a more casual look.

Cutting out
Cut out all the pieces to the sizes given in the cutting list, taking particular care to ensure that the legs are all the correct length. You will find it easier to sand all the separate members at this stage, rather than when the chair is assembled. Use coarse sandpaper, then fine, and take off the sharp edges but do not round them.

The joints
You can follow one of two procedures to cut out the joints. You can either cut out all the mortises at once, then all the tenons, or you can work in strict order and make each matching mortise and tenon before going on to the next. The second method is more suitable for the home carpenter as it allows you to check each joint for fit as it is cut. (See the Techniques section for the method of cutting mortises and tenons.)

Start by putting all four legs together with the bottom ends exactly level. Then square lines across them to mark the positions of the upper and lower rails. This will ensure that all the mortises are in line with each other. You can either set out all the mortises together or one at a time using the squared lines for getting the correct position.

The lower rails do not have tenons cut in them, they simply slot straight into the mortise holes. The lower rails are 8½in (216mm) from the bottom of the leg to the bottom edge of the rail. Cut the mortises to a depth of ¾in (19mm), and when the waste wood has been removed, trial assemble the lower rails to the legs and, if necessary, trim to fit.

Now cut the joints for the upper side rails. These are more complicated but, if care is taken, should present no real problems. Begin by cutting out the mortises for the side rails in the front legs. These mortises are 1¼in (32mm) deep, 1in (25mm) long, ½in (13mm) wide and are located ¼in (6mm) below the top edges of the front legs. Then cut the corresponding tenon joints on the front ends of the side rails. In this case these joints are haunched tenons, which are cut in such a way that they lock into the corresponding joints cut into the upper front rail.

To cut the haunched tenons, first cut out a conventional tenon ½in (13mm)

thick and 1in (25mm) wide. Then, using Fig. 1 as a guide, cut a ¼in (6mm) strip off the top of the tenon. Next, form the haunch by cutting a piece ⅝in (16mm) square out of the top edge of the tenon.

When the side rails have been completed, cut the mortises for the front and back rails. The tenons are the same as for the front rails, but the haunch is reversed so that it will interlock with the side rail tenons. Fit all the joints dry to ensure that they are tight and that the rails are parallel.

The back rest
First cut out mortises 4in (102mm) long, ¾in (19mm) deep and ¼in (6mm) wide in the rear legs. These mortises are located so that their top edges are 1½in (38mm) from the top ends of the rear legs. Make corresponding tongues on the plywood back, as shown in Fig. 1. Take the two wood blocks and cut them out to the shape shown in Fig. 1. Glue and screw the blocks to the plywood back, then glue and screw the hardboard back to the blocks. This hardboard back is then held in a curved position by pinning it, at the centre, to the plywood back panel.

The seat
This part is assembled in the same way as the back rest. A ¼in (6mm) plywood panel is situated on battens which are glued and screwed to the top rails (Fig. 1), and to this panel are fixed full-length, shaped blocks and a curved hardboard seat panel.

Final assembly
With all the joints cut, assemble the chair in the following order. Glue one of the lower side rails into the front and back legs. Before the glue sets, add the upper side rail. Lay this assembly on its side and fix the upper front and back rails into position, followed by the lower front and back rails.

Leave this assembly while you make up the other side rails and legs. Then fix them to the chair assembly and add the back rest. Allow the glue to set and, if possible, use clamps to hold each member in its correct position. When the glue has set add the seat assembly.

Covering the chair
Both the back rest and the seat are covered with 1½in (38mm) thick rubber foam. You can choose a whole range of materials for final covering, ranging from a variety of fabrics to leather. Depending

on what wood you have used, you can give the chair a varnish, paint, or natural finish.

Chair B
Popularly called a carver chair, the design of this chair differs in that it includes a pair of arm rests. There are some other modifications, including a longer, upper front rail and shorter front legs.

To make it, first cut out all the pieces to the sizes given in the cutting list. The rear of the chair (including the back rest), the lower rails and the seat are assembled in exactly the same way as described for chair A. Where the front construction differs is in the assembly of the front legs to the top front rail, and the addition of the arm rests.

The front legs are joined into the top front rail and are located so that their outside edges are 3in (76mm) from the ends of the front rail. The joints used are haunched mortises and tenons and these lock into corresponding joints cut in the upper side rails (Fig. 2). The arm rests are supported at the front on two members which are through mortise and tenoned into the front rail, as shown in Fig. 2. Mortise and tenon joints are also used to joint the arm rests to the supports.

A different jointing technique is employed to fix the arm rests to the rear legs. Two holes are bored in the narrow edges of the arm rests where they coincide with the rear legs. Matching holes are then bored in the rear legs, and short lengths of dowelling glued into the matching holes to form a secret dowelled joint.

Final assembly follows the same order as that employed for chair A, and the chair can be finished in the same way.

Chair C
This sling-back chair uses the same basic framework as the previous chairs, but its appearance is transformed by the substitution of a canvas slung seat for the rigid wooden seat. Apart from this feature, the only other modification is that the upper side and back rails have the same dimensions as the lower rails, and are jointed into the legs in the same way. This makes the assembly of this chair much easier, as there are no complicated haunched mortise and tenons to cut.

Begin by cutting out all the pieces to the sizes given in the cutting list. Make the joints as detailed above. In place of the upper front rail is a ¾in (19mm) diameter chrome tube which is glued into

Dining chairs

Fig. 2   Chair B

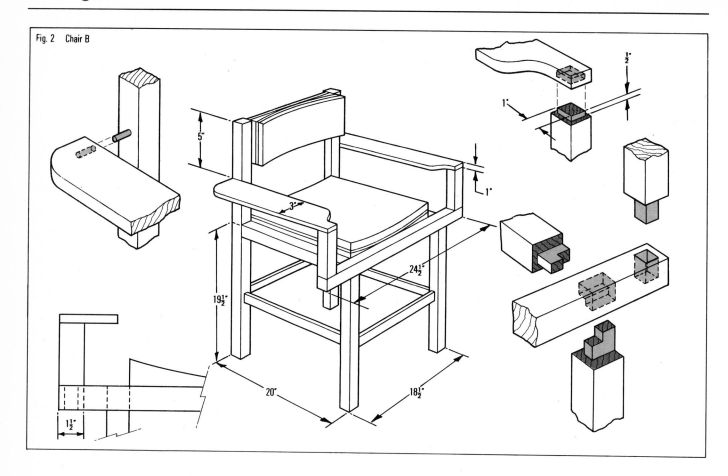

Fig. 3   Chair C

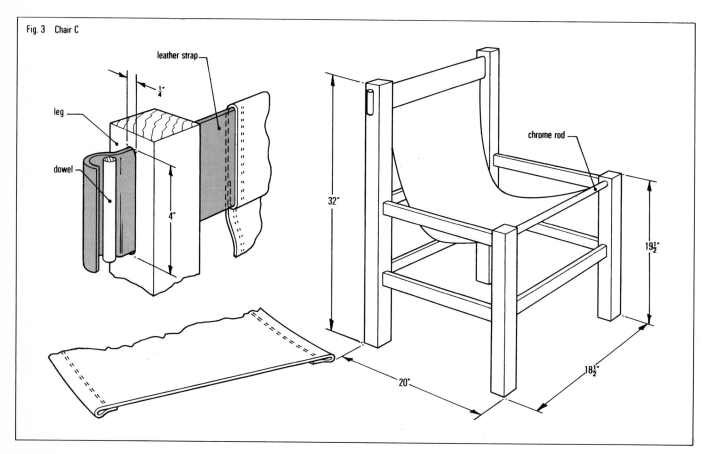

holes bored into the front legs, as shown in Fig. 3. Then cut out slots (or through mortises) in the back legs to take the hide strap. The latter acts as a back rest. These slots, which are illustrated in Fig. 3, are located ¾in (19mm) below the top ends of the back legs, and should be just wide and long enough to take the hide strap.

When the framework of the chair has been assembled, fix the back rest in position. This is done by first passing the hide strap through the slots so that an equal length of strap protrudes from both slots. Then, take lengths of dowel just longer and wider than the slots, and sew or stud the strap round the dowel and back

on itself, as shown in Fig. 3.

The slung seat can be made from a strong fabric, such as stout canvas, or from leather or some synthetic material. Before fitting it, turn it back and sew the long edges as shown in Fig. 3 to prevent it tearing under the weight of a person. Attach it first to the hide strap, as shown in Fig. 3, then gauge the amount of slack needed before fixing the other end round the chrome tube.

Depending on what material you choose for the seat, this chair can be used for a variety of purposes. Fitted with a leather seat it makes an elegant and unusual dining chair. If a colourful canvas seat is chosen, it can be used in the kitchen or garden.

Fig 2. Chair B showing details of the construction.

Fig 3. Illustration of Chair C and the supporting leather strap.

Cutting list: Chair A

Solid wood	standard	metric
2 back legs	32 × 1½ × 1½	813×38×38
2 front legs	19½ × 1½ × 1½	495×38×38
2 lower side rails	18½ × 1 × ½	470×25×13
2 upper side rails	18½ × 1½ × 1½	470×38×38
2 lower cross rails	17 × 1 × ½	432×25×13
2 upper cross rails	17 × 1½ × 1½	432×38×38
4 battens	15 × ½ × ½	381×13×13
2 wood blocks	7 × 1½ × 1½	178×38×38
4 wood blocks	17 × 1½ × 1½	432×38×38
Plywood		
1 back panel	17×7×¼	432×178×6
1 seat panel	17×15½×¼	432×394×6
Hardboard		
1 seat panel	17×15½×¼	432×394×6
1 back panel	15½×7×⅛	394×178×3

You will also require:
Rubber foam padding. Carpenter's glue. ½in (13mm) panel pins.

Cutting list: Chair B

Solid wood	standard	metric
2 back legs	32 × 1½ × 1½	813×38×38
2 front legs	18 × 1½ × 1½	458×38×38
1 upper front rail	24½ × 1½ × 1½	622×38×38
2 arm rests	20×4×1	508×102×25
2 arm rests supports	7½ × 1½ × 1½	191×38×38

All other members are the same dimensions as the corresponding members of Chair A.

Cutting list: Chair C

Solid wood	standard	metric
2 back legs	32 × 1½ × 1½	813×38×38
2 front legs	21 × 1½ × 1½	534×38×38
4 side rails	18½ × 1½ × ½	470×38×13
3 cross rails	17 × 1½ × ½	432×38×13

You will also require:
1 ¾in (19mm) diameter chrome tube 17in (432mm) long. Hide strap 22½in × 4in × ¼in (572mm × 102mm × 6mm). Leather or fabric 36in × 19in (915mm×482mm).

Dining chairs

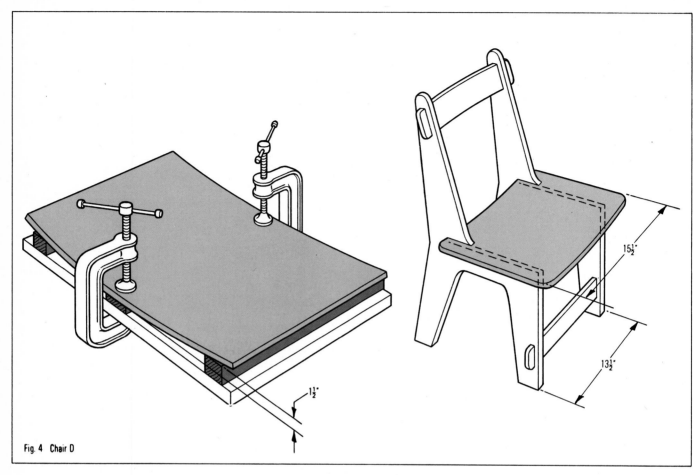

Fig. 4 Chair D

Fig 4. Construction details of chair D. Also shown is the method used to curve the plywood for the back and seat. It is always a good idea to use waste blocks between the shoes of the cramps and the work to prevent bruising of the wood.

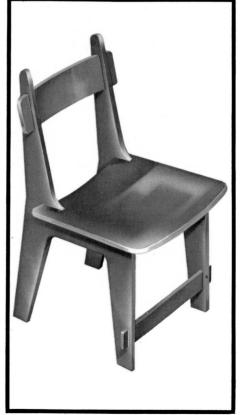

Chair D

If you want to make a matching set of chairs easily and cheaply, this design is ideal. The material used is $\frac{5}{8}$in (16mm) birch plywood – the sides being cut from one sheet of ply 25in × 32in (635mm × 813 mm), while the seat, back rest and rail are cut from one sheet 15$\frac{1}{2}$in × 21in (394 mm × 533mm). Note that an allowance must be made for saw cuts.The seat and back rest are slightly curved to fit the contours of the body. To curve plywood, first apply a heavy coating of water-based wood glue to the wood, then fix it in the desired shape with a G cramp, as shown in Fig. 4. Leave in a warm place for 48 hours by which time the glue will have set and will hold the curve. Final assembly is by glueing the pieces together to the plan shown in Fig. 4.

Finish the chair by rubbing it down with coarse sandpaper, especially around the edges, then finishing off with a finer one. Then, paint it, first with an undercoat then with two coats of polyurethane gloss.

The finished chair is both attractive and robust enough to make an ideal kitchen chair for the family.

Fold~down table with cupboard

The design

The table and cabinet consist mainly of 7 panels of $\frac{3}{4}$in (19mm) birch plywood, all cut from one standard-sized 4ft × 8ft (1.22m × 2.44m) sheet as shown in Fig. 1. Parts A and B are shaped to fit together and joined with strap hinges, then screwed to the wall to form the table when A is dropped down (Fig. 5). Panel A drops down to rest on battening fixed to the front or sides of the cabinet; an exploded view of this arrangement is shown in Fig. 2. The cabinet, in turn, is screwed firmly to panel B.

A small ball catch is fitted in the top edge of panel B, and the cup for this at the point where panel A butts against it. This holds panel A, in position when it is folded against the wall out of the way.

All the cabinet joints are simply butted, glued and screwed. If the unit is to be painted, the screw heads are counter-sunk flush with the surface and filled over with a proprietary cellulose filler, which is then sanded down to give a perfectly smooth finish. But if you want to stain or varnish the unit, the screw heads must be sunk deeper and the holes filled with matching plugs of timber cut from dowelling of a suitable size.

Fold~down table with cupboard

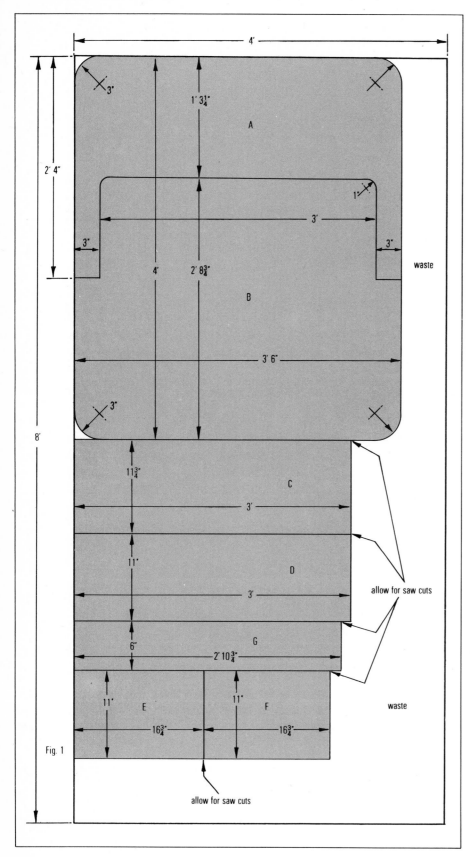

Fig. 1

Materials and tools

The unit will require one 4ft × 8ft (1219mm × 2438mm) sheet of ¾in (19mm) birch plywood; one length of 3ft × 1½in (914mm × 38mm) hardwood ½in (13mm) thick; two large 12in (305mm)

strap hinges with mounting screws; one ball catch no wider than ⅝in (15mm); two dozen 1½in (38mm) No. 8 countersunk head screws; and woodworking adhesive. You will also need paint or varnish.

Cutting out

Mark out the large sheet of ply, using the dimensions in Fig. 1 as a guide. To ensure that the table top will fit properly over the top of the cabinet when dropped down, it is essential that you commence marking in a particular order.

First mark out panel C. This panel has two square corners, and two rounded corners.

Where radiused corners are required, mark two points 3in (75mm) along each edge, from the corner. Link these two points with lines drawn at right angles to the edges to make a 3in (75mm) square. The inner corner of this square will be the centre for the curve, which should be drawn with a pair of compasses. Then, mark out the rest of the ply sheet, but not the dividing line that will separate panels A and B.

With the jig saw, carefully cut round the outline of panel C. When this has been done, finish the cut edges of the panel with the bench plane (fine set) along the straight edges, and the spokeshave at the radiused corners.

Mark out the dividing line between panels A and B, using panel C as a template for the central piece. This is done to ensure that when the table top is dropped down it will fit exactly over the top of the cabinet, which will be panel C.

Making the cabinet

This is constructed from panels C, D, E, F and G, fastened together with glued and screwed butt joints.

Trial assemble the cabinet panels as shown in Fig. 2 to check that all the edges butt neatly. Where they do not, plane the high spots down. Then finish off all the edges that will be visible at the front of the unit. Trial assemble again to ensure that the cabinet is square and that all parts fit correctly.

Drill screw holes at 2in (50mm) intervals through the ends of the top and bottom panels and C and D. Spread adhesive along the top and bottom of the side panels (F and E), then erect the carcase in the shape shown in Fig. 2, and drive the screws home into the side panels.

Before the glue has set, lightly mark a horizontal line with a try square half way down the outside of each side panel and drill screw holes along the lines at 2in (50mm) intervals to take the shelf G. Trim shelf G to fit in between the side panels, spread adhesive along each of its ends, place it in position and drive the screws home. Check that the cabinet is square, then leave it while the glue sets.

Assembling the unit

This is relatively simple except that care is required to make the table flap drop accurately over the cabinet top.

Lay panels A and B down on a flat surface and fit the strap hinges (Fig. 4) to link them as shown in Fig. 5. Lay the cabinet on its back, on top of panel B, in the approximate position where it will eventually be fixed. Lift the table flap up to a vertical position and adjust the position of the cabinet until the top fits neatly into the cut-out of the flap. When the cabinet is in the right postion, lightly mark a line round its top, base and sides onto the surface of panel B.

Take the cabinet off, then drill screw holes at 2in (50mm) intervals round the inside of the marked line. Each hole should be drilled inside the line at a distance equal to half the thickness of the plywood used for the cabinet carcase. Lay sections A and B on a table, place the cabinet in position again, ease part of panel B over the edge of the table to expose some of the screw holes underneath, then drive several screws in. Repeat this until the cabinet has been screwed all round and is securely fixed to panel B.

Finally, fit the flap-stop. This is the 3ft (1m) length of hardwood. Place it in position underneath panel C so that one third of its width protrudes beyond the front of the panel. Mark a line along the front edge of C on to the flap-stop. Remove the stop and drill holes at 2in (50mm) intervals at a point halfway between this marked line and the back of the stop. Replace the stop and screw it in position.

Fixing and finishing

Fill any cracks or holes with filler, allow it to dry, then rub the surfaces down.

To avoid getting any paint on the walls, it is best to paint the unit before fixing it to the wall. When the paint is dry, all that remains is to fix the unit to the wall with screws and wall plugs.

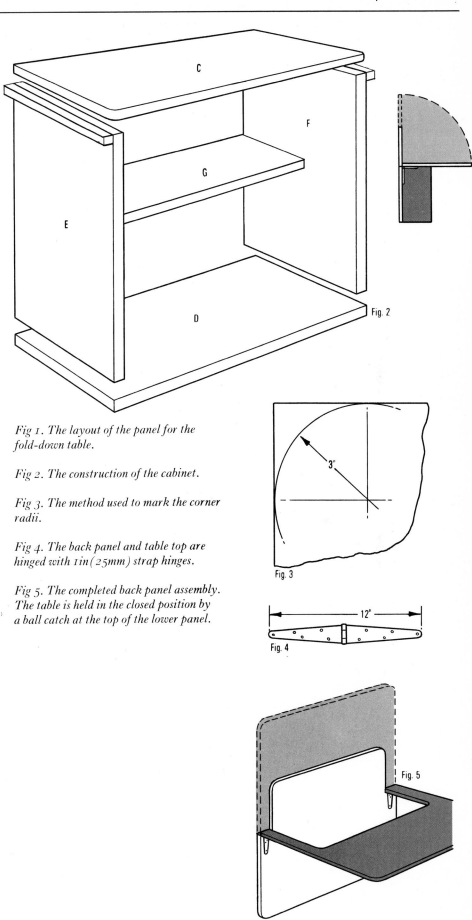

Fig 1. The layout of the panel for the fold-down table.

Fig 2. The construction of the cabinet.

Fig 3. The method used to mark the corner radii.

Fig 4. The back panel and table top are hinged with 1in (25mm) strap hinges.

Fig 5. The completed back panel assembly. The table is held in the closed position by a ball catch at the top of the lower panel.

Made~to~measure kitchen unit

Shop-bought kitchen units are expensive and do not always fit the general layout of your kitchen. This made-to-measure unit can be adapted to your own particular requirements.

The unit has been designed to avoid unnecessary work in the kitchen. The wide, corner sub-assembly, clearly illustrated in Fig. 1, is ideal for a work surface directly adjacent to a cooker. The rest of the unit is fitted with drawers or cupboards and is designed to have a sink recessed into the work surface. The advantages of this system are clear. Food can be prepared next to the cooker and dirty dishes can be stacked on one side of the sink and, when washed, can be placed on the other side to drain. All washing materials and utensils can be stored in the adequate drawers and recesses, for immediate access. In conjunction with a wall-mounted unit for holding foodstuffs, you have a complete and labour-saving system for your kitchen.

There is no reason why the dimensions of the unit cannot be altered to individual requirements. The length of the unit is limited only by the space available; its depth can be adjusted if, for example, you wish to incorporate a fridge or dishwasher into a recess. The height of the unit, as shown on the plan, is 34in (863mm) which is suitable for the smaller person. Standard kitchen furniture is 36in (914mm) high; but the height of the unit can be adjusted to suit your own requirements.

Preliminaries

Before embarking on the construction of a large piece of furniture like this kitchen unit, you are advised to bear several factors in mind. When assembled, this unit will not pass through conventional doorways so, unless you have the freedom of the kitchen for a few days, you must temporarily assemble the unit in the workshop and, when all cutting is complete, transfer it for final assembly to the proposed site. As the unit comprises a large number of individual members, you are advised to consult the cutting list and group similar materials into the same sizes where possible. This makes the job of ordering the materials much easier and prevents wastage.

The materials

You can choose the materials for the unit to match the style of your existing kitchen. Those given in the cutting list have been chosen for their good looks, economy and hard-wearing qualities, but suitable alternatives can be substituted. Thus, while ¾in (19mm) blockboard is recommended for the main work surface, an alternative would be veneered or plain chipboard. Blockboard or plain chipboard should be covered with a hard-wearing veneer. As well as being used for the working top, blockboard is recommended for the end and division panels. All other panels, including the doors and drawers, are cut from ⅝in (16mm) thick veneered chipboard.

Frame members, which include the ground-level kick boards, are of softwood, planed all round. The backs of both sub-assemblies are made from hardboard, as are the drawer bottoms which are covered by a veneer. All the drawer battens and stops are cut from a hardwood such as teak.

Construction

When making a large unit comprising many parts, it is best to work in a strict order of procedure. You can either build each sub-assembly separately, or you can cut out and assemble similar parts of the sub-assemblies together. Remember though, that if you are making the wide corner sub-unit, it must be constructed either on the site, or trial assembled elsewhere.

Begin by cutting out the four main panels for the sink unit to the plans in Figs. 2 and 3, using an electric circular saw with combination blade. Cut the cut-outs in the panels with a jig saw. The two ends have cut-outs made at the top corners to house the two upper long rails. Another cut-out, at the front lower corner, houses the kickboard. Cut-outs similar in size and location to those on the top edge of the end panels are made on the two intermediate divisions, but the lower edges of these panels are cut to a different plan which is shown in Fig. 2. If the unit is to house a standard size kitchen sink, you will have to cut the intermediate divisions to accommodate it. The exact size and shape of such a cut-out will depend on the design of your sink.

Now cut out the lower shelf and then the two top 3in × 1in (76mm × 25mm) softwood rails to the sizes required. Lay the rails on top of the shelf so that they are parallel to its long edges and are ¾in (19mm) from each end; and mark the position of each division.

Screw and glue 1in × 1in (25mm ×

25mm) jointing members to the inside surface of the two ends. Their exact location is shown in Fig. 1.

At this stage, before beginning assembly, add veneer or laminate strips to all the exposed front edges of the divisions and lower shelf.

With all exposed edges laminated, fix the intermediate divisions to the lower shelf by glueing and screwing through the shelf. Then turn the unit over and fix the top rails, referring to the previously marked positions of the divisions to give their exact location.

Before fixing the ends, add the hardboard back panel by pinning and glueing it to the rear edges of the intermediate divisions and the top, rear rail.

Now that the addition of the back panel has given greater stability to the unit, you can glue and screw the ends into position. Check at this stage that the pieces are square to each other.

Turn the unit right way up and fix the kick board into position. This piece is recessed into the housings cut in the bases of the ends and extends the whole length of the sub-assembly. It is held in position by being fixed to a 1in (25mm) × 1⅜in (35mm) batten which is glued and screwed to the underside of the lower shelf. When assembled correctly this member is overlapped by the doors. As added support, timber reinforcement brackets (cut to the shape shown in Fig. 4) are screwed into the internal right angles made by the kick board/bottom shelf joint. There are four of these brackets and each is located at a corner of the unit.

Shelving

You can choose shelving to suit your individual needs. In this unit the sink is recessed onto only one of the intermediate divisions, and the cupboard space that it occupies, i.e. the cupboard formed by the end and first intermediate division, is left clear so that it can store large items such as buckets and washing bowls. The space between the intermediate divisions is fitted with a single shelf situated about half-way up the cupboard. The space between the second division and the other end is used for four drawers. Obviously you can modify this arrangement as necessary.

The easiest method of fixing the shelves is to simply rest them on 1in × 1in (25mm × 25mm) hardwood battens glued and screwed to the division panels. This method allows you to remove shelves for

Made~to~measure kitchen unit

Fig 1. Exploded view of the fitted kitchen unit.

Fig 2. The end panels of the unit. These are the only two panels which are full depth.

Fig 3. The intermediate panels finish at the unit base. The dotted line shows the cut-out which must be made to accommodate the sink unit.

Fig 4. The brackets supporting the kick board are clearly illustrated, as are the top rails and the position of the shelf.

Fig 5. Front view of the end unit showing position of the drawers and runners.

Fig 6. Plan view of the end unit.

Fig 7. Side elevation of the end unit.

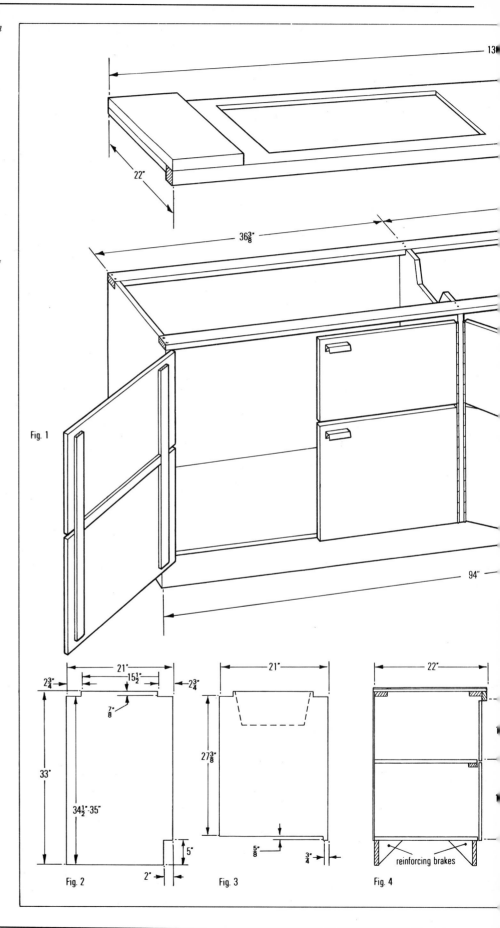

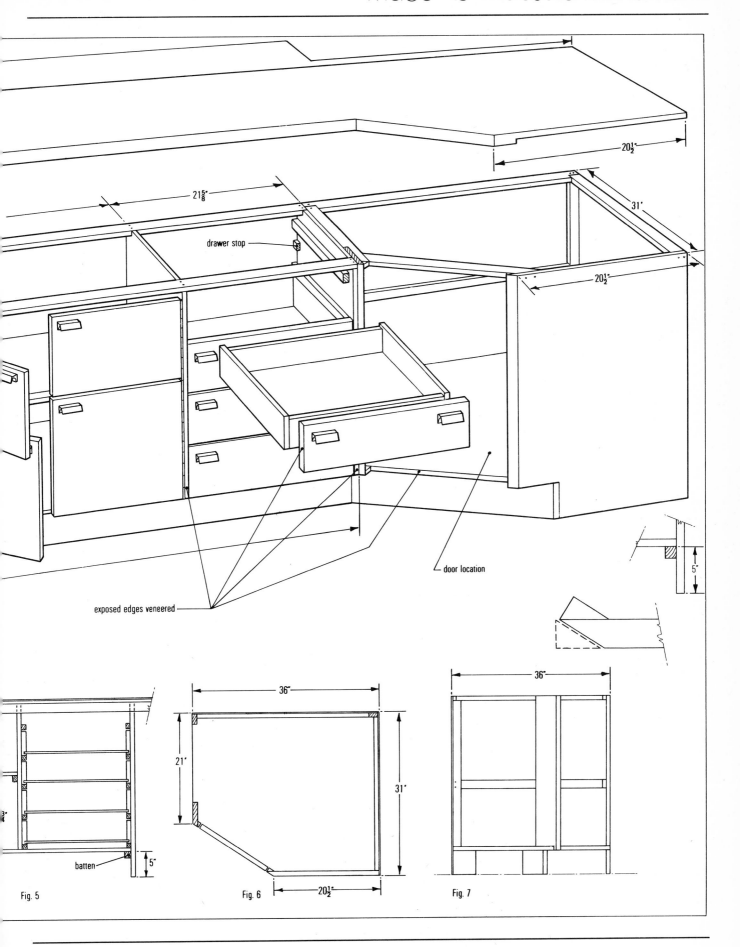

drawer stop

$20\frac{1}{2}$"

$21\frac{5}{8}$"

31'

$20\frac{1}{2}$"

5"

door location

exposed edges veneered

Fig. 5

batten

5"

$\frac{3}{4}$"

Fig. 6

36"

21'

31'

$20\frac{1}{2}$"

Fig. 7

36"

Made-to-measure kitchen unit

cleaning. Under the weight of heavy kitchen utensils, a chipboard shelf will bend. To prevent this, glue and screw a 2in × 1in (51mm × 25mm) batten under each shelf, flush with the front edge as shown in Fig. 4.

Drawer construction

In a unit of this size, there is a possibility that the finished dimensions will deviate slightly from those given in the cutting list and Fig. 1. As a result, you are advised to use the dimensions of the drawer members given in the cutting list as a guide, and to take the exact measurements for the drawers from the unit itself. Aim for a ⅛in (3mm) clearance between the drawer sides and the division panels.

Make up the drawers to the plan shown in Fig. 1, after cutting out the pieces for a good fit. The two centre

Below: The finish of the unit is a matter of personal taste. Here, wood veneer has been used but the unit can be painted or covered with a plastic laminate. The handles and hinges should be chosen to suit the finished unit, so decide on the finish before buying the hardware.

drawers are larger than the top and bottom drawers. All the drawer bottoms are cut from laminate covered hardboard and fit into ¼in (6mm) deep grooves cut into the sides ¼in (6mm) above their bottom edges. The sides are simply butt jointed to the front and back and secured with glue and 1½in (38mm) panel pins. A false or decorative front, cut from veneered chipboard is added to each drawer front, but before fixing this piece in position, check that the main drawer bodies fit satisfactorily.

To do this, glue and screw the lower pair of hardwood drawer runners into position on the lower shelf, tight against the division panels. Slide one drawer into position, slip a piece of cardboard onto its upper edges to give the correct clearance, then mark out the position of the next pair of drawer runners and fix them into position on the division panels. Repeat this procedure with the other two drawers and, when you are satisfied that each drawer fits well, add the false drawer fronts.

Note that the lower drawer front is wide enough to extend below the bottom of the drawer to cover the main unit

lower shelf edge. When fitted correctly, the other drawer fronts should just have a working clearance between each other, and the top drawer front must clear the front edge of the working top.

Door construction

The dimensions of each door will depend on the arrangement of the internal shelving. Door sizes given in the cutting list are ideal for the unit shown. Having cut all the door panels to size, check for fit, remembering that each panel is hung on the inside faces of the divisions on full-length, piano-type hinges. Where internal shelving is fitted (as in the centre cupboard, shown in Fig. 4), upper and lower door panels are fitted separately. But where no shelf is fitted, door panels should be joined by ¾in or ½in (19mm or 13mm) battens, glued and screwed to the rear surfaces, as shown in Fig. 1.

Cut the piano hinges to length, and then screw them into position on the edges of the doors. Mark the correct position of the hinges on the divisions and screw the doors to the unit. Finally, fit each door with a magnetic-type catch and add the handles of your choice.

Corner sub-assembly construction

As stated previously, the dimensions and shape of this sub-unit will depend on individual preference and the existing scheme of your kitchen. Remember, a unit of this size is too large to fit preassembled through the average kitchen door.

If you intend to make the sub-unit as shown, cut the lower main shelf to the shape and size shown in Fig. 6. All the corner unit parts are assembled using simple butt or housing joints, but you may experience some difficulty in cutting out the two panels which have angled long edges. Having examined Fig. 1 to discover the precise arrangement of the various members, use direct measurement to mark up the pieces. To angle the edges of the panels, first mark out the correct angle on the upper and lower edges of each. Then, using a marking gauge and pencil, draw a line along the inside surface of each panel between the marked points. Cut the wood down to this line. Do not discard the off-cut; it is used to provide a right-angled edge on which the door is hung, as shown in detail in Fig. 1. When you have cut out the panels, fix them to the base.

Build up the rest of the frame from

2in × 1in (51mm × 25mm) softwood. The two rear vertical members simply butt onto the base and onto the underside of the top rails which are joined in a modified lap joint.

Add the kick board and the support blocks and then the two hardboard back panels. Cut the door to size and hang it between the two angled off-cuts as described previously. Shelving can be added if desired.

Working top construction

Measure the working top against the assembled units. If you wish to incorporate a recess between the sub-assemblies you must allow for this. The dimensions of the top given in the cutting list apply only if the two sub-units are butted together.

Glue and screw the 1in × 1¼in (25mm × 32mm) softwood, front edge thickener under the top, so that its front edge is flush with the front edge of the working top. Then cover the whole surface with a resistant plastic laminate, using a suitable adhesive. Add a hardwood work block to the surface in a convenient position.

Now you must cut out a space in the work top to receive the sink and its surround. Assuming that you want to fit a new sink with an integral draining board, you must make sure that its dimensions will fit the top of the unit. Most sink/draining units come complete with fixing instructions and, provided you make a watertight seal between sink and work top, you should experience little difficulty in fitting a sink unit. You can cut the necessary hole using a jig saw. The area of wall behind the sink will have to be covered with a splash-proof surface of some kind. One of the most attractive materials for this purpose is ceramic tiling. The only other modification to the work top that may be required is the boring of holes to take taps.

When you have checked the precise location of the sink in relation to the unit and have cut away the necessary areas of the work top, it can be fixed into position by special clips provided with the sink. Any plumbing and sealing processes should be carried out now.

Although the construction of the unit will have entailed a lot of work, the finished result more than justifies it. The kitchen unit will save time in the kitchen, aid hygiene and introduce a contemporary touch to what is often a neglected part of the home.

Cutting lists
Main sink unit

Wood	standard	metric
2 blockboard ends	33 × 21 × ¾	838 × 533 × 19
2 blockboard intermediate partitions	28 × 21 × ¾	711 × 533 × 19
1 veneered chipboard lower shelf	92½ × 20¼ × ⅝	2349 × 514 × 16
1 veneered chipboard centre shelf	35¼ × 20¼ × ⅝	895 × 514 × 16
4 veneered chipboard upper doors	17½ × 11½ × ⅝	445 × 292 × 16
4 veneered chipboard lower doors	17½ × 15 × ⅝	445 × 381 × 16
8 veneered chipboard drawer sides	20 × 5½ × ⅝	508 × 140 × 16
8 veneered chipboard drawer ends	19½ × 4½ × ⅝	489 × 114 × 16
2 veneered chipboard drawer fronts	20½ × 7¼ × ⅝	521 × 184 × 16
2 veneered chipboard drawer fronts	20½ × 6⅛ × ⅝	521 × 156 × 16
1 veneered chipboard kick board	95 × 5 × ⅝	2413 × 127 × 16
2 blockboard rear supports	5 × 5 × ¾	127 × 127 × 19
4 blockboard kick board reinforcements	5 × 5 × ¾	127 × 127 × 19
2 softwood top main battens	90 × 3 × 1	2286 × 76 × 25
1 softwood shelf front edge	35¼ × 2 × 1	895 × 51 × 25
10 hardwood drawer runners	20 × ¾ × ½	508 × 19 × 13
4 hardwood door joining battens	26 × ¾ × ½	660 × 19 × 13
2 hardwood door joining battens	13 × ¾ × ½	330 × 19 × 13
4 laminated hardboard drawer bases	19¾ × 20	502 × 508
4 hardwood jointing and shelf supports	19 × 1 × 1	483 × 25 × 25
1 hardboard back	94 × 28 × ⅛	2388 × 711 × 3

Corner sub-unit

Wood	standard	metric
1 veneered chipboard lower shelf	36 × 31 × ⅝	914 × 787 × 16
1 blockboard angled panel	33 × 22 × ¾	838 × 559 × 19
1 blockboard angled panel	28 × 5 × ¾	711 × 127 × 19
2 softwood frame members	26⅜ × 2 × 1	670 × 51 × 25
1 softwood horizontal frame member	36 × 2 × 1	914 × 51 × 25
1 softwood horizontal frame member	34 × 2 × 1	863 × 51 × 25
2 softwood horizontal frame members	29¼ × 2 × 1	743 × 51 × 25
1 softwood horizontal frame member	21 × 2 × 1	533 × 51 × 25
1 softwood horizontal frame member	22 × 2 × 1	559 × 51 × 25
1 softwood jointing batten	17 × 1 × 1	431 × 25 × 25
1 veneered chipboard kick board	22 × 5 × ⅝	559 × 127 × 16
1 veneered chipboard lower door	16¼ × 15 × ⅝	413 × 381 × 16
1 veneered chipboard upper door	16¼ × 11½ × ⅝	413 × 292 × 16
4 blockboard support blocks	5 × 5 × ¾	127 × 127 × 19
2 hardwood door joining battens	26 × ¾ × ½	660 × 19 × 13
1 hardwood door jointing batten	13 × ¾ × ½	330 × 19 × 13

Working top

Wood	standard	metric
1 blockboard top	130 × 31 × ¾	3300 × 788 × 19
1 blockboard working top block	22 × 12 × ¾	559 × 305 × 19
1 softwood edging strip	114 × 1¼ × 1	2896 × 31 × 25
2 softwood edging strips	22 × 1¼ × 1	559 × 31 × 25
2 softwood edging strips	10 × 1¼ × 1	254 × 31 × 25

You will also require:

Plastic laminate, ⅝in (16mm) veneer strips. Door handles. Woodworking glue. 144 1½in (38mm) panel pins and wood screws. Laminate adhesive.

Kitchen unit with oven and hob

Above: The attractive lines of the kitchen oven and hob unit are shown here to good advantage. Some adjustments to the dimensions given here may be required to accommodate the units used and the size of your particular kitchen.

This kitchen unit comprises a recessed sink and hob unit which butts onto an eye-level oven unit. The design is practical and good-looking. Buying an equivalent unit will be an expensive purchase. This is not a difficult construction if you follow the instructions carefully.

Plastic-covered material – ContiPlas – is used for the carcase of both sub-assemblies of this kitchen unit. This is obtainable in standard width panels and consists of a high-density chipboard core, covered on both surfaces and long edges with a tough melamine coat. There are many

alternative materials, but whatever type you choose, ensure that the laminate covering is heat resistant. Blockboard is used for the working top – again, when choosing a laminate covering, check that it is heat resistant.

You may wish to modify the dimensions of the unit to suit your kitchen; the simplicity of the design allows this. One cautionary word, however, before you start construction – check the oven and hob plate manufacturer's instructions and specifications and amend the design shown where necessary.

The hob/sink unit

Use an electric jig saw with a fine 3in (76mm) blade for cutting. A straightedge will help you cut accurate, straight pieces. Cut all the long sections with a circular saw. Begin by cutting out the two ends to the outline shown in Fig. 2. These have cut-outs at the top corners to accommodate the two upper long rails. Another cut-out, at the front lower corner, houses the kick board. Now cut out the three intermediate divisions to the shape represented by the dotted line in Fig. 2. Again, these pieces have cut-outs similar to those made on the top edges of the ends but as they rest flush on the bottom shelf, they do not house the kick board. Having decided on and checked the locations of the fitted hob and sink, make cut-outs in the intermediate divisions to accommodate these fixtures.

Next, cut out the lower shelf and then the two 2in × 1in (51mm × 25mm) upper long rails to the sizes given in the cutting list. Lay the rails on top of the shelf so that they are parallel to its long edges and overlap both ends by ⅝in (16mm). Mark in the position of each division on the rails, and shelf, as shown in Fig. 1.

Turn the intermediate divisions upside down and referring to the previously marked locations, pin the lower shelf to their bottom edges. Secure the divisions with 1½in (38mm) No.6 screws. Set the structure right way up and add the long rails into the appropriate housings. At this point, add the ends by pinning and screwing, and, when you have checked that the unit is square, fit the hardboard back panel.

Now you can add the kick board. First fix a full-length 1in × 1in (25mm × 25mm) softwood batten to the underside of the lower shelf at the location shown in Fig. 2. The kick board butts·onto this member and is fixed between the ends. Screw it with 1½in (38mm) No.6 screws.

The top front panel is butt jointed to the front edges of the divisions and ends at the location shown in Figs. 1 and 2.

Shelving

You can choose shelving to suit your individual needs, remembering that the recessed sink and hob will not leave very much space under them. The simplest method of fixing any shelves is to rest them on 1in × 1in (25mm × 25mm) hardwood battens glued and screwed to the divisions This method allows you to remove shelves for cleaning. Remember that under the weight of heavy kitchen utensils even chipboard can bend. To prevent this, glue and screw a 2in × 1in (51mm × 25mm) batten under each shelf, flush with the front edge.

Once any shelving is in place, you must effectively fireproof the area round the hob location. Different hobs require different treatment, so before starting work consult the manufacturers' instructions or, if you do not possess these, the manufacturers themselves. Asbestos is the most effective fireproofing material in common use. Cut it to size with a fine-toothed saw and fix it to those areas where it is needed.

Drawer construction

Drawers are fitted at one end of the unit only. When marking out the individual drawer members, use the dimensions given in the cutting list as a guide and take the exact measurements from the unit itself. Aim for a ⅛in (3mm) clearance between the drawer sides and the division panels.

When you have cut out each piece, make ¼in (6mm) deep grooves in the drawer sides to accommodate the hardboard drawer bottoms. The bottom edges of the grooves are located ¼in (6mm) from the bottom edges of the sides. Once the drawer bottom has been glued into position, add the front and back which simply butt between the sides. Secure them by driving screws through the bottom panel into their lower edges.

An additional false front is added to each drawer, but before fixing this piece in position, check that the main drawer bodies fit satisfactorily. To do this, glue and screw a pair of hardwood drawer runners into position on the lower shelf, tight against the division. Slide one drawer into position, slip a piece of cardboard onto its upper edges to give the correct clearance, then mark out the position of the next pair of drawer runners and fix them into position. Repeat this procedure with the other two drawers and, when you are satisfied that each drawer fits well, add the false fronts.

Door construction

Having cut out all the door panels to size, check for a good fit, remembering that each panel is hung on the inside faces of the formers on full-length, piano-type hinges. Cut these hinges to length and then screw them into position on the edges of the doors. Mark the correct position of the hinges on the division and end

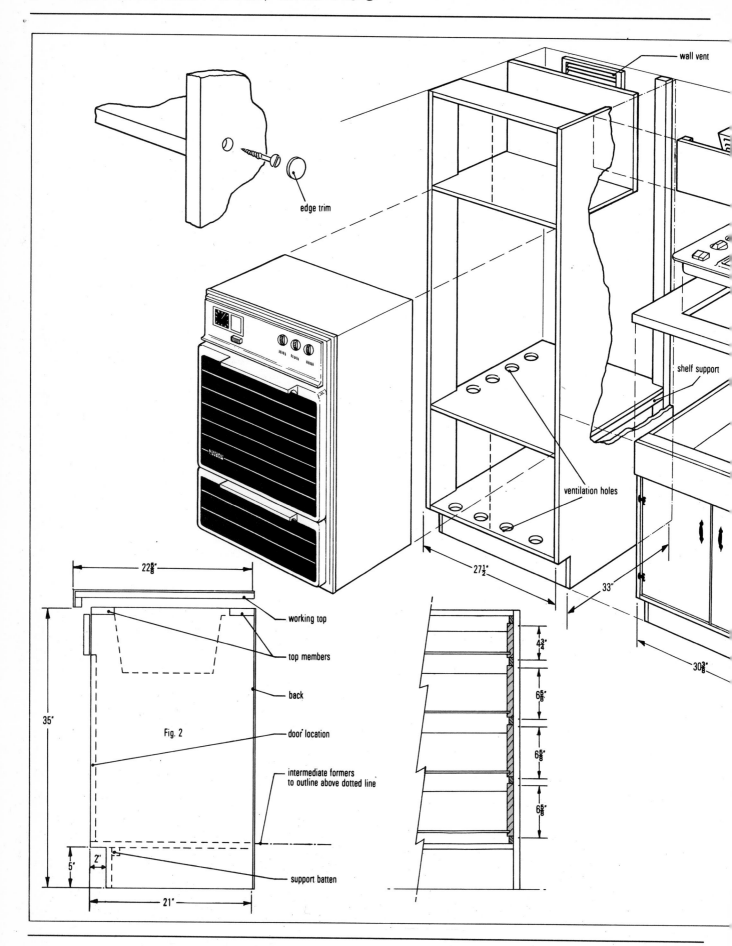

edge trim

wall vent

shelf support

ventilation holes

27½"

33"

30⅜"

working top

top members

back

door location

intermediate formers
to outline above dotted line

support batten

22⅝"

35"

Fig. 2

5"

2"

21"

4¾"

6⅝"

6⅝"

6⅝"

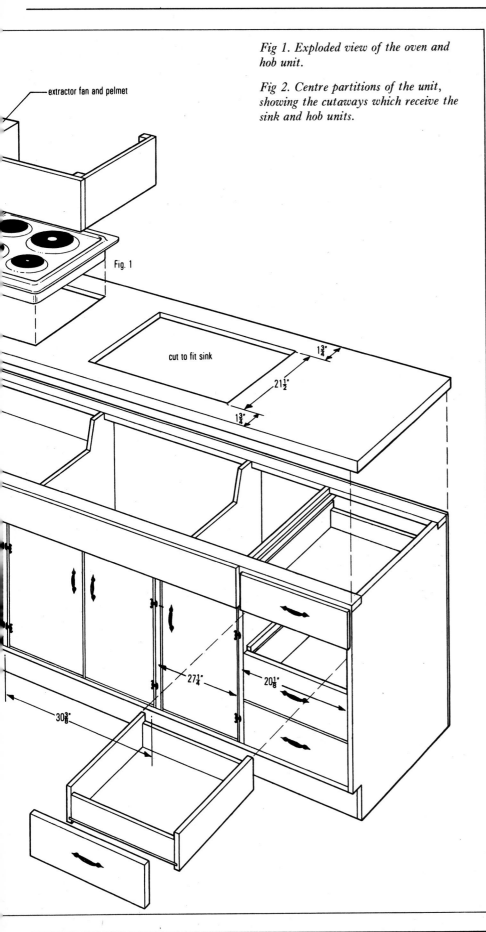

Fig 1. Exploded view of the oven and hob unit.

Fig 2. Centre partitions of the unit, showing the cutaways which receive the sink and hob units.

panels and screw the doors to the unit. Finally, fit each door with a magnetic-type catch and add the handles of your choice.

Working top construction

Cut the working top and glue and screw a 1in × 1in (25mm × 25mm) softwood strip to the front and right-hand edge of this piece, as shown in Fig. 2. Then cover the surface with a resistant plastic laminate.

Now cut out spaces for the sink and the hob to the manufacturers' specifications. When you have made the cut-outs, fix the working top in position by glueing and screwing it to the upper long rails – driving the screws through the rails into the top. Carry out any plumbing or electrical work at this point and then cover the area of wall immediately behind the sink with a splash-proof material.

Making the oven unit

Before starting to build the unit, you must check the dimensions of your oven against the dimensions of the unit shown and, if necessary, modify both the design and sizes of the various parts of the unit. Then cut out the two side members and the shelves. Take the two lower shelves and make cut-outs at one corner to accommodate the narrower side member. These shelves also house the rear 2in × 1in (51mm × 25mm) vertical support batten and cut-outs must be made in their rear edges to accommodate this member. The top shelf also houses the narrower side member, but butts directly onto the support batten. Before fixing this shelf to the main structure, glue and screw the back panel to it.

With all the pieces cut out, begin assembly by glueing and screwing the side members to the shelves. Add the recessed kick board and the top cross member. Next, stand the unit on its proposed site and mark out on the wall the locations of the support battens. Fix these in place, using wall plugs, and screw the unit to them. Before fitting the oven in place on the centre shelf, add 1in × 1in (25mm × 25mm) reinforcing battens as shown in Fig. 1. Then bore out ventilation holes in both the bottom and centre shelves.

Doors are fitted in the same way as described for the sink/hob unit. They should be equipped with handles to match the sink unit. If you intend fitting extractor fans above the oven and hob, you can increase their efficiency by building a simple pelmet onto the oven unit. The method of construction is clearly illustrated in Fig. 1.

In order to achieve a good finish, all exposed screw heads can be covered by small laminate discs cut from matching iron-on edge trim. Any exposed door edges must also be trimmed.

The construction and fitting of this unit will transform your kitchen and make it a more pleasant place to work in. Once you have experienced the advantages of this system you may wish to make matching units to hold foodstuffs and kitchen equipment. By using the basic designs described in this chapter, this should present no problem, and the resulting scheme on your kitchen will more than match expensive, manufactured kitchen systems.

Cutting lists
Sink/hob unit

Wood	standard	metric
Laminated chipboard		
2 ends	$35 \times 21 \times \frac{5}{8}$	$889 \times 533 \times 16$
3 intermediate divisions	$30\frac{3}{8} \times 21 \times \frac{5}{8}$	$771 \times 533 \times 16$
1 lower shelf	$96 \times 21 \times \frac{5}{8}$	$2438 \times 533 \times 16$
5 doors	$25\frac{1}{8} \times 15 \times \frac{5}{8}$	$638 \times 381 \times 16$
1 top drawer front	$18 \times 6\frac{1}{4} \times \frac{5}{8}$	$457 \times 159 \times 16$
2 centre drawer fronts	$18 \times 7\frac{1}{4} \times \frac{5}{8}$	$457 \times 184 \times 16$
1 bottom drawer front	$18 \times 7\frac{3}{4} \times \frac{5}{8}$	$457 \times 197 \times 16$
1 top front panel	$77\frac{1}{4} \times 7 \times \frac{5}{8}$	$1962 \times 178 \times 16$
1 kickboard	$96 \times 5 \times \frac{5}{8}$	$2438 \times 127 \times 16$
Blockboard		
1 working top	$98\frac{1}{4} \times 22\frac{5}{8} \times \frac{3}{4}$	$2495 \times 575 \times 19$
Softwood		
2 top rails	$97\frac{1}{4} \times 2 \times 1$	$2470 \times 51 \times 25$
1 front edge	$98\frac{1}{4} \times 1 \times 1$	$2496 \times 25 \times 25$
1 front edge	$21\frac{5}{8} \times 1 \times 1$	$549 \times 25 \times 25$
Hardboard		
1 back	$97\frac{1}{4} \times 35 \times \frac{1}{8}$	$2470 \times 889 \times 3$
4 drawer bottoms	$19 \times 17\frac{1}{2} \times \frac{1}{8}$	$483 \times 445 \times 3$
Plywood		
6 drawer sides	$19 \times 6\frac{5}{8} \times \frac{1}{2}$	$483 \times 168 \times 13$
2 top drawer sides	$19 \times 4\frac{3}{4} \times \frac{1}{2}$	$483 \times 121 \times 13$
2 top drawer ends	$17 \times 3\frac{1}{2} \times \frac{1}{2}$	$432 \times 89 \times 13$
6 drawer ends	$17 \times 5 \times \frac{1}{2}$	$432 \times 127 \times 13$
Hardwood		
10 drawer runners	$20 \times \frac{3}{4} \times \frac{1}{2}$	$508 \times 19 \times 13$

You will also require:
Plastic laminate. Fireproofing material. Door handles. Woodworking glue. 144 $1\frac{1}{2}$in (38mm) panel pins and No.6 screws. Edge trim.

Oven unit

Wood	standard	metric
Laminated chipboard		
1 side panel	$80 \times 21 \times \frac{5}{8}$	$2032 \times 533 \times 16$
1 side panel	$80 \times 6 \times \frac{5}{8}$	$2032 \times 152 \times 16$
2 bottom shelves	$31 \times 21 \times \frac{5}{8}$	$787 \times 533 \times 16$
1 top cross member	$30\frac{3}{8} \times 6 \times \frac{5}{8}$	$771 \times 152 \times 16$
1 top shelf	$31 \times 17 \times \frac{5}{8}$	$787 \times 432 \times 16$
1 top back panel	$31 \times 24 \times \frac{5}{8}$	$787 \times 610 \times 16$
2 top doors	$16\frac{1}{4} \times 15 \times \frac{5}{8}$	$413 \times 381 \times 16$
2 bottom doors	$18 \times 15 \times \frac{5}{8}$	$457 \times 381 \times 16$
1 kickboard	$29\frac{3}{4} \times 5 \times \frac{5}{8}$	$756 \times 127 \times 16$
Softwood		
1 vertical support batten	$80 \times 2 \times 1$	$2032 \times 51 \times 25$
2 centre shelf battens	$20 \times 1 \times 1$	$508 \times 25 \times 25$

Kitchen wall cupboard

Although kitchens require more storage space than any other rooms, they are often too small to allow adequate standing units to be installed. One satisfactory solution is to build a spacious wall mounted cupboard, purpose built for your own kitchen.

This kitchen wall cupboard has been designed to take advantage of the ever-increasing range of pre-finished and laminated materials suitable for furniture construction. The material used for this unit consists of a high grade chipboard core, covered on both surfaces and long edges with a tough melamine facing. All laminated materials have the advantage of being ready for use without preliminary sanding and finishing, and do not require subsequent decoration. If desired, the unit can be built of conventional solid wood, but this involves more work in

finishing and is not so easy to clean—an important consideration for kitchen furniture.

The design of the cupboard
The dimensions of the unit are suitable for most kitchens, but can be modified to suit individual requirements. Details of the shelving are not included, but the methods of fixing shelves to the unit are described.

A feature of this cupboard is the angled end, which has been designed to fit a corner of an existing kitchen. Obviously this angled corner is unsuitable for most kitchens, but details of its construction are included to show the techniques involved in making a fitted cupboard. It is a simple job to modify the design to give a conventional square ended unit.

Above: The completed unit in position. The dimensions of the unit may be adapted to fit your own kitchen.

Kitchen wall cupboard

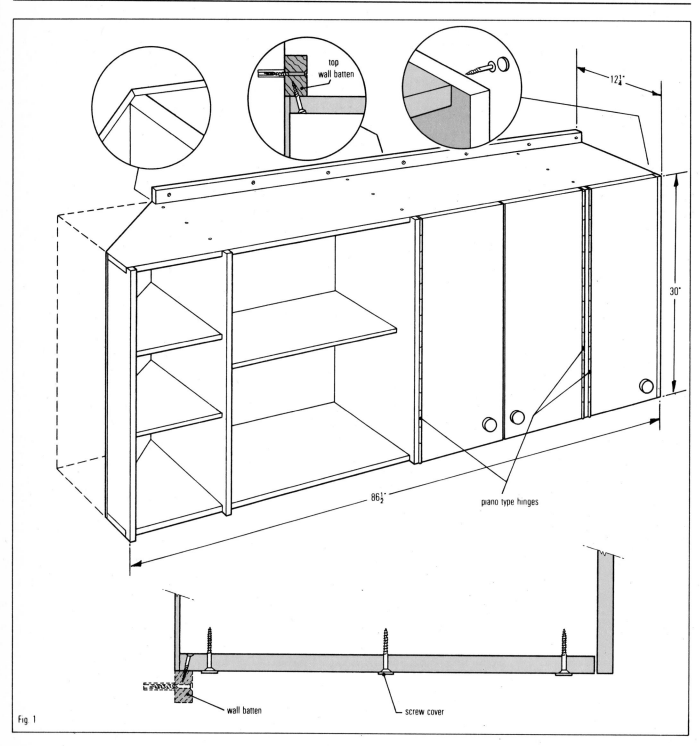

top wall batten

12¼"

30"

86½"

piano type hinges

wall batten

screw cover

Fig. 1

Fig 1. Details of the construction of the cupboard.

Working laminated materials

Laminated materials must be handled and worked with care to preserve their finish, and to prevent the chipboard core breaking and the laminate splintering. The following general rules must be observed when cutting out the pieces for the kitchen cupboard.

When cutting the laminated material, support it adequately on both sides of the intended cut to avoid the possibility of the last inch or two of the uncut material breaking under the weight of the unsupported panel. Whether you are using a hand or power saw, ensure that the tool is sharp and correctly set. To ensure a clean cut when using a hand saw, first score along the proposed cutting line with a sharp laminate cutting knife to

the depth of the laminate.

Cutting out

The uncomplicated design of the cupboard means that the number of different sections to be cut is kept to the minimum. Because of this, and the fact that the material is pre-finished, you should devote more care to marking and cutting each piece accurately. Once the cutting is complete, assembly is straightforward,

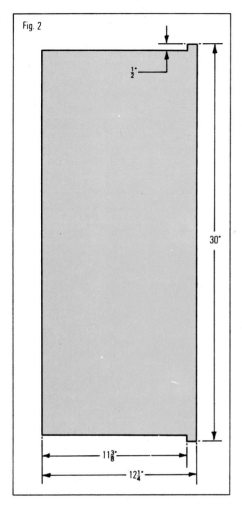

Fig. 2

$\frac{1}{2}$"

30"

$11\frac{3}{8}$"

$12\frac{1}{4}$"

Fig 2. The dimensions of the panels for the kitchen unit. The ends of the panels are cut away so that the top and bottom fit flush with the full depth doors.

the inset to Fig. 1 (opposite).

Now clean up all the internal cut edges by lightly sanding them, and mark the locations of the vertical panels on the top and bottom of the unit. The easiest way to do this is to lay the top onto the bottom, so that all the edges are flush, and then mark both at once.

First, mark out the location of the vertical end panels, then work inwards. The cupboard is fitted with two single 12in (305mm) doors, located at each end, and two double 30in (762mm) doors located in the centre. The vertical panels are, therefore, positioned to allow for the width of these doors plus their $\frac{1}{8}$in (3mm) hinge or hinges, and a working clearance of $\frac{1}{16}$in (2mm) between closed doors.

Assembling the unit

Before commencing assembly, lay a sheet of hardboard on the ground to prevent damage to the pieces. Initially, the unit is fitted together using $1\frac{1}{2}$in (38mm) panel pins and glue, before final fixing with screws. In order to make strong glued joints, first 'key' the laminate with coarse sandpaper where the joints occur, then apply a laminate adhesive. Allow the glue to set then add the panel pins.

Use only two pins for each joint, and locate these adjacent to where the screw holes are to be drilled. When the unit has been pinned together, drill for $1\frac{1}{5}$in (31mm) No. 8 twinfast screws, using a combination drill/countersink bit. It is essential, when drilling laminated materials of this type, that a pilot hole be drilled to take the screw threads. Fix the screws in position and remove any glue left on the exposed surface.

Fitting the back

Roughen the finished surface of the hardboard back where the glue joints occur, and glue and pin it into position. If the cupboard is to incorporate an angled end, the hardboard must be cut to shape and two edges mitred as shown in Fig. 1.

With a wall-fixed unit of this type, the hardboard edges do not normally show once the unit is fixed. The lower edge is hidden by a supporting batten and generally the top edge is above eye level. However, should it be necessary to disguise the top edge, a length of $\frac{1}{2}$in (13mm) quadrant moulding can be fixed after the unit has been mounted. The

Fig 2. The dimensions of the panels for the kitchen unit. The ends of the panels are cut away so that the top and bottom fit flush with the full depth doors.

as there are no complicated joints or time-consuming finishing processes.

Following the general rules laid out above, mark out and cut all the pieces to the sizes given in the cutting list.

The carcase of the unit is constructed from two 96in (2440mm) lengths of 24in (610mm) wide board cut lengthwise to make two pieces $11\frac{3}{8}$in (289mm) wide and $86\frac{1}{2}$in (2197mm) long for the top and bottom. The remaining two $12\frac{1}{4}$in (311mm) wide boards are cut into five 30in (762mm) long panels to make the vertical partitions and ends. Unless you wish to incorporate the angled or mitred end, cut all these pieces as square ended panels.

The top and bottom of the unit fit into recesses cut in the vertical panels. These recesses are $\frac{1}{2}$in (13mm) deep and $11\frac{3}{8}$in (289mm) long as shown in Fig. 2.

Cut the recesses carefully and trial assemble the panels to check that all the rear edges of the unit are flush. If you are making the unit with an angled end, cut the rear (long edge) of one vertical panel at the correct angle as shown in upper supporting batten of 2in x 1in (51mm x 25mm) softwood should be attached at this point by screwing through from the inside of the unit.

Only the doors and shelving need to be added, but before fixing these, carefully trim the hardboard back flush with the laminate surfaces and cover the screw heads. These screw covers are cut from edge trim material and are fixed by laying them in place and running a warm iron over them.

The cupboard doors

At least one cut edge of the door panels will expose the composition board core and should be covered with an edge trim. Various types of trimming are available, but perhaps the longest lasting is iron-on edge trim. Cut this trim to size, and glue it to all cut edges.

It is easier to add the door handles at this stage. These may be chosen according to taste, but when fixing handles which require a hole to be drilled through the door, remember to cramp a waste piece of timber to the drill exit surface in order to avoid splitting the laminate.

The doors are hung on full length piano type hinges, which are widely available in plastic or metal. One advantage of this type of hinge over conventional door hinges is that it does not need to be recessed into the edge of the door frame. To fix the hinges in position, first mark out their location on the edge of the door and the vertical panels. Screw the hinge to the door edge after having first pre-drilled for $\frac{3}{4}$in (19mm) No. 4 brass screws. Now hang the doors to the unit using $\frac{1}{2}$in (13mm) screws.

To complete the construction of the doors, fix 5lb (2.2kg) magnetic catches to the edge of the top panel. In order to reduce noise when closing the doors, a small rubber disc can be glued adjacent to the catches.

Shelving

Shelving should be fitted according to individual requirements. The ideal width of shelves for this unit is 9in (225mm). Each shelf should be supported on manufactured plastic stops, or battens, glued and screwed to the vertical panels.

Wall fixing

Kitchen cupboards, when filled with utensils or foodstuffs, are heavy and require adequate support if they are to be fixed to a wall. The best way to provide this support is to fix a full length batten to the wall on which the unit rests. First, decide where the cupboard will be located, then fix the batten firmly into position with plugs and screws in the wall. Rest the cupboard on the batten, but before fixing it to the wall, check that the wall surface is flat and true. If it is not, it will be necessary to insert packing between the wall and the unit, to prevent distorting the structure as the wall screws are driven home.

When you are satisfied that the cupboard is positioned true to the wall, fix it with screws through the top batten. These screws are fixed at 18in (457mm) intervals.

The kitchen wall cupboard is now ready for use. As the need arises, you can build other kitchen units in the same materials, using the same techniques. In this way you can provide a complete and attractive storage system, tailor-made for your own kitchen.

Cutting list

Laminated chipboard	standard	metric
1 top panel	$86\frac{1}{2} \times 11\frac{3}{8} \times \frac{1}{2}$	$2197 \times 289 \times 13$
1 bottom panel	$86\frac{1}{2} \times 11\frac{3}{8} \times \frac{1}{2}$	$2197 \times 289 \times 13$
5 vertical panels	$30 \times 12\frac{1}{4} \times \frac{1}{2}$	$762 \times 311 \times 13$
4 door panels	$30 \times 15 \times \frac{1}{2}$	$762 \times 381 \times 13$
2 door panels	$30 \times 12 \times \frac{1}{2}$	$762 \times 305 \times 13$
Hardboard		
1 back panel	$86\frac{1}{2} \times 30 \times \frac{1}{4}$	$2197 \times 762 \times 6$

You will also require:

6 30in (762mm) plastic/metal piano type hinges. 6 door handles. Shelving and shelving battens to individual requirements. Edge trim for door edges. 4 5lb (2.2kg) magnetic catches. 2 full-length supporting battens. Waste hardboard. Laminate for trimming. 30 $1\frac{1}{2}$in (38mm) panel pins. 50 $1\frac{1}{2}$in (38mm) No.8 Twinfast screws. 30 $\frac{3}{4}$in (19mm) No.6 screws. Laminate adhesive.

Bunk beds

Bunk beds

These bunk beds can be varied in length by replacing the side rails and inserting an additional strip to the plywood base.

This means that if the bunks are wide enough – at least 2ft 6in (762mm) – they can be made, initially, for children, and 'grow' with them. You will end up with adult bunk beds that are useful space-saving units for guests.

Construction details

The beds illustrated are made in teak, although any hardwood will do. If you intend to paint or varnish the finished product, buy timber that has been kiln dried; an undried wood, because of its moisture content, can sometimes cause the paint to 'lift' and peel.

The unit basically consists of two rectangular carcases, with plywood bases, mounted between four upright members as shown in Fig. 1. Both pairs of upright members or legs – the front and rear pairs – are joined across the bottoms by a 'skid' or runner as shown in Fig. 2. This not only makes the frame more rigid but also enables the unit to be moved easily.

Various joints are used in construction: a halving for the inside of the box frames; mortise and tenon for the top and bottom rails and the ladder; a single dovetail for the leg/skid joint; stub mortise and tenon for the head box joint; a mitred secret dovetail for the box corners at the bottom of the bunks; and a housing for the side rails.

The mitred secret dovetail (Fig. 10) is widely held to be one of the most difficult joints in woodwork, but this is not quite true. While it certainly takes a little patience and care to make, as long as the fit is reasonably snug, any imperfections will be covered by glue and hidden under the surface of the wood, unlike the open dovetail where any inaccuracies are instantly visible.

Upholstery details have been omitted here, because of the vast numbers of permutations possible. The mattresses can be purchased ready made, or you can make them yourself from foam rubber or plastic with or without a fibre filling such as Dacron or Terylene, and cover them in a suitable fabric.

The materials

A complete list of materials is given in the cutting list. Buy your timber planed to size, but slightly overlength as there will be a certain amount of wastage in finishing. Do not overdo this as it is only necessary to order each piece about 1in (25mm) longer than the final length intended.

Cutting and marking

With a pencil, lightly mark each piece of timber so that you know where it fits in the unit – there is nothing more annoying than making a perfect joint, only to discover that it has been cut on the wrong piece of wood.

Carefully mark the length of each piece of timber. When marking pieces of identical timber, such as the four uprights, cramp or wedge the pieces together and mark them together so that each length will be consistent. Measure carefully several times before you mark and cut. Time spent on accurate marking is never wasted.

As most of the unit is held together by slot-type joints, it is advisable to cut these first. This will enable you to check your progress as you go along by fitting the various parts together in jig-saw fashion to make sure the dimensions are correct.

Mortise and tenon

Two types of mortise and tenon are used here. The cross bearers and ladder use the basic type as shown in Fig. 5, but the joints between the boxes and legs are mortise and tenons which have been haunched in the middle, as in Fig. 6.

Mark out all the tenons on the bearers first. Set the marking gauge to $\frac{3}{16}$in (5mm) (in order to mark out a $\frac{3}{8}$in [10mm] tenon), and run this along the ends of the pieces as in Fig. 5. Run it along all four edges and you will have marked out an area $\frac{3}{16}$in (5mm) deep (inwards) all round. The tenon will stand $\frac{3}{4}$in (19mm) proud, so measure this distance down from the end of the timber and mark a line right round. Now mark out the mortise outlines on the legs by laying the tenon over the leg at the correct place and direct marking. The tenon of the joints can be made with an electric drill and power circular saw.

Next, mark out and cut the haunched mortise and tenon for the boxes and legs. Here again the tenon is $\frac{3}{8}$in (10mm) wide, but the shoulder is not the same width all round. It is cut $\frac{1}{2}$in (13mm) inwards at the edges and $\frac{3}{16}$in (5mm) along the sides. The haunched portion is a $1\frac{7}{8}$in × 1in (48mm × 25mm) rectangle cut from the centre of the leading edge as in Fig. 6. When you have finished these joints, put them together to check that they fit.

Dovetail

A single dovetail is cut out of both ends of each skid, which is fitted to the foot of each leg.

Mark out the dovetails on the skids as shown in Fig. 8. The shoulder is $\frac{1}{2}$in (13mm) wide and the slope is 1 in 7 – but this is not critical. Cut the dovetails and use them as templates for transferring the outline to the legs. In this way each joint will be fitted individually, ensuring a better fit. Clearly mark each pair of joints so that the correct match can be made easily when assembling the unit later.

Stub mortise and tenon

The stub mortise and tenon joins the corners of the head box. The head board is added when the bunks are finished. The stubs, as shown in Fig. 7, are $\frac{1}{2}$in × $\frac{3}{4}$in (13mm × 19mm) tenons. They are not cut away at the sides of the timber and are only $\frac{1}{2}$in (13mm) deep. The top and bottom tenons are set $\frac{1}{2}$in (13mm) inside the edges of the boards and the mortises are $\frac{3}{4}$in (19mm) from the ends of the boards. Once again, temporarily fit the joints together to check the fit.

Mitred secret dovetail

This joint fits the corners of the foot box and the dimensions for making it are shown in Fig. 10.

First, mark each board to what will be its finished length. Next, butt the box together and check with the try square that it is square. The small dovetails on one side (Fig. 10D) are called pins, and the opposite dovetails are tails. The pins are cut first, and this section is used as a template for marking the tails.

Using the diagram in Fig. 10A, mark out a rebate $\frac{9}{16}$in wide and $\frac{3}{16}$in deep (14mm × 5mm) on the timber. Cut the rebate and you will have a section as

Fig 1. Side elevation of the bunk beds.

Fig 2. End elevation of the beds.

Fig 3. Construction details of the ends of the units. It is the rails which screw to the end boxes of the beds that give the units their ability to 'grow'. They may be cut short to accommodate children when they are small, and replaced later with larger components.

Fig 4. Exploded view of the bunk bed unit. Only one end is shown, as the other end is identical except for the headboard extension.

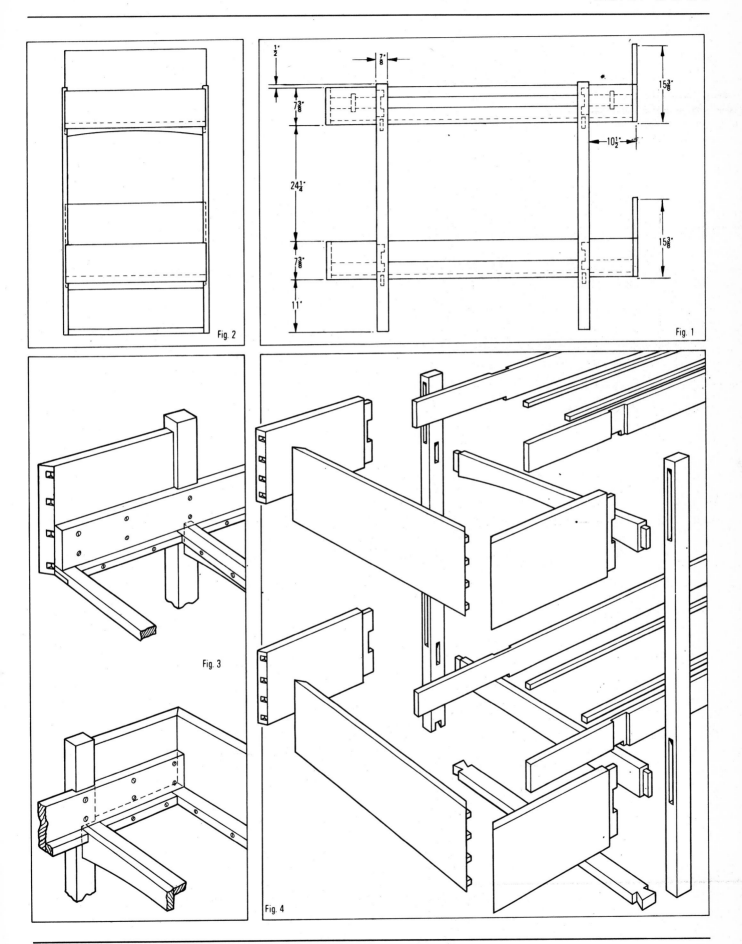

Fig. 2

Fig. 1

Fig. 3

Fig. 4

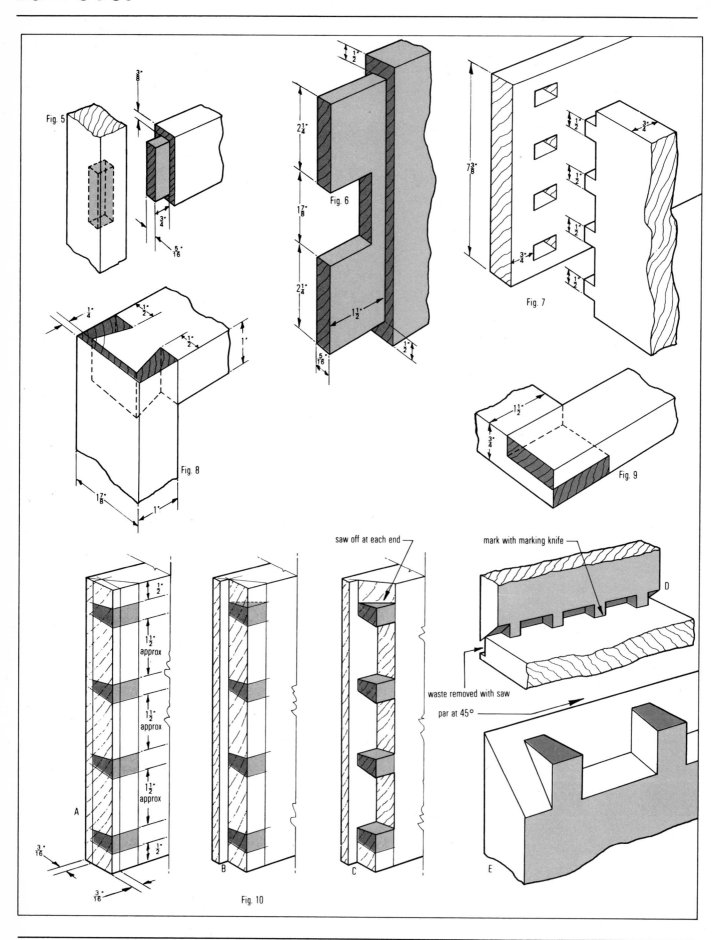

Fig. 5

Fig. 6

Fig. 7

Fig. 8

Fig. 9

saw off at each end

mark with marking knife

D

waste removed with saw

par at 45°

A

B

C

E

Fig. 10

shown in Fig. 10B. Now mark out the pins; these are at approximate $1\frac{1}{2}$in (38mm) intervals and $\frac{1}{2}$in (13mm) from each edge. With a tenon saw and chisel cut the sloping recesses for the tails, leaving the pins proud as in Fig. 10C. Finish off by sloping the remaining lip of the rebate with a paring chisel as in Fig. 10E.

Now cut an identical rebate in the opposite timber and, using the pin joint as a template, transfer the markings for the tails as in Figs. 10D and E. The tails can now be formed by cutting out the pin recesses.

When the joint is complete, mark each piece so that you can match it later. Make the joint for the opposite corner of the foot box.

The joints for the corners of the inside box frames are of the simple halving variety shown in Fig. 9. Housing joints (see Fig. 3) are used to join the legs to the side rails.

Assembling the units

The unit, from the assembly aspect, consists of two frames, each consisting of two legs, two struts or bearers, one skid, and two foot or head boxes – an example of the head frame is shown in Fig. 3. The two frames are stood upright, and joined by the side rails, which are screwed to the inside of the boxes and legs as shown in Fig. 4. An internal box framing, which is virtually battening round the inside, is then screwed round to support the edges of the plywood panel which is the base for the mattress.

First, glue, fit and cramp the head frame as shown in Fig. 4. Lay the assembly down on a flat surface for this, and constantly check all angles for squareness. It is best to complete all the head frame at the same time – if you make the boxes separately, the tenons might not fit into the mortise slots when the glue is dry. Repeat this for the foot frame.

When the adhesive has thoroughly set on both frames, place them on their sides so that the open ends of the boxes are facing the middle, lay the rails along the inside and mark out the housing joints to fit over the inside of the legs as in Fig. 3. Cut the housing joints and screw the side rails in position to the legs and boxes which are on the floor. Carefully lift the frame over so that the opposite side is on the floor, and mark. Cut and screw the remaining side rails in position.

Fit and screw the box frame battening round the inside of the bunks as in Fig. 3. Then, fit and screw the plywood mattress bases to the top of the battening.

The guard rails for the top bunk can be fitted in the same way as the rails. This is recommended for children because they cannot remove the guard rails. However, there are many fitments which provide for easy removal of the guard rail and this might be an advantage for adults. One such method consists of brass rods sunk and glued into the bottom edge of the guard rail and fitted into holes drilled in the top edge of the side rail.

The headboards are simply cut away at the lower outside edges to provide recesses for the protruding corners of the sides of the head boxes, and then screwed to the top of the head box.

The ladder

This consists of five rungs fitted into the sides by means of mortise and tenon joints, and is simple to construct. Radius the tops of the rungs slightly.

The ladder hooks can be made from mild steel strip, but there are many proprietary types on the market.

Finishing

Sand down all surfaces using an orbital finishing sander with a grade 'o' glass-paper, wipe with a cloth dampened with turpentine to remove the wood dust, and varnish with a clear polyurethane diluted 50/50 with turpentine. When dry, rub down with a grade 'o' steel wool, wipe it down and finish with polyurethane.

Fig 5. The basic stopped mortise and tenon used in the construction of the bunk beds.

Fig 6. The end boxes joint to the uprights using a mortise and tenon haunched in the middle.

Fig 7. The head boxes are jointed using stub mortise and tenons.

Fig 8. The stopped dovetail which joins the skids to the uprights.

Fig 9. The half lap used to join the inside corners of the box frame.

Figs 10 A-E. The method of cutting the mitred secret dovetails.

Cutting list

Solid wood	standard	metric
Teak		
4 legs	$50\frac{1}{2} \times 1\frac{7}{8} \times 1$	$1283 \times 47 \times 25$
2 skids	$32 \times 1\frac{7}{8} \times 1$	$813 \times 47 \times 25$
4 cross bearers	$32 \times 3 \times \frac{3}{4}$	$813 \times 76 \times 19$
4 foot boxes	$12 \times 7\frac{3}{8} \times \frac{3}{4}$	$305 \times 187 \times 19$
2 foot boxes	$31\frac{3}{4} \times 7\frac{3}{8} \times \frac{3}{4}$	$806 \times 187 \times 19$
4 head boxes	$12 \times 7\frac{3}{8} \times \frac{3}{4}$	$305 \times 187 \times 19$
2 head boxes	$31\frac{3}{4} \times 7\frac{3}{8} \times \frac{3}{4}$	$806 \times 187 \times 19$
4 side rails	$31\frac{3}{4} \times 3\frac{1}{2} \times \frac{3}{4}$	$806 \times 89 \times 19$
2 safety rails	$31\frac{3}{4} \times 1\frac{3}{4} \times \frac{3}{4}$	$806 \times 45 \times 19$
2 ladder sides	$49\frac{1}{2} \times 1\frac{1}{2} \times \frac{3}{4}$	$1257 \times 38 \times 19$
5 ladder rungs	$12\frac{1}{2} \times 1\frac{1}{2} \times \frac{3}{4}$	$318 \times 38 \times 19$
Hardwood		
4 internal battens	$44 \times 1\frac{1}{2} \times \frac{3}{4}$	$1118 \times 38 \times 19$
8 internal battens	$10 \times 1\frac{1}{2} \times \frac{3}{4}$	$254 \times 38 \times 19$
8 internal battens	$32 \times 1\frac{1}{2} \times \frac{3}{4}$	$813 \times 38 \times 19$
Plywood		
2 mattress bases	$64 \times 29\frac{3}{4} \times \frac{1}{2}$	$1626 \times 756 \times 13$
2 head boards teak or chipboard	$32\frac{1}{2} \times 15\frac{3}{8} \times \frac{3}{4}$	$826 \times 390 \times 19$

Bed platform

Below: Installing a bed platform is an ingenious way of making extra space in a small living area.

A proportion of today's houses consist of buildings 40 years or more old. By modern standards the ceilings in such homes are high, and the top part of each room is just wasted space. This bed platform enables you to use some of this otherwise wasted area – and add interest as well as utility to your sleeping space.

This particular structure has been designed to provide a platform, some 7ft (2.1m) high, covering a sufficient area for sleeping space for three adults. A large room is required for this, but you can alter the dimensions to suit your room. For example in a smaller room you could build the storage/desk unit with single bed above, as shown in Fig. 1. In a small flat this could be the sleeping accommodation for the occupant, while in a larger home, it might be used for the occasional visitor.

The boarded-in area at the base could provide even more sleeping space – in which case this particular section would be nothing more than a large pair of bunk beds – but here it is used as a table of sorts, with storage space underneath that is reached by doors at one side. Alternatively you could use this as a desk in which case one of the doors should be left out to provide a recess for your knees.

Construction

The main supports consist of 3in × 2in (76mm × 51mm) timbers. The two rectangular frames shown in Fig. 4 are of 2in × 2in (51mm × 51mm) timbers, with ½in (13mm) T&G boarding fixed around the inside of the end framing and the inside of one side. The other side, the front, is fitted with two doors, made of the same size timber framing and boarding, as shown in Fig. 4.

The top, or platform, has a framing of 4in × 1in (102mm × 25mm) rails bolted to the vertical supports. The method of doing this is shown quite clearly in Fig. 2 which is a 'top floor' plan.

The floor of the platform consists of 1in (25mm) thick T&G boarding supported on 1in × 1in (25mm × 25mm) battening screwed round the inside of the rails as shown in Fig. 6.

T&G boarding, used for the floor, is secured across the narrow width, of each frame. If laid along the length it would give too much in the middle. For this reason, where a frame is wider than 3ft (914mm), the underside of the flooring should be reinforced every 3ft (914mm) along the diagonal line of the frame, as in

Fig. 7 with 2in × 1in (51mm × 25mm) battens.

A major safety point to note is that the combined unit, as shown in Fig. 2 is a self-supporting structure. But if you wish to build only the main unit as shown in Fig. 1, the vertical supports should be bolted, or otherwise secured to the wall. This is necessary because the weight of an adult, when climbing on and off, could cause the structure to sway and possibly topple over if it were not firmly fixed to the wall.

The main frame

The main frame as illustrated in Fig. 1 is constructed by cutting the side rails 7ft (2134mm) long out of 4in × 1in (102mm × 25mm) and the end rails 3ft (914mm) long. The uprights 8ft (2438mm) long are cut and the end frames assembled.

Measure 5in (127mm) down from the top of the uprights and drill a hole in each of the rear uprights for screws or bolts into the wall. Fix the end rails to the front and rear uprights using bolts or large screws.

Next cut the lower end rails out of 2in × 2in (51mm × 51mm). These rails will be 4in (102mm) shorter than the top rails. The lower rails are fixed into position with lost-head nails and then holes are drilled at an angle so that screws can be driven 'on the skew' into the uprights (the upper rail being 2ft 3in [685mm] above floor level). When the framing has been made up it should be checked for square by measuring the diagonals.

When the framing is square, the boarding can be fixed to the inside of the lower rails. The completed framework should then be lifted into place and plumbed up so that the position of the top hole can be marked and the wall plugged ready for the screws.

Screw the frames into place against the wall and then fix the long rails. The rear rails are skew-nailed and screwed as before, but the front rails butt against the ends and are screwed to the inside face of the uprights.

Boarding is also screwed to the inside of the rear rails using two No.8 screws in each board, taking the measurements directly from the framing.

Two doors are hung between the lower front rails, or one is left open if it is to be a desk. The doors are frames of 2in × 2in (51mm × 51mm) timber, mitred, glued and screwed at the corners, with vertical T&G boarding at the rear. A good wood-

Bed platform

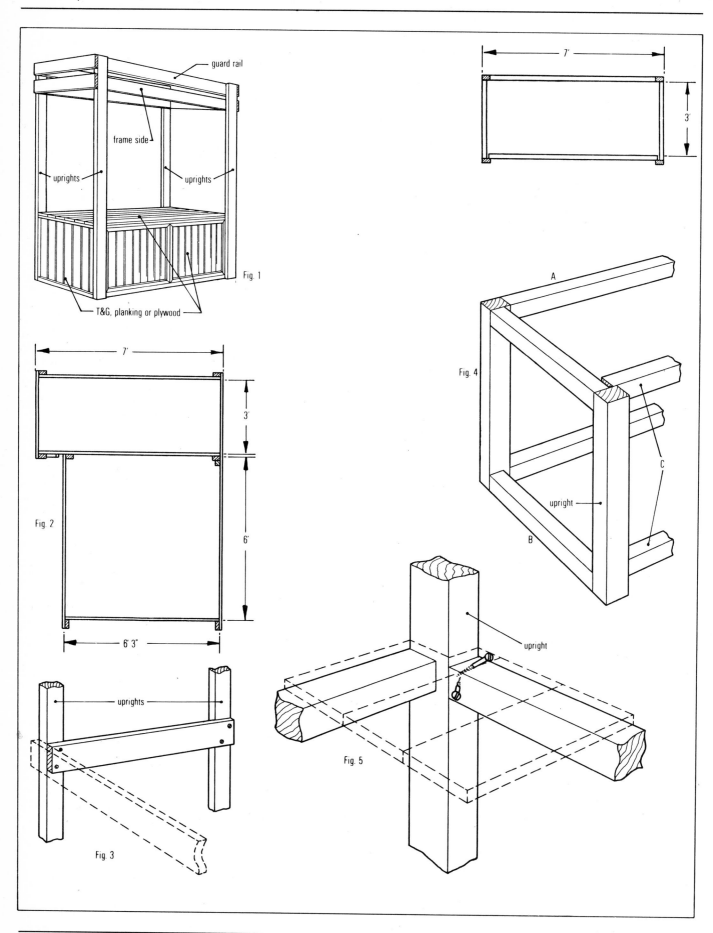

guard rail

frame side

uprights

uprights

T&G, planking or plywood

Fig. 1

7'

3'

7'

3'

6'

6' 3"

Fig. 2

uprights

Fig. 3

A

Fig. 4

C

upright

B

upright

Fig. 5

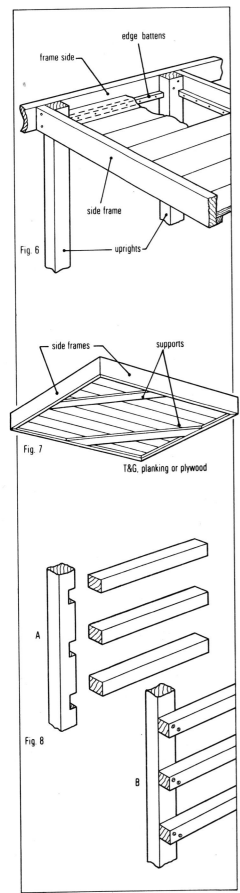

Fig. 6

edge battens

frame side

side frame

uprights

Fig. 7

side frames

supports

T&G, planking or plywood

A

Fig. 8

B

working adhesive is spread in the groove of each board before the tongue is inserted. When the glue has set, the run of boarding will be sufficiently strong and rigid not to require cross bracing behind. Every part of the doors should be direct fitted, because almost certainly the space it will be filling will not be a perfect rectangle.

The base is finished by laying the boarding over the top. This runs from edge to edge across the narrow width, as shown in Fig. 1. The method of fixing means that the end-grain of the boarding along the sides of the base will be visible. End-grain is not very attractive at best, so ensure that the boards are cut with a fine-toothed panel saw to make as clean a cut as possible. If you prefer, the boarding can be laid along the length of the base, but in this case you will need a cross member added between top timbers A and C. This is secured at each end by skew-screwing into timbers A and C.

To complete the platform above, screw 1in × 1in (25mm × 25mm) battening round the inside faces of the bottom rails. This battening should be secured with countersunk 1½in (38mm) wood screws at 3in (76mm) intervals.

Then lay the 4in × 1in (102mm × 25 mm) T&G boarding to be the 'floor' of the platform. As with the boarding lower down, this is secured with two screws at each end and a dab of glue. But here the screw holes are drilled only ½in (13mm) inwards from the ends of the boards. As each board is fitted, spread a little woodworking adhesive in the grooves to make the floor more rigid.

It only remains to fit the side and end guard rails round the top. These are made of 3in × 1in (76mm × 25mm) timber, and are bolted to the supports in the same way as the side and end planks immediately below.

The side unit

This is really only an extension of the main frame. Here it has been made wide enough to accommodate two sleeping adults, but the dimensions can easily be altered.

The method of construction is identical to that of the main unit. As shown in Fig. 2, two uprights are bolted to one side of the main unit, and these provide fixing points at one end for the side planking of the unit, with the two remaining supports placed at the far end as shown in Fig. 6.

When a side unit is added to a main

Fig 1. The basic unit. If this is to be used on its own, the uprights must be secured to a wall, otherwise the weight of a person climbing into it may cause it to topple over.

Fig 2. Plan view of the unit with extension. In this form the bed platform is free standing.

Fig 3. Method of fitting the platform rails to the uprights.

Fig 4. The cupboard construction with plan view of the same. Note the way in which the front horizontal fits inside the uprights.

Fig 5. The top of the cupboard unit must be notched round the uprights as illustrated here. Note the method of screwing the horizontals to the uprights.

Fig 6. Method of constructing the side unit.

Fig 7. The base of the side unit requires support whichever method of construction is used.

Figs. 8A-B. The two alternative methods of constructing the ladder.

unit the guard rail separating them is omitted to allow easy access to both sides.

If you make a side unit as large as the one shown here, then you will have to fit underfloor supports under the T&G boarding so that it will not sag in the middle. Use two pieces of $2in \times 1in$ ($51mm \times 25mm$) timber fixed diagonally (Fig. 7). Each end is bevelled to fit snug against the sides of the platform and is secured to the sides with screws at each end. Where the supports run across the boarding, drill holes so that a screw can be driven into each board.

The ladder
This ladder has rungs that are housed into the side supports as shown in Fig. 8A. To do this, cut all rungs to an exact length and direct mark; then cut and fit so that each rung houses perfectly.

Then, you must secure the joints with glue and screw through the outside of the side supports into the end grain of the rungs.

A simpler version is shown in Fig. 8B. Here the rungs are laid directly over the side rails and secured at each joint with glue and two screws.

Whichever method you use, when you have finished the construction you must carefully round off the tops of the rungs with a spokeshave. This will make them easier on your feet.

Cutting list Solid wood Main unit	standard	metric
4 uprights	$96 \times 3 \times 2$	$2438 \times 76 \times 51$
4 lower frame sides	$78 \times 2 \times 2$	$1981 \times 51 \times 51$
4 lower frame ends	$36 \times 2 \times 2$	$914 \times 51 \times 51$
Lower frame boarding		
21 tops (T&G)	$36 \times 4 \times \frac{1}{2}$	$914 \times 102 \times 13$
42 sides (T&G)	$27 \times 4 \times \frac{1}{2}$	$686 \times 102 \times 13$
18 ends (T&G)	$27 \times 4 \times \frac{1}{2}$	$686 \times 102 \times 13$
Platform materials		
2 sides	$84 \times 4 \times 1$	$2134 \times 102 \times 25$
2 sides	$84 \times 3 \times 1$	$2134 \times 76 \times 25$
2 ends	$36 \times 4 \times 1$	$914 \times 102 \times 25$
2 ends	$36 \times 3 \times 1$	$914 \times 76 \times 25$
2 edge supports	$84 \times 1 \times 1$	$2134 \times 25 \times 25$
Battens		
2 edge supports	$36 \times 1 \times 1$	$914 \times 25 \times 25$
21 flooring (T&G)	$36 \times 4 \times 1$	$914 \times 102 \times 25$
Side unit		
4 uprights	$96 \times 3 \times 2$	$2438 \times 76 \times 51$
Platform materials		
2 sides	$75 \times 4 \times 1$	$1905 \times 102 \times 25$
2 sides	$75 \times 3 \times 1$	$1905 \times 76 \times 25$
1 end	$72 \times 4 \times 1$	$1829 \times 107 \times 25$
1 end	$72 \times 3 \times 1$	$1829 \times 76 \times 25$
2 edge supports	$75 \times 1 \times 1$	$1905 \times 25 \times 25$
Battens		
2 edge supports	$72 \times 1 \times 1$	$1829 \times 25 \times 25$
19 flooring (T&G)	$72 \times 4 \times 1$	$1829 \times 102 \times 25$
2 underfloor supports	$84 \times 2 \times 1$	$2134 \times 51 \times 25$
The ladder		
2 sides	$84 \times 2 \times 1$	$2134 \times 51 \times 25$
10 rungs	$12 \times 2 \times 1$	$305 \times 51 \times 25$

You will also require:
2 brass 3in (76mm) angle brackets. At least 24 $3\frac{1}{2}$in (88mm) long $\frac{1}{4}$in (6mm) bolts, with nuts. Wood screws, No.8 $1\frac{1}{2}$in (38mm) and 3in (75mm). Lost head nails, $1\frac{1}{2}$in (38mm). Wood adhesive.

Fitted wardrobe

This built-in cupboard is simple to construct and a great space-saver.

This wardrobe has been built into a corner, but it could equally well have been built against a wall or into an alcove. The dimensions can be altered to suit the space you have available. For this reason no cutting list has been included. As long as the timber sections are adhered to, there should be no problems.

General construction details

The construction outline, with exploded views of the joints used, is shown in Fig. 1. When making fitted units such as this you have to design according to the room you are fitting. For instance this unit is 7ft 5in (2260mm) at the back, because of the slope of the ceiling.

Main supports consist of three 2in × 2in (51mm × 51mm) vertical members, but a wardrobe built against a wall would require four supports, or only the two front ones if built into an alcove. Timbers of the same dimensions are used for the front top and bottom rails. The middle rail 2in × 1½in (51mm × 38mm) acts as the main support for the lower sliding doors, which are cut from panels of ¾in (19mm) blockboard.

The top part of the structure is a compartment with two hardboard sliding doors set between two runners. A sectional view of the runners for both sets of doors is shown in Fig. 2. Runners and fittings for both upper and lower doors are proprietary fitments. There are many different types on the market and the ones shown here are just two examples. Your local retailer will show you the kinds that are readily available.

Fitted wardrobe

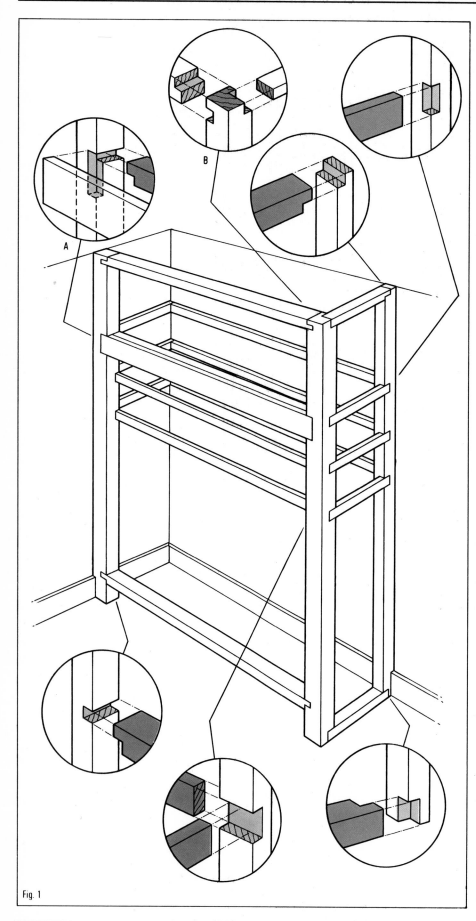

Fig. 1

Fig 1. Construction details for a wardrobe built into the corner of a room. The third upright is unnecessary in this case. The unit is simply built—all joints being of the ordinary housing type.

The fittings of the lower runners are hidden from view by a 4in × ½in (102mm × 13mm) timber pelmet as shown in Fig. 2. This pelmet is housed into the vertical supports at each end and also acts as a strengthening support for the middle rail.

The frames for the three shelves consist of 2in × 1¼in (51mm × 32mm) timbers. The wardrobe is a floor-to-ceiling structure and is secured to the walls at two points. If you are building in a corner or alcove, it is not necessary to screw the top and bottom members to the floor and ceiling, but this will have to be done in the case of a unit with two free-standing sides as in Fig. 4.

The receiving wall

It is essential for the supports on each side of the doors to be absolutely vertical. The rear supports, if any, can be screwed to a wall that is out of true, and the joints adjusted to fit. But if the front supports are not plumb the doors will not close flush with the sides of the wardrobe.

The easiest way of fixing a timber support vertically to a 'leaning' wall is to stand the support so that it is touching the wall at one end.

Use a plumb line or spirit level to ensure that the timber is vertical. Then measure the space between the timber and wall at the 'open' end. Put the timber aside and screw a block of wood, the same thickness as the space and as wide as the timber, to the wall. The timber can then be screwed to the block at one end and to the wall at the opposite end, and the wedge-shaped space between it and the wall filled with plaster. When the plaster has set, drill holes through the support and plaster, into the wall, and screw the support firmly in place. This method is the one to use if the wall is an inch, or less, out of true.

If your wall is more than an inch out over the length of the timber support, it would be better to cut a wedge-shaped fillet to shape as shown in Fig. 5. A piece of timber, as wide as the support but thicker, is placed vertically against the wall, with a 1in (25mm) piece of batten at the 'narrow' end (the batten can be dispensed with if a skirting board is there).

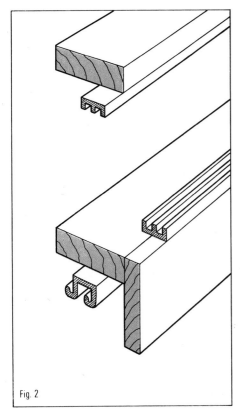

Fig. 2

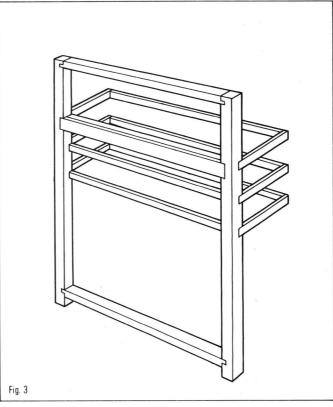

Fig. 3

Fig 2. The type of door runners used is a matter of personal choice.

Fig 3. If the wardrobe is to be built into an alcove, the rear uprights may be dispensed with altogether. The basic construction remains the same in all cases.

Ensure that the support is vertical and place a block into the wide end as shown in Fig. 5. Now measure the gap between the edge of the timber nearest the wall and the wall itself at regular intervals and lightly mark the timber at these points. Lay the timber on the ground and mark off each measurement along the timber. Draw a line along the ends of these as shown by the dotted line in Fig. 5, and cut the timber along the line. This is easily done with a circular saw on the bench stand. There is a special way of doing this called firring. See the chapter on power sawing in the Techniques section.

When the cut-out portion that has the markings is turned end for end, it should fit the incline of the wall perfectly. If there is a skirting board at floor level, the bottom of the fillet will have to be sawn off level with this so that the fillet can be screwed directly to the wall.

Building the main frame

With chalk, mark out the outline of the wardrobe base on the floor. This wardrobe will only require two lines – side and front. Make sure that the area is square by measuring the diagonals and checking that both measurements are identical. Using a plumb line, transfer the marks to the ceiling.

Measure the height of the uprights –

they should all be about the same length, so cut them to the shortest measurement. Put the two front uprights together and mark the positions of the rails. Cut the housings and then cut the rails to length. Mark the shoulders of the joints by placing the rails together and squaring the lines across all three timbers. This will ensure that the uprights will be parallel.

Cut the joints and fit the frame together dry, to check that all the dimensions are correct. Then, glue the joints, fit them together and pin them to hold them while the glue sets.

Before the glue sets, measure the diagonals to ensure that they are the same length and that the frame is square. Then tack a temporary batten from the middle of the top rail across the middle rail and to about the middle of the upright. This will hold the frame square until it is fixed in place.

Mark the end joints, putting the third upright against the frame flush at the top and bottom, and squaring the lines across the two timbers. Then cut out these housings. Cut the end rails and glue and pin them into the housing of the third or back upright. The front frame can then be lifted up and the end section glued and pinned to it. The pelmet timber can be either fixed now or later when the doors and tracks have been fitted. The latter

may be the best as it will give more freedom to fit the doors.

Now you can put the whole framework into position and mark the walls so that they can be drilled and plugged. Three screws to each upright should be sufficient. The front frame is square; so if you level the bottom rail, the sides will be plumb. Use a little packing if necessary. Measure the end frame and the distance from the back wall to the face of the front frame at both ends to ensure that the front frame is parallel to the back wall.

Measure and cut the shelf-supporting battens and plug and screw them to the wall finding their position by levelling from the top of the end rails.

Shelves and side

Each shelf top is marked out and cut individually. You can do this by taking several length and width measurements for each shelf space and transferring them to the panel of hardboard or plywood from which they will be cut. If you are using hardboard for the shelving, then this must be nailed all round the shelf supports with panel pins. If you are using plywood, it is a good idea just to rest the shelf panels on the shelf supports. This way you can remove them easily if you want to alter the internal layout, or perhaps to repair the sliding door runners.

Fitted wardrobe

Fig 4. A free-standing unit requires a different approach. Four uprights are necessary to provide adequate support for the structure.

Fig 5. Walls are rarely absolutely true and vertical. The uprights need to be trimmed accordingly, using a spirit level to ensure that the timber is plumb.

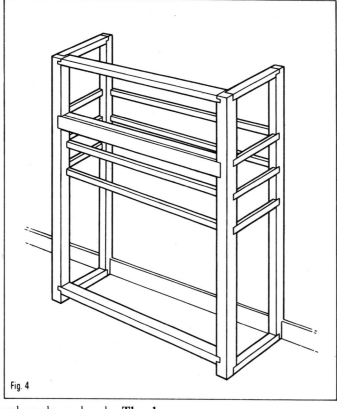

Fig. 4

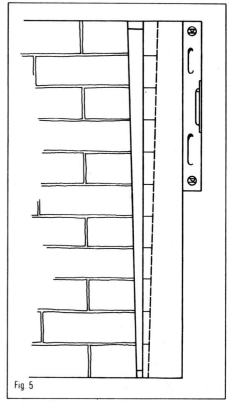

Fig. 5

Fitting the hardboard or plywood end will need a paper template, but if you cannot make one, cut the ply to the height of the framework and a little wider than the end framework. Put it in position with one side against the wall and the other parallel with the face of the front frame. If when the front edges are parallel the ply does not fit the wall you can scribe it by taking a small piece of wood or ply about $\frac{1}{4}$in (6mm) wider than the widest part of the gap to make a guide. Slide this piece of timber down the wall making a mark on the plywood side with a pencil held against the outer edge of the timber guide. The result should be a line that is parallel with, and as uneven as, the wall. Cut the ply along this line and prop in place again; this time measure how much to take off to fit flush with the front frame.

Pin the panel to the framework with panel pins with their heads punched below the surface and the holes stopped with suitable filler.

A length of skirting board will cover the joint at the bottom of the end panel and this board can be continued around the front of the frame to meet the skirting on the other wall. Alternatively, you can fit a piece of board to the inside of the front frame, at the bottom to make a toe space.

The doors

Sliding doors of the type used for the lower part of this wardrobe are in fact much easier to fit than conventional hinged doors. They are merely hung on the top runners and dropped into a slotted plate below. The runners shown in Fig. 2 are fairly typical, but they do vary in fitting. Pay particular attention to the instructions that come with your runners.

Some aspects of fitting sliding doors on runners are applicable to all makes. The bottom slots into which the door bottoms will fit, for example, must be directly underneath the runners. Otherwise the doors will not hang properly. Fit the top runners first, then use a plumb line to ensure that the bottom plate is fitted properly underneath the runners.

Fitments to allow the doors to hang on the runners, and slide from side to side, must be fitted to the tops of the doors, it is only when this has been done, and the doors hung in place, that you should consider any alteration in the dimensions of the doors. This can be done by planing the sides or bottom.

The top sliding doors are more simple and consist of two lengths of grooved wood into which sheets of hardboard are fitted as shown in Fig. 2. The strips or runners are nailed in position at the top and bottom of the upper compartment, and flush with the front of the wardrobe. The top grooves must be twice the depth of the bottom groove. The two doors are cut from a sheet of hardboard, slightly oversize at first, and then cut accurately using direct marking. The doors must be fractionally higher than the distance between the runners, so that each door can be eased into the top recess, straightened, then dropped into the bottom recess.

For both sets of doors, ordinary door handles would, of course, be impossible to fit because they protrude and would stop the doors sliding. But there are many recessed handles for sliding doors on the market that your local retailer will show you.

Finishing

Smooth down any bumps or rough patches in the woodwork with a plane. Using a spatula and cellulose filler, fill in any visible holes or cracks. Apply the filler generously, so that it dries proud of the hole or crack. Then smooth the filler down level with the surface with fine glasspaper. Rub the entire surface of the wardrobe down to a smooth finish and apply a layer of undercoat. If necessary, rub down again, then finish with two coats of paint.

Fitted dresser

The simple design of this dressing table is adaptable to any size of bedroom. The unit is very functional, giving ample drawer and shelf space. The dressing table is made mostly from ¾in (19mm) thick plywood, but any softwood that can be sanded to a smooth finish is suitable. The dressing table top, the shelf panel and the bottom and top panels of the upper component are made from plywood; as are the bottoms of the drawers. The drawers run on strips of hardwood fixed under their outside bottom edges.

The only joints used in the construction are simple butt joints, which are held together with glue and panel pins. The central shelf is held up by standard plastic shelf supports fixed to the vertical dividing pieces. The wall at the back of the shelf area is covered with plastic laminate, and the area above the dressing table with mirrors. These are fixed with screws positioned so that they are not conspicuous when the unit is installed. In this way, you can save the trouble of making a back for the unit itself. No cutting list has been included in this project because all dimensions are variable to suit individual requirements.

The sides of the unit

The dimensions of the unit's sides are shown in Fig. 2. These pieces are fixed to the wall first, and the horizontal pieces of the unit fitted between them.

First, cut the ends and vertical dividers to the length and width required and square their ends. Lay them on a level surface and mark the position of the top piece, the facing strip of the middle shelf and the dressing table top. The facing strip of the shelf is housed into the front of the side pieces for a neat appearance.

From the top of the ends and dividers measure downwards a distance of 10in (254mm). This indicates the top of the housing. The housing is ¾in (19mm)

Above: The completed dresser unit in position. It is both functional and attractive and the dimensions can be varied to individual requirements.

Fitted dresser

Opposite page: This dressing table has been made mainly from plywood, but any softwood that can be sanded down to a smooth finish is suitable.

Fig 1. Construction details of the fitted dresser. The supports for the table top also provide a guide for the drawers.

deep and $2\frac{3}{4}$in (70mm) long. Mark the depth of the housing with a marking gauge and use a try square to mark the ends of the housing. Cut the ends with a tenon saw and chisel the housings out to the correct depth.

The next step is to fix the ends and dividers to the walls. On the walls, mark where the bottom of the ends and dividers will come. These points are 23in (584mm) from the floor on each wall. This will make the dressing table top $27\frac{7}{8}$in (708mm) high – adequate for a person of average height. Raise or lower it if required.

Now fasten the ends and dividers to the wall. The original of this unit was fixed between two end walls, so the sides did

not need to be screwed on through the back edge. They were just screwed in place through their flat surfaces, with the screws arranged to fall behind the horizontal pieces as so not to show. If your unit is to be in the middle of a wall, mount the ends and dividers on pieces of metal angle strip which are plugged and screwed to the wall.

The top of the unit

A top for the unit is made out of $\frac{5}{8}$in (16mm) plywood fixed to a timber framework. Cut two lengths of $2\frac{3}{4}$in $\times$ 1in (70mm $\times$ 25mm) to the full length of the unit. Cut four pieces of $1\frac{1}{2}$in $\times$ $\frac{3}{4}$in (38mm $\times$ 19mm) $6\frac{3}{4}$in (171mm) long and two the same length out of $2\frac{3}{4}$in $\times$ 1in (70mm $\times$

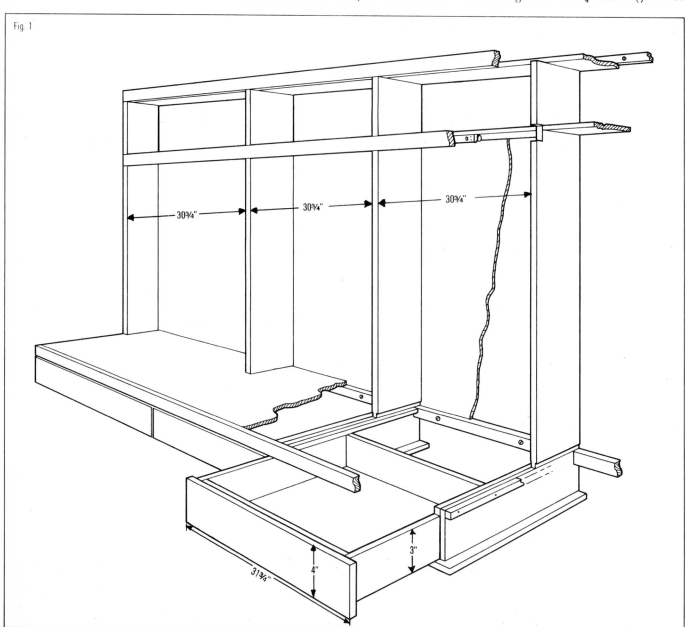

Fig. 1

30¾"   30¾"   30¾"

3"

4"

31¾"

25mm). Mark the positions of the dividers onto the plywood top piece. If the plywood top has to be made of more than one piece of wood, try to make the joint over the top of one of the dividers. The plywood top will be $6\frac{3}{4}$in (171mm) wide, and is set out to take the four intermediate pieces of timber and the two ends.

Glue and nail the intermediate timbers into place flush with either side of the plywood panels. Then fix the ends and the front and back members by glueing and nailing them to the ends of the intermediate pieces and the edge of the ply. Then, lift up and screw the top section to the tops of the dividers and plug and screw it to the wall.

The table top

The table top is made from $\frac{3}{4}$in (19mm) plywood. At the front, a strip of $1\frac{3}{4}$in $\times$ $\frac{3}{4}$in (45mm $\times$ 19mm) timber is glued and pinned to it. The back of the table top, which butts against the wall, is supported by, and fitted to, a strip of 2in $\times \frac{3}{4}$in (51mm $\times$ 19mm) softwood plugged and screwed to the wall. The plywood top of the table is supported at the ends and dividers by the same method. You will not be able to get a single board of the length required for the top, so use two or more boards. Make sure that the ends of the boards that are to butt against each other are perfectly square. The joins will be less conspicuous if they occur parallel to and in line with the slots. The

table top can now be fixed to the wall and vertical units.

Cut the battens for supporting the top to length and glue and screw them to the side of the dividers flush with the top of the L-shaped projection. Next, cut the facing strip to length and fix it in the same way to the front of the dividers. The table top can then be laid on and scribed to the back wall.

Slots will have to be cut in the table top to fit around the dividers. If you can make $\frac{1}{8}$in (3mm) deep housings in the sides of the dividers to take the cut-out in the table top it would make a better fit. Glue the table top to the surrounding battens and to the front facing strip. The front edge of the top should be flush with the front of the facing strip.

The facing strip for the central shelf is housed in notches cut into the front edge of the dividers $12\frac{3}{8}$in (314mm) from the top of the dividers. This notch is $\frac{3}{4}$in (19mm) deep and $2\frac{3}{4}$in (70mm) long.

The shelf

The central shelf is made up from $\frac{5}{8}$in (16mm) plywood panels which extend between pairs of vertical dividing pieces. They are supported where they meet these pieces by small proprietary nylon shelf supports screwed in place. The front facing strip, which is housed into the dividing pieces, should be fitted with these nylon supports too, so that it supports the front edge of the shelf. The supports should go $\frac{5}{8}$in (16mm) below the upper edge of the facing.

Cut the facing strip to length and glue and pin it in place. Cut the plywood shelf panels to size. When they are fixed, their front edge should be flush with the rear surface of the facing strip. Fix the shelf supports and place the shelves on them.

The drawers

The unit has four drawers made from $\frac{5}{8}$in (16mm) timber. The four sides of the drawer are butted, glued and screwed together. A front panel is glued to the front side of each drawer and screwed on from the inside. These panels protrude below the bottom edge of the front side and beyond the end of the front side.

The dimensions of the drawer components are shown in Fig. 1. Cut the four sides to length and square their ends. Drill screw holes in the pieces, lay them on a level surface and apply adhesive to the ends of the two short sides. Screw the pieces together. Check that the construct-

Fitted dresser

ion is square and lightly sash cramp it (or use string twisted tight with pegs if you do not have any sash cramps). The drawer base may be made from thin ply or hardboard and rests on $\frac{1}{2}$in × $\frac{1}{2}$in (13mm × 13mm) battens which are glued around the edge of the drawer flush with the bottom edge.

The drawer facing protrudes below the bottom edge of the front of the drawer by 1in (25mm). The length of each front piece is the length of the unit divided by four, so that in the finished unit the end of one drawer almost butts against that of the next one.

Lay each front piece on a flat surface with its inner face uppermost. Mark from each end the distance it protrudes beyond the front side of the drawer. Lay the partially finished drawer between these two points and draw around this outline. Apply adhesive to the front piece between the pencil lines and on the front side of the drawer. Next, you must screw the pieces together from the inside of the construction.

The drawer runners

The drawer runners are glued and screwed to the underside of the dividers. Cut hardwood strips, $2\frac{1}{2}$in × $\frac{3}{4}$in (64mm × 19mm), as long as the L-shaped projection of the table top supports. Then glue and screw them into place, positioning them centrally so that they will carry a drawer on each side of the divider.

Finishing the unit

Sand all the surfaces smooth. Knock any panel pin heads that are conspicuous below the surface of the timber. Fill the holes with wood filler. Apply several coats of polyurethane varnish to the unit sanding down carefully between coats.

The mirror

The mirror is fixed in place with mirror screws positioned 1in (25mm) from the corners of the mirrors. Your glass merchant will supply mirrors cut to size and ready-drilled, The plastic laminate can be glued to the wall.

Fig 2. The method of laying out the panel from which the vertical partitions are cut.

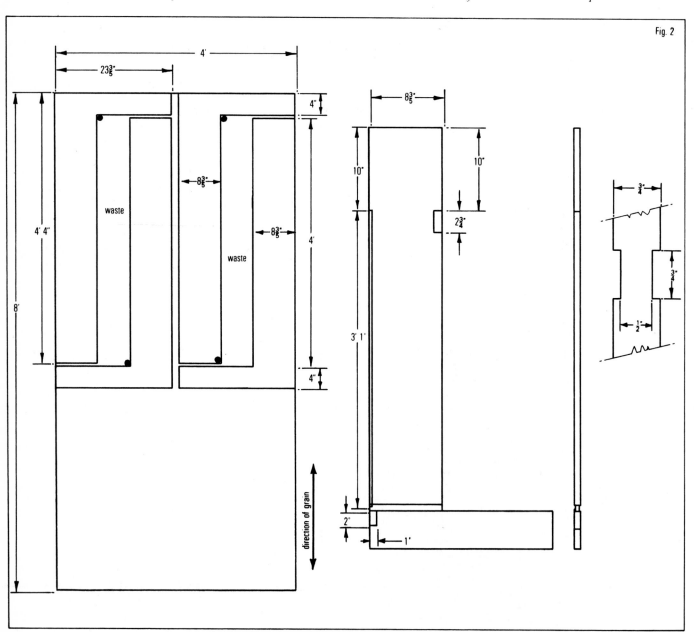

Four-poster bed

Four poster bed

Fig 1. The panels for the four poster bed are all cut from three sheets of plywood. The layout for the first of these is shown here.

Figs 2-3. The layout for the other two sheets. An allowance must be made for the sawcuts and great care must be taken when cutting these to ensure that they are straight and true.

Fig 4. Detail of the ends of the panels where they meet the uprights at the foot of the bed.

Fig 5. The dimensions for the headboard.

Fig 6. View of the rear of the headboard showing the position of the batten.

Fig 7. View of the front of the headboard showing the position of the lower batten.

Fig 8. Lower side panel of the bed and position of the support batten.

Fig 9. Lower end panel of the bed showing position of the support batten.

Fig 10. The top panels of the bed showing positions of the battens.

The four-poster bed is the aristocrat of bedroom furniture. It has the flavour of history and an element of prestige. Unfortunately, four-poster beds are not sold by most furniture shops. Where they are, only traditional designs are available and these are expensive. Instructions are given here for making a four-poster of modern design that does not cost the earth. If you prefer, you could provide a traditional touch by adding curtains.

Construction

This bed consists of four upright wooden posts of red deal – you could use another timber if you wish – supported and kept vertical by eight panels, four at the base and four at the top.

The panels are of plywood and, at the base butting to the floor, there are two side panels and one foot board. The panel at the head end is raised to provide support and to act as a head board.

The four panels or fascia running round the tops of the uprights provide rigidity for this part of the structure, but are also used for decoration. They can be painted, covered with fabric, or fitted with a curtain rail.

Plywood rarely has an attractive surface, and the end-grain or cut edges look unsightly. For this bed, therefore, the plywood panels have been covered with felt, but you could use some other material, or paint. If you prefer a natural wood finish, then the plywood would have to be replaced with $\frac{3}{4}$in (19mm) solid wood planking, but this would be much more expensive. If you do decide to do this, then each base panel will be replaced with four solid planks as wide as the panels they replace. The solid planks can be glued and cramped together to form solid panels, or left as individual planks. The main advantage of the former method is that it prevents the planks from buckling out of line.

Support battening is fixed all round the upper inside of the base side panels. This provides support for the slats, which in turn makes the frame more rigid and provides the support area for the mattress. These slats are part of the structural design, and should not be replaced with anything less rigid.

Materials

The timber for the uprights should be ordered 'dressed', this ensures that the timber will arrive with a good surface finish. This is essential because in this design, the uprights are the only part of the woodwork that is visible.

The rest of the solid timber can be of a cheaper wood. This consists of the slat supports and edge battens, which are of 2in × 2in (51mm × 51mm) timber, and the slats, which are of 6in × 1in (152mm × 25mm) timber.

All the panels are cut from $\frac{1}{2}$in (13mm) plywood, but if you want to replace these with solid wood planking, then this should be of $\frac{3}{4}$in (19mm) timber, because solid timber is more likely to warp than plywood. All the plywood panels can be cut from three large sheets of plywood as shown in Figs. 1 to 3

Where screw heads are visible, brass screws with screw cups are used, but elsewhere ordinary steel screws with countersunk heads are just as good, and cheaper.

Cutting the panels

All the $\frac{1}{2}$in (13mm) thick plywood panels can be cut from three large sheets of plywood, and the cutting plan for this is as described. This will avoid the cost of having to pay for the panels to be cut to specific sizes. But this only applies if you have done some carpentry and have access to a bench power saw. Cutting long straight lines in wood is no job for the inexperienced carpenter. So if you have never done this sort of work, order the plywood already cut into eight individual panels according to the dimensions shown in Figs. 1-3.

First, prepare the two base side panels. Each panel has two recesses cut in one end, as shown in Fig. 4. The recesses shown are $5\frac{1}{4}$in (133mm) wide and $3\frac{1}{2}$in (89mm) deep. Mark out the outline of the recesses, using a try square to ensure that all lines are straight, then cut out the recesses with a fine-toothed saw. When you have finished, you will have two identical panels like the one shown in Fig. 8.

Next, cut the recesses in the foot board. These recesses are identical to those cut in the side panels. Stand one of the side panels on edge, in the position shown in Fig. 8. Do the same with the foot board, as in Fig. 9, and then mark the positions of the tenons on the foot board and jig saw the two together so that the protruding parts of one panel slide into the recesses in the opposite panel. Now add the remaining side panel to the opposite end of the foot board in the same way.

Fix the two 73in (1853mm) battens to

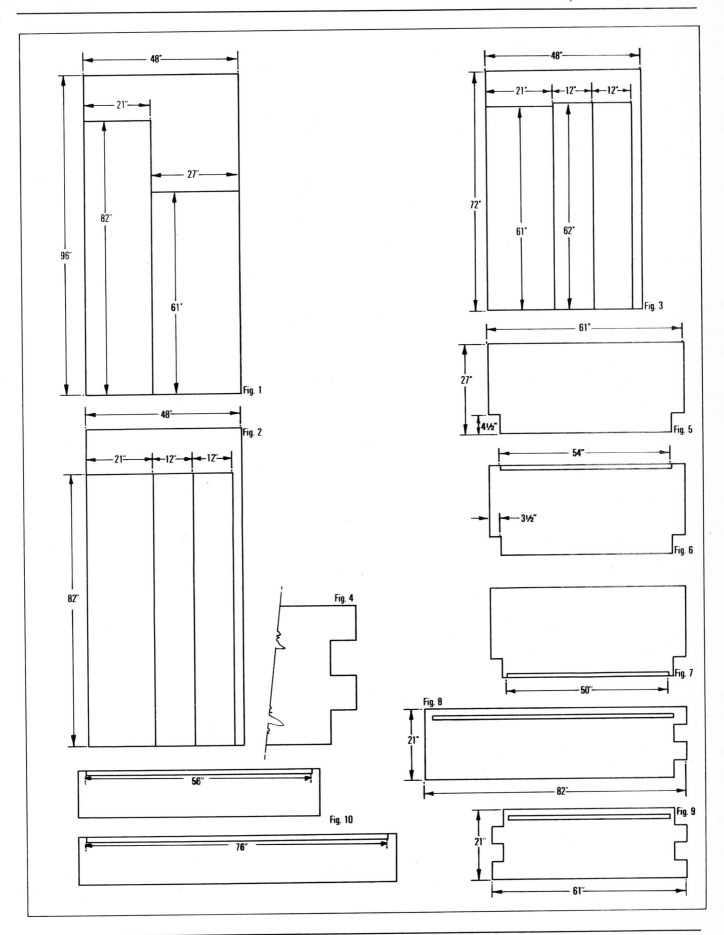

Fig. 1

Fig. 2

Fig. 3

Fig. 4

Fig. 5

Fig. 6

Fig. 7

Fig. 8

Fig. 9

Fig. 10

the side frames, $2\frac{1}{2}$in (63mm) down from the edge of each inside face, and the 54in (1371mm) batten in the same position on the foot board. Figs. 8 and 9 show the battens in position.

Mark and cut the two recesses in each bottom corner of the head board. Each recess is $3\frac{1}{2}$in (89mm) wide and $4\frac{1}{2}$in (114mm) deep, as shown in Fig. 5. Glue and screw a 54in (1371mm) batten along the top of one side of the head board, and a 50in (1270mm) length along the opposite, at the bottom. Figs. 6 and 7 show these in place.

Fix one length of 76in (1930mm) battening along one side of each of the top side panels. The batten should be flush with one edge, and centrally placed so that there is a space of 3in (76mm) between each end of the batten and the ends of the panel the same as with the back of the head rest. Repeat this with the top end panels and the 56in (1422 mm) battens.

Assembling the main frame

You are now ready for a dry run, to check that everything fits, and to mark and fit the slats. Do not apply glue to any of the joints at this stage and do not drive the screws in too tightly. This is because each panel will have to be removed, covered with felt, and replaced before the slats are finally screwed in place and the bed is ready.

Assemble the two base side panels and the foot board so that the three panels are free-standing.

Where the panels interlock, the ends will protrude, forming a V at each corner. Stand an upright in one of these, so that the panel ends overlap two sides of the upright, then screw them together, through the panelling into the upright. Repeat this at the other end. The uprights for the foot end are now in position.

Now fit the uprights at the head end. Stand an upright at the outside end of a side panel, in exactly the same position as the upright at the opposite end. Screw this in position through the inside of the panel. Repeat this procedure with the remaining upright on the opposite panel. Stand the head board in position on the edges of the side panels, backing on to the uprights, and screw it to the uprights through the front of the head board.

The base frame is now assembled, and you can check the various panels for fit. You can also check the top frame. It is not necessary to assemble this, it should be sufficient to hold each panel up (you will need help) to check that it fits.

Mark, cut and fit the slats. Do this by direct marking, and as you cut and fit each one, number it on the slat and the butting batten, so that each slat will be fixed in the same place when you assemble permanently. Do not screw the slats in place – it is only necessary to drop each one into position to see that it fits.

Carefully dismantle the unit. The panels can now be covered with felt, and the bed can then be assembled permanently. A bedspread can be made to fit, and, if required, curtain rails fixed around the inside of the top frame so that the curtains enclose the bed.

Cutting list

Solid wood

	standard	metric
4 uprights	$84 \times 3 \times 3$	$2134 \times 76 \times 76$
11 slats	$54 \times 6 \times 1$	$1371 \times 152 \times 25$
2 slat supports	$73 \times 2 \times 2$	$1853 \times 51 \times 51$
2 edge battens	$54 \times 2 \times 2$	$1371 \times 51 \times 51$
1 edge batten	$50 \times 2 \times 2$	$1270 \times 51 \times 51$
2 edge battens	$76 \times 2 \times 2$	$1930 \times 51 \times 51$
2 edge battens	$56 \times 2 \times 2$	$1422 \times 51 \times 51$

Plywood

	standard	metric
2 basic side panels	$82 \times 21 \times \frac{1}{2}$	$2083 \times 533 \times 13$
1 foot panel	$61 \times 21 \times \frac{1}{2}$	$1549 \times 533 \times 13$
1 head board panel	$61 \times 27 \times \frac{1}{2}$	$1549 \times 686 \times 13$
2 top side panels	$82 \times 12 \times \frac{1}{2}$	$2083 \times 305 \times 13$
2 top end panels	$62 \times 12 \times \frac{1}{2}$	$1575 \times 305 \times 13$

You will also require:

Brass screws, with cups, for the visible screw heads. Ordinary countersunk head steel screws can be used for screws that are not visible, such as the securing screws for the slats. Woodworking adhesive.

Linen chest

The linen chest is made from high quality polished pine with the exception of the base, which is made from plywood. The sides, front and back are dovetailed together at the corners. The lid rests on two pieces of softwood and between the sides. The base rests on similar pieces glued to the insides of the front and back at the bottom of the chest.

Preparation of the wood

The sides of the chest are 18in × 18in (457mm × 457mm) and the front and back are 38in × 14½in (965mm × 368mm). Select wood planks that have grain patterns which are attractive and work well together.

Plane the planks to the required thickness of ¾in (19mm), and the bottom edges exactly square. Use a jack plane to do this – a smoothing plane will simply follow the contours of the wood. Check that the faces and edges are level with a straightedge and use a try square to check that they are exactly at right angles to each other.

Then butt the planed edges together. Mark them as shown in Fig. 3. This will enable you to match the grain, easily later on.

With the boards still together square a line down the face close to one end. From this line measure the length of the components in the following sequence: front 38in (965mm), side 18in (457mm), back 38in (965mm), side 18in (457mm). Add ¼in (6mm) to each of these measurements to allow for waste.

Glueing the planks

To form the components of the chest glue the planks together along the planed edges. You will need a number of sash cramps – at least one for every 18in (457mm) of the length of the planks – and a PVA adhesive. If you do not have enough sash cramps or room to work with two planks as long as this, cut them across their width down the line that marks off one set of side and end panels from the other.

To enable you to join the planks quickly once the adhesive has been applied, pre-set the cramps to the correct length by cramping the boards together dry with blocks of waste wood between the shoes of the cramps and the edges of the planks. This will protect the edges of the planks from damage and will spread the cramping pressure more evenly. If you have cut the boards across

their width, three cramps is the minimum number to use, although four is ideal.

Release the cramps and spread adhesive evenly on the edges of the planks that are to butt. Cramp them together again with the bars of the cramps alternatively on the top surface of the panels and on the underside of the panels.

It is essential that the planks fit together perfectly and the surface is completely level. If one plank is slightly higher than the other slacken the cramps a little. Place a piece of waste wood on the raised plank and bang it with a mallet. this will force the raised plank downwards, until its surface is flush with the other plank.

Tighten the cramps and wipe every trace of excess adhesive off the face of the planks with a soft damp cloth. Run your finger along the join to check that there are no irregularities in it. Allow adequate time for the adhesive to set – 12 hours is usually sufficient, but follow the manufacturer's recommended times. It is better to be overcautious than to spoil the join and have to do the work all over again.

When the adhesive has set, cut the joined planks along the marked lines. Plane the two shorter lengths (the sides) to a width of 18in (457mm). Then take the two longest pieces (the front and back) and mark off their final width of 14½in (368mm). To do this, measure half this distance from the join and on both sides of it. (This will keep the join running continuously around the finished box.) Draw lines through these points parallel with the join. Then cut the wood to the waste side of these lines and plane the planks square and to width.

Making the dovetails

The side panels are joined to the front and back panels with dovetailed joints. But first, you must cut and plane the boards to their final length. From one end of each board mark off approximately ⅛in (3mm) for waste. Square a line through this point on the surface of each board and on the edges.

From these squared lines measure and mark the exact length of the sides, front and back. Square lines through these points. The next step is to plane away the wood to these lines marked on both ends of each board. Use a sharp smoothing plane to do this, but use it carefully or you will damage the corners.

There are several ways of preventing

this from happening. A waste piece of wood can be sash cramped to the planks with its tip flush with the tops of the planks. Then any wood that is split away during planing will be from the waste timber. Another way is to chisel away the corner at the end to which you will be planing – but be careful not to chisel away any wood below the square line. Planing the wood from its outside edges inwards towards the middle will also prevent damage.

When the boards are of the exact length required and the ends are square,

Fig 1. Construction details of the linen chest. Note the position of the battens which prevent the lid from warping.

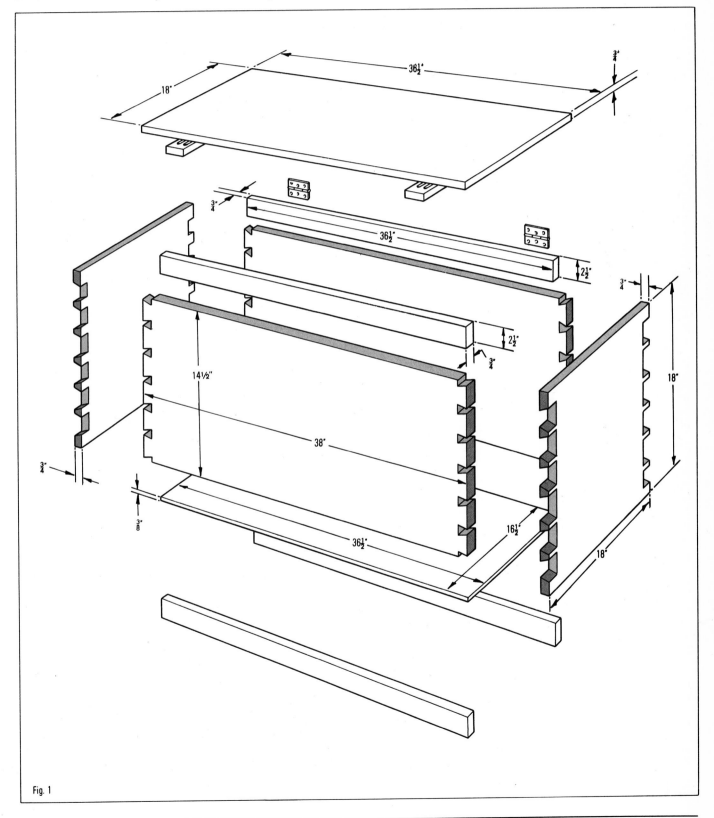

Fig. 1

Linen chest

A large plane is used to smooth the planks.

Method when planing end grain.

Sash cramping the planks together.

Make sure that the planks fit together perfectly and the surface is level.

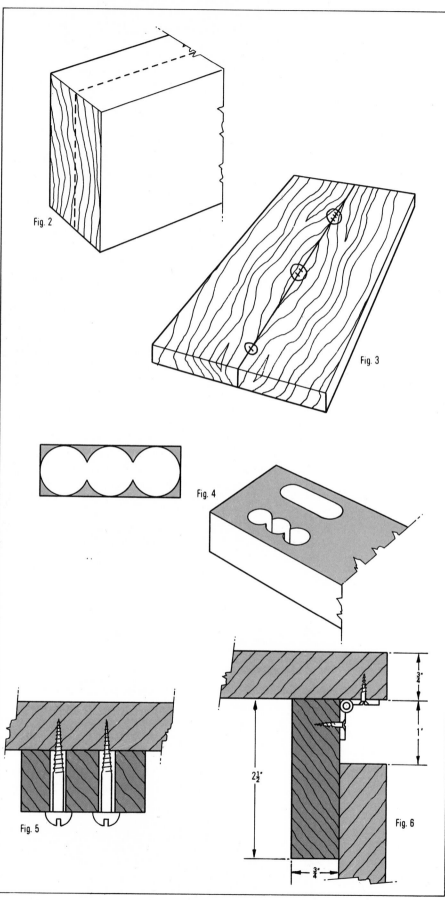

Fig. 2

Fig. 3

Fig. 4

Fig. 5

Fig. 6

Chest components may be cut from a plank 1¾in (44mm) thick (Fig 2). Resulting planks are opened and glued as shown (Fig 3), creating a mirror image. The under-lid battens require slots to allow for wood expansion, cutting waste as shown (Fig 4). Brass round-head screws are used to fix the batten to the lid, if there is expansion. (Fig 5). Hinging the lid (Fig 6).

for waste. Square a line through this point on the face of each board and on the edges.

From these squared lines measure and mark the exact length of the sides, front and back. Square lines through these points. The next step is to plane away the wood to these lines marked on both ends of each board. Use a sharp smoothing plane to do this but use it carefully or you will damage the corners.

There are several ways of preventing this from happening. A waste piece of wood can be bar clamped to the planks with its tip flush with the tops of the planks. Then any wood that is split away during planing will be from the waste lumber. Another way is to chisel away the corner at the end to which you will be planing—but be careful not to chisel away any wood below the square line. Planing the wood from its outside edges inward towards the middle will also prevent damage.

When the boards are of the exact length required and the ends are square, mark a line to indicate the depth of the dovetails. Set a marking gauge to ¾in (19mm)—the width of the wood. Score the line inward from both ends of all four boards. Mark this line very lightly as it will have to be planed out later.

Then measure and mark a point 1¾in (45mm) down from the top of both side pieces. Do this at each end. This will indicate the point at which the top of the front and back pieces join the sides. Mark out the dovetail between this point and the width of the front and back panels. Cut the tail (wider pieces) of the dovetails first. Then direct-mark and cut the pins. Ensure that the tops of the front and back pieces are level with the point marked on the sides. Trial assemble, then glue the sides together.

Refer to the Techniques section for the two methods of cutting the dovetail. By using the dovetail attachment you will achieve much greater accuracy, although you may feel that this is not worth the expense just for one project. In which case, try the jigsaw method, practising on a scrap piece of lumber first. To make dovetails without using power tools, a tenon saw and wood chisel can be used. Trial assemble the cut dovetails before gluing the sides together.

Making the lid

The lid for the chest is 36½in (927mm) long and 18in (457mm) wide. Two planks have to be butted together to form a surface this wide. Cut the lumber for the lid so that it splits down the middle. Plane the edges and butt and glue them to form a plank in the same way as for the side components.

A board of this size which is fixed along one edge only is unlikely to stay perfectly flat and level. The underside is, therefore, strengthened with battens. Cut two 1in x 2in (25mm x 51mm) battens to a length of 12in (305mm). The battens are not screwed in the normal way. Instead, the holes through the battens which accommodate the shanks of the screws must be elongated to allow for any movement in the wood caused by variation in temperature and humidity.

Mark the positions on the battens through which the screws will pass; four pairs of screws for each batten is sufficient. Drill holes at these points. Drill another hole of the same size on either side of every original hole (Figs. 4 and 5). Chisel out the wood around each pair of holes to form a rectangular opening.

Use round head 1½in (38mm) No.8 brass screws to fix the battens to the lid. Before using these screws pre-cut the thread in the lid with steel screws. This ensures that when you screw in the brass screws they will not snap in the hole and the head will not be damaged.

Finger hold and baseboard

To make the finger hold and the baseboard and their balancing pieces at the back you will need four pieces of ¾in x 2½in (19mm x 64mm) pine. Cut and square these to a length of 36½in. (927 mm). Glue the two struts at the top of the insides of the front and back panels so that 1in (25mm) of their width is visible from the exterior of the chest. Position the bottom struts so that 2in (51mm) is visible. The base of the chest can now be cut to rest on the bottom struts and glued into place.

The lid of the chest rests on the top struts and between the side panels, flush to their tops. Plane the lid to the required size but ensure that the fit is not too tight. If you can slide a thin coin between the end edges of the lid and the sides the fit is ideal.

Fix the lid to the back strut with three 2in (51mm) brass butt hinges and some ½in (13mm) brass screws. The plates of the hinges when fixed are at right angles to each other (Fig. 6). The exact position of the hinges is not really important provided one is in the middle and the other two are placed near the ends.

Finishing the chest

Clean up the surfaces with a sharp smoothing plane and sand them perfectly smooth with your orbital sander, or by hand, using fine paper. Use a clear polyurethane or cellulose varnish so as not to obscure the grain. Rub down the finish after each coat with steel wool until you have achieved a completely smooth finish.

Cutting list

Solid wood	standard	metric
Sides, front and back:		
1 piece	1¾ x 9 x 9ft 4in	45 x 229 x 2.7m
Lid:		
1 piece	1¾ x 9 x 36½	45 x 229 x 927
Battening:		
2 pieces	1 x 2 x 12	25 x 51 x 305
Scuff board and finger hold:		
4 pieces	¾ x 2½ x 36½	19 x 64 x 927
Base:		
⅜in (10mm) plywood	18 x 36½	457 x 927

These measurements do not include any allowance for waste. To get the net 9ft 4in (2.8m) you will need a piece about 10ft (3m) long.

You will also require: 3 2in (51mm) solid brass butt hinges, 1½in (38mm) roundhead brass screws, ½in (13mm) No. 8 brass screws and white glue.

Garden bench

A garden bench can be an attractive feature of any garden. Unlike a lot of garden furniture, this design is not only attractive and comfortable, it is also sturdy enough to be used as a permanent feature all year round and to give a lifetime's use.

The garden bench has been designed specifically for DIY construction. No special tools, other than a tube spanner and a protractor, are required and all the joints are simple. At the same time the bench is very sturdy and, provided the timber has been properly treated with preservative, is suitable for outdoor use throughout the year.

One major attraction of the design is that it can easily be modified to make a bench of a different size, or even an individual garden chair. The construction processes would remain exactly the same, the only difference being that the main timbers for a chair should be reduced in section from 4in × 2in (102mm × 51mm) to 3in × 1½in (76mm × 38mm). By adapting the design you can build a complete set of matching garden furniture.

Choosing a suitable wood

There is a wide range of woods suitable for use. Among the softwoods, pine is the most readily available and is easy to work. It requires treatment with an exterior wood preservative, even if you intend to paint the finished structure. Of the hardwoods, elm, oak, teak and makore are the most suitable, but they all have different properties and the home carpenter should make his choice after a consideration of their individual characteristics. Oak is strong and highly weather resistant, but its extreme hardness makes it difficult to work. Elm is suitable for most outdoor uses – its only drawback is that it tends to split more easily than the other woods listed. Perhaps teak combines all the most desirable properties. It is a very attractive wood, which is relatively easy to work and, unlike the other woods, is so oily that it does not need any special treatment with a preservative. Unfortunately, it is fairly costly, although this high initial cost is offset by its long life.

Treating the timber

Most timber merchants will undertake to supply pre-treated timber to your order at a small additional cost. The type of wood preservative to be used depends not only on the species of timber, but also on the intended location of the finished structure. A horticultural grade wood preservative is best suited for application to the garden bench, as not only does it prevent timber rot, but also its non-toxic nature means that no damage is done to plants in the vicinity of the bench.

Generally, hardwoods are left unpainted in order to show off their distinctive grain. Softwoods, such as pine, can be stained or painted – after the preservative dressing has soaked well into the timber.

The end sections

Each end section comprises an arm rest, a front and back leg, and end rail and a rear, vertical back support. These members are assembled by glueing and jointing; final fixing being by galvanized coach screws countersunk below the surface. When finished, these two sections should match exactly, so great care must be taken in marking and cutting out.

Begin by marking and cutting out the pieces for the two end sections to the dimensions given in the cutting list. All these pieces with the exception of the arm rests, are ½in (13mm) overlength at this stage, to enable the angled ends (shown in Figs. 3 and 4) to be cut out accurately.

Now take one of the front legs and mark a point 22in (559mm) along one long edge. With the aid of a protractor, set a sliding bevel gauge at an angle of 83°, lay the gauge against the mark and draw a line to the opposite edge. Cut along this line with a tenon saw to give the completed leg. Repeat this procedure on the other front leg member and, when it has been cut out, match the 'paired' legs and, if necessary, trim them so that they are of an identical size.

The rear legs are angled at both ends. To cut them accurately, first mark lines ¼in (6mm) from each end with a try square. Lay the sliding bevel, preset to 70°, on the front edge of the leg to coincide with the mark at one end and draw the angled line. Reset the sliding bevel to 75° and mark this angle from the back of the leg at the other marked point. Now cut along the angled lines to make a rear leg.

Next, take the two rear, vertical back support members, and mark a line ½in (13mm) from one end of each. With the sliding bevel set at 102°, draw the angled ends as detailed previously and cut the members to shape. Round off the top ends with a jig saw or band saw, according to the pattern shown in Fig. 4. Do not cut out the halved joints at the bottom of these members yet, instead, cut out the other component pieces of the end sections.

Take the end rails and, using a try square, mark a line ½in (13mm) from one end of each. Set your sliding bevel to 70° and, referring to Fig. 4 as a guide, mark the angled ends. Cut these ends with a tenon saw. Bevel the front end as shown in Fig. 3. The upper edges of the end rails are hollowed out with a bow saw or jig saw to the shape shown in Fig. 3.

The last parts of the end sections to be cut out are the arm rests. Round off 2in (51mm) at the front ends of these pieces and, with a spokeshave make 'nosings' on these ends. At the other ends, cut the lapped joints which house the vertical back supports.

Cutting the end section joints

The back supports and the end rail are joined together by means of a halving joint. This is an easy joint to make, but it has to be set out at an angle as shown in the illustrations. Measure 6in (152mm) along the bottom edge, from the back, of the end rail, then mark a line at an angle of 102°. Measure the width of the back support at right angles to this line and make another angled line to mark the other side of the cut-out. Refer to Figs. 3 and 4 as a guide and when you are satisfied that you have marked out correctly, cut out the joint.

Both the front and top horizontal rails are housed in the end rail and rear support respectively. These housings are 2in (51mm) wide and ¾in (19mm) deep; their exact locations are given in Figs. 1 and 4.

When all the joints have been cut, trial assemble all the pieces and, if necessary, trim for a good fit.

Assembling the end sections

Initially these pieces are joined by glueing and nailing, final fixing being by coach screws. Begin by glueing the front and rear legs to the arm rests, according to the plan shown in Fig. 4. Then glue the end rails inside the legs, so that their angled ends lie flush with the back edges of the rear legs, and their lower long edges are 10¾in (273mm) from the bottom of the front legs. To complete the assembly, glue the vertical back supports into the housings on the arm rests and end rails

Garden bench

Fig 1. Exploded view of the garden bench.

Fig 2. Front elevation of the bench showing positions of the slats.

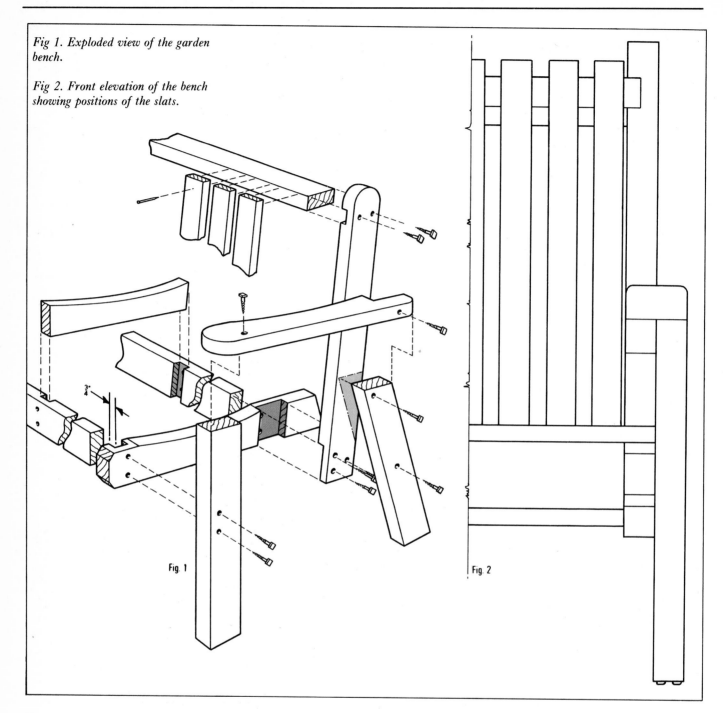

Fig. 1

Fig. 2

Fig 3. The ends of the seat are shaped as shown. The inside curve at the top of the component may be cut with either a spokeshave or a rasp.

so that their lower ends are flush with the bottom edges of the end rails. When the glue has dried, use 3in (76mm) galvanized nails, driven in from the inside faces, to secure the structure. Do not fix with screws just yet.

The seat and back
Three rails connect the end sections. One

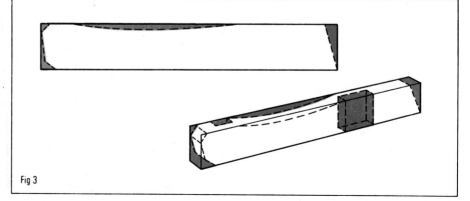

Fig 3

Cutting list

Solid wood	standard	metric
Main frame timber	$408 \times 4 \times 2$	$10363 \times 102 \times 51$
Back slat timber	$312 \times 4 \times \frac{3}{4}$	$7924 \times 102 \times 19$
Seat slat timber	$420 \times 1\frac{3}{4} \times 1$	$10668 \times 45 \times 25$

Cut to give:

2 front legs	$22\frac{1}{4} \times 4 \times 2$	$565 \times 102 \times 51$
2 rear legs	$22 \times 4 \times 2$	$559 \times 102 \times 51$
2 arm rests	$23 \times 4 \times 2$	$584 \times 102 \times 51$
2 end rails	$28 \times 4 \times 2$	$711 \times 102 \times 51$
2 vertical back supports	$31\frac{1}{2} \times 4 \times 2$	$800 \times 102 \times 51$
1 front rail	$57\frac{1}{2} \times 4 \times 2$	$1460 \times 102 \times 51$
1 top rail	$57\frac{1}{2} \times 4 \times 2$	$1460 \times 102 \times 51$
1 back rail	$56 \times 4 \times 2$	$1422 \times 102 \times 51$
1 centre rail	$16 \times 4 \times 2$	$406 \times 102 \times 51$
11 back slats	$28 \times 4 \times \frac{3}{4}$	$711 \times 102 \times 19$
7 seat slats	$60 \times 1\frac{3}{4} \times 1$	$1524 \times 45 \times 25$

You will also require:

18 6in (152mm) galvanized coach screws. 2 $1\frac{1}{2}$in (38mm) galvanized coach screws. 1lb 2in (51mm) galvanized nails. $\frac{1}{2}$lb 3in (76mm) galvanized nails. Waterproof woodworking glue. Waterproof stopper. Wood preservative.

of these is glued and screwed into the housings on the front of the end rails, another is butted to the rear of the end rails in line with the front of the back supports, and the third slots into the housings cut in the top of the vertical back supports. Before fixing them in position, cut the housings for the centre rail at the midpoints of the two seat rails. These housings are 1in (25mm) deep and 2in (51mm) wide.

At this stage, cut the centre rail to shape using Fig. 1 as a guide. Use a bow saw or jig saw to hollow out the upper edge of the centre rail and check that this hollow corresponds exactly to those cut on the end rails. Now glue and nail the front rail into position.

When the glue has set, fit the back rail. This piece is fixed between the end rails at the same angle as the vertical supports. Its exact location is shown in Fig. 4. Finally, glue the top rail into the housings on the vertical supports.

Fixing with coach screws

Figs. 1 and 4 show the location of the coach screws. Use 6in (152mm) screws to secure the end section members to the main rails, and 3in (76mm) screws at all other joints. Pre-drill for the screw threads, taking care to avoid nails, and allowing an extra $\frac{1}{4}$in (6mm) for countersinking the screw heads. Insert the screws and fill the exposed cavities with timber plugs which can be cut either from waste wood with a plug cutter, or, if you do not possess this tool, from dowel of the correct diameter.

Adding the slats

This is the easiest part of the construction. Begin by nailing the vertical rear slats to the rear and top rails, after marking the centre location of each. To help you space the slats evenly, allow about $\frac{7}{16}$in (11mm) between each one. Now nail the horizontal seat slats in position, allowing about $\frac{1}{2}$in (13mm) between them. With a spokeshave, round off the edges of the seat slats and make a 'nosing' on the leading edge of the front seat slat. Finally, smooth the whole structure with sandpaper and apply another dressing of preservative.

Your garden bench is now complete: the work involved will be amply rewarded by the pleasure the bench will give throughout the year.

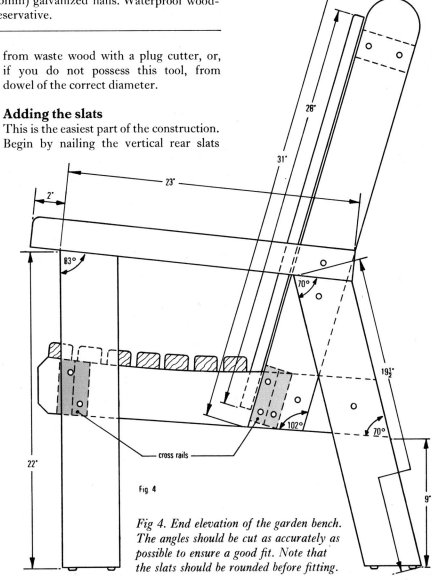

Fig 4. End elevation of the garden bench. The angles should be cut as accurately as possible to ensure a good fit. Note that the slats should be rounded before fitting.

Garden seat/planter

This timber seat planter makes an attractive addition to any garden, either as a major feature in a small area, or as part of a large landscaped garden. The centre of the unit can be used to display flowers or shrubs, or you can build the seat round a tree trunk so that the branches will provide shade. This structure is also ideal for patio or small paved areas which need an eye-catching focal point.

General construction details

The unit is a hexagonal or six-sided garden seat, the centre of which has a well that is filled with soil and planted out with a display of some sort.

The main framework consists of 2in × 1in (50mm × 25mm) softwood members, clad with 4in × ¾in (100mm × 18mm) cedarwood tongued-and-grooved treated boarding; you will require 60 lengths of 1ft 8in (508mm) boarding for the base, and 80 lengths of 9in (229mm) for the top. All other timber members, such as the seat boards, soil support and base corner plates, are of either 1in or ½in (25mm or 13mm) marine plywood.

All timbers must be treated with a horticultural grade of wood preservative such as Cuprinol. In addition the internal top lining of the T&G boarding, and parts O, H and J must be coated with a bitumen-based preservative such as Aquaseal to prevent damp soil from rotting the wood.

The outside supports consist of six outer base frames D joined with halving joints, Fig. 3. These form the outer hexagon. Six inner base frames E provide the internal support, and these radiate from the middle and are joined to the outer frames. The inner frames are constructed with bridle joints to provide greater strength vertically.

The inner hexagon, which houses the soil, is formed by six rectangular frames, clad both sides, and with an internal base of ½in (13mm) marine plywood (Figs. 1 and 9).

If you prefer to build the seat round a tree, then you will have to omit the centre base plate, and replace it with six

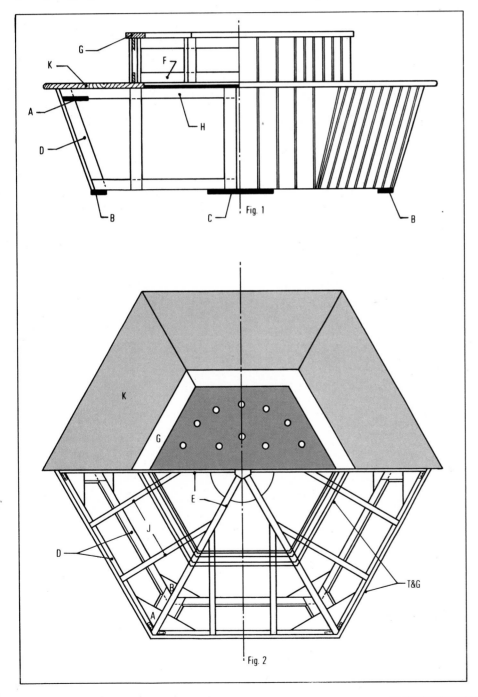

Fig 1. Side elevation of the garden seat and planter.

Fig 2. Plan view of the seat. If the unit is to be constructed round a tree the centre section will require a certain amount of modification.

Garden seat/planter

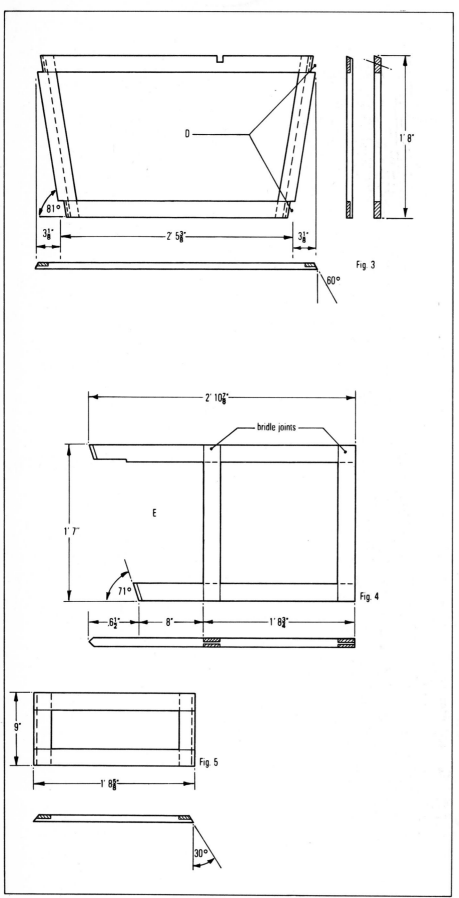

Fig. 3

Fig. 4

Fig. 5

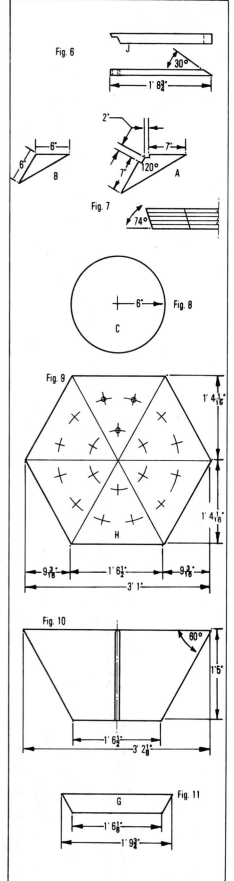

Fig. 6

Fig. 7

Fig. 8

Fig. 9

Fig. 10

Fig. 11

blocks of ½in (13mm) thick marine ply, one under each inner base frame, to keep the structure off the ground and to keep it level with the base corner plates. The soil container will obviously have to be left out of the design. These alterations will not weaken the unit, because the missing pieces are needed only as a support for the soil.

All joints must be screwed – use non-ferrous screws such as brass or galvanized ones to prevent unsightly rust stains – and glued with a waterproof woodworking adhesive. Remember, though, that not all combinations of wood preservative and wood adhesive will allow a secure join. Make sure you buy an adhesive that will adhere well to wood that has been treated with preservative. Your local supplier will provide you with details from the data sheets that the manufacturers send out.

The ground underneath the unit must be level. Otherwise it will be set at an unsightly angle and you will be sitting on a sloping seat. You will usually be able to level the area with a shovel. However, if the ground slopes too much you might have to raise the structure on a concrete foundation.

Outer base frames

First, make up the six outer base frames as shown in Fig. 3D. Each frame consists of four members, with halving joints at each corner. The edges of the two vertical sides or vertical members are bevelled or mitred so that the frames will butt together and form the hexagonal shape shown in Fig. 2.

The joint has to be angled, because the corners are not square. This is done using the same technique, except that the angles are marked out using a bevel gauge.

The next step is to mitre or bevel the edges. With the bevel gauge, mark out the angle on the end-grain of each end, then draw with a marking gauge and pencil a line along the inside of the timber between each marked point. Cut the wood down to this line, preferably using a power bench saw. If one is not available, the angle can be cut with a rip saw. Place the timber vertically in a wood vice. To prevent the wood from vibrating while sawing, start with only about a 10in (254mm) length of wood above the vice and gradually raise the member as the cut is made. The last few inches can be cut by reversing the member in the vice and

continuing from the opposite end. Alternatively a jack plane may be used to do the job.

Assemble the frame and check that the angles are correct. To do this, measure the side members and check that they are identical in length, then measure the diagonals. Each measurement must be identical. Glue and screw the joints and leave for the adhesive to set.

When the glue has set, cut the notches to house the ends of the inner base frames. (The housing recesses on the top that will take the outside ends of the seat support members J [Fig. 2] can be cut later after marking out by direct marking.) Make up the other five frames in the same way.

Inner base frames

The construction outline of these is shown in Fig. 4E. Each frame consists of a top and bottom member, and two vertical members – one centrally placed and one at the side, creating, in effect, one 'open' and one closed side. The open end of the frame is housed into notches cut into the corners of the outer base frames.

The frame is secured with bridle joints. These are the best joints to use when vertical timbers are under compression – as these will be when supporting the amount of soil required.

The bridle joints should be marked with a mortise gauge, which is similar to an ordinary marking gauge except that it has two scribing points or spurs, one of which is adjustable to give varying widths of mortise or tenon. To set the gauge, first loosen the stock setting screw and slide the stock back. Next, adjust the width – in this case $\frac{5}{16}$in (8mm) – and set the gauge so that the distance between the points locates in the centre of the member. Check that it does, by measuring the distance from each scribed line to the edge of the timber. Each measurement must be identical.

After marking out, cut the joints. Cutting techniques are similar to those used for a mortise-and-tenon joint. Trial assemble the frame and check the diagonals for squareness, then glue and screw. Do not worry too much about the lengths of the top and bottom members at the open end. They can be finished off by direct marking at a later stage.

Top frames

These are simple rectangular frames with a halving joint at each corner. Full con-

Fig 3. The outer frames of the garden seat are built to this pattern. A total of six is required. Note the angle at the top edge of the units.

Fig 4. Six frames to pattern E are required. Note the shape of the ends of the frames. These butt to the ends of frames D.

Fig 5. The inner frames of the planter itself. Again, six are required to pattern F.

Fig 6. Pieces J form the braces and seat supports and are cut to pattern J.

Fig 7. Triangles A and B are the corner braces. These are cut to the pattern shown. Piece B fits at the angle which joins pieces F. Piece A fits at the joint between pieces E and F underneath in the cut-out provided in piece E. Note the angles cut to accept the uprights of D.

Fig 8. Piece C is the centre base plate. It is not absolutely necessary that this piece be circular.

Fig 9. The base of the planter. It is this component which carries the soil and drainage holes must be drilled so that excess water can drain away.

Fig 10. The pattern for the seat panels.

Fig 11. Pieces G are the top combing of the planter.

Garden seat/planter

Opposite page left to right.

Top row: The method of using the marking gauge for marking the bridle joints.

The joint is cut with a tenon saw and the waste chopped out with a chisel.

The other component of the bridle joint. Again the first cuts are made with a tenon saw and the waste is removed with a chisel.

Middle row: Completed frame E. The bridle joint is used to retain the strength of the vertical members.

The method of marking the bevels at the ends of pieces D.

Once the angle has been marked on the end grain, the gauge is set to the measurement and a line is scribed down the length of the upright.

Bottom row: The waste is removed, either with a bench power saw or with a jack plane.

Close-up of the finished basic frame before the corner braces are fitted.

Plan view of the completed frame.

struction details are shown in Fig. 5F. These frames form the walls of the soil container and are boarded over on the outside to provide the seat back. They can, if necessary, be built at a much later stage.

Other components

The centre base plate is a disc of ½in (13mm) marine plywood as shown in Fig. 8C. It is not essential for this piece to be circular, and if you want to save some time you can just as effectively use a 12in (305mm) square of plywood.

You may, however, prefer the neatness of the circle. In this case lay a piece of 12in × 12in (305mm × 305mm) ply on a table. Lightly tap a nail about one third of the way into the centre of the board, and tie a 6in (152mm) long piece of string to the nail. Tie the other end to a pencil, stretch the string out and draw a circle on the board. Then cut out the circle with a jig saw or bow saw.

The soil support is the hexagonal base for the soil and is shown in Fig.9H. It is cut from a 37in × 32½in (940mm × 826mm) sheet of ½in (13mm) ply. Lay the ply on a level surface and mark a line lengthways down the middle. Along each *long* side *only*, mark off a point $9\frac{3}{16}$in (234mm) away from each corner. This will give you two marks along each long edge. Mark a line from each of these marks to the nearest end of the middle line, and you have your hexagon ready for cutting out, in four cuts, with a panel saw.

Corner plates are triangles of wood that provide bracing for the outer frames. They are easily cut from sheets of ½in (13mm) plywood by following the diagrams in Figs. 7A and B.

Coping pieces are run around the rim of the top frame to protect the end-grain of the boarding and conceal the boarding/ framework join. Each one is cut from a $21\frac{3}{4}$in (553mm) length of 3in × ½in (76mm × 13mm) ply as shown in Fig. 11G.

Seat supports – the cutting details for these pieces are shown in Fig. 6J – are housed at one end into the top of the outer frames, and butted at the opposite end, at an angle, to one side of the top member of an inner frame and screwed in place.

The seats are cut from 1in (25mm) ply as shown in Fig. 10K. The top surface should be lightly planed and sanded down, and the front edge radiused slightly with a plane to provide comfortable seating.

Assembly

There are several ways in which the unit can be constructed, but the following method is one of the easiest ways to assemble it. Part of the structure is built upside down.

Place the soil support on level ground. Mark out the frame positions on it, place two adjacent inner frames in position and skew nail them in position (leave the heads protruding slightly in case the positions need adjusting). This will allow one of the outer frames to be fitted in position. Repeat this procedure until the hexagon is complete, glueing and screwing each piece into place when you are sure of the fit. Each outer frame is joined to its adjacent outer frame by screws through the inside of the side members. While the unit is still upside down, screw the centre base plate and all the base corner plates in position.

Carefully turn the structure right way up and, using direct marking, mark out, cut and fit the seat support members. Trial assemble the top frames round the soil support and when you are sure that the fit is correct, screw the top frames to the tops of the inner frames, and to one another as for the outer frames.

Trial assemble the seats. When you have made sure they fit (by planing a few edges if necessary), secure them by screwing from underneath through the inner base frames or seat supports.

Mark out, cut and fit the boarding for the bottom section. Skew nail each T&G board through the tongue at each end so that the nail heads do not show. Repeat this for the top section.

Trial assemble the coping pieces round the top lip of the well and, when the fit is accurate, skew nail them in position using lost head nails and punching the heads down.

Filling the planter

The well of the seat planter can now be filled with soil. If you can afford to do so, use one of the peat-based composts. These are only a fraction of the weight of soil and, apart from easing the strain on your back, will lessen your watering problems because peat retains much more water than soil.

If you intend growing shrubs in the well, make sure that you do not plant ones that tend to deep-root. The depth of the growing medium is only about 9in (229mm) making it unsuitable for some shrubs.

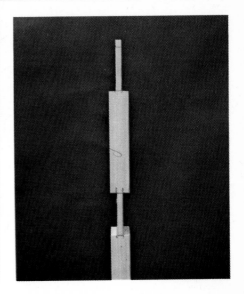

Garden gates

The garden gate is one of the most noticeable yet most often neglected features of a house. The gate illustrated here is not expensive and its design and dimensions can easily be adapted to your own requirements. Sturdily built, its classically simple lines are easily achieved with a minimum of carpentry know-how.

Wooden garden gates, however well-made and painted, inevitably decay and need replacing after some years. Wood merchants generally stock replacements in a range of sizes. Unfortunately, gate posts, particularly those of old houses, do not always conform to the standard sizes. If, under those circumstances, you want a new gate, you will either have to have one purpose-built – which can be expensive – or make one yourself.

If you do choose to make your own gate you will have complete control over the design instead of having to make do with what you can buy. A few variations on a simple, basic design are given here, but all use the same woodworking techniques, and so will almost any versions that you design yourself.

A garden gate has to stand up to considerable wear and tear, including children swinging on it. So it must be stoutly made, with the same standard of accuracy and finish that you would use for a piece of indoor furniture. Only then will it last for a reasonable length of time.

The cheapest material for a gate is ordinary softwood. Provided it is factory-treated with preservative, or properly primed and painted it will last for years. But the more you are prepared to spend on timber, the longer-lasting the job will be. Oak, at three or four times the price of softwood, and teak, which is even more expensive, are particularly durable.

The gate design given here uses T&G boarding, which is often not obtainable in hardwood. Fortunately, its use is not essential. You can use plain boards.

Nails used for outdoor work should be sheradized and galvanized to resist rust and screws should be of the black japanned type. This is particularly important if you are making a hardwood gate, because the natural acids in the wood attack bare metal.

The hinges for the gate can be of several types (Fig. 3). Ordinary tee hinges up to 18in (457mm) are quite strong enough for a medium-sized gate up to about 36in (914mm). A larger gate will need the stronger bands and hooks. These are available with either normal fixings for wooden posts or special flat plates for bedding in the mortar joints of brick pillars. This gate would need 24in (610mm) bands and hooks or 30in (762 mm) if it is made in heavy hardwood.

If you want your gate to fold back flat against the wall you will need cranked hinges which have offset pivots.

Measurement and planning

The first step is to measure the site and note the condition of the existing gate posts. They will probably need replacing at the same time as an old gate. If you are installing a new gate between existing posts, the total width of the gate must be about 1in (25mm) narrower than the space between the posts, and perhaps more for a large gate. This gap allows for the extended dimension of the diagonal which is presented as you begin to open the gate, and for the inevitable swelling of the timber in winter.

Once you know the height and width of the gate, draw up a plan of the design you want. This need not be full size, but it must be to scale to enable you to work out the dimensions of everything.

Note that planed 4in × 2in (102mm × 51mm) timber is actually about 3½in × 1¾in (89mm × 45mm), and that other sizes are proportionally smaller.

Whether you are adapting the gate shown in Fig. 1 or designing one of your own, some dimensions will be the same in all cases. These include the sizes of the mortise and tenons and of the rebates into which the T&G boards are set.

The mortise-and-tenon joint

This joint is very strong and reasonably simple to make. But it must be made accurately, for it is worse than useless if it is a loose fit. The mortise-and-tenon joints are held tight with small wooden wedges.

Begin by cutting the timber to length for the various pieces allowing ½in (13mm) extra for waste. At the same time, cut twelve small wedges from scrap of the same type. Lay the two stiles, (the vertical outside pieces) face to face and mark off ¼in (6mm) at one end and then from that mark set out the positions of the mortises. Square these lines around the timber, then add an extra ⅛in (3mm) to the top and bottom of the mortise hole on the outer edge of the stile widening the mortise to make room for the wedges.

The mortises should be one third the thickness of the timber and you can mark them by setting a gauge to that measurement and scribing a line from each side of

Right, top to bottom: Scrap wood is used to raise the gate to the correct height. The gate post is then drilled using the hinge as a template. The outer gatepost is set upright using a spirit level and the gate is then ready for use.

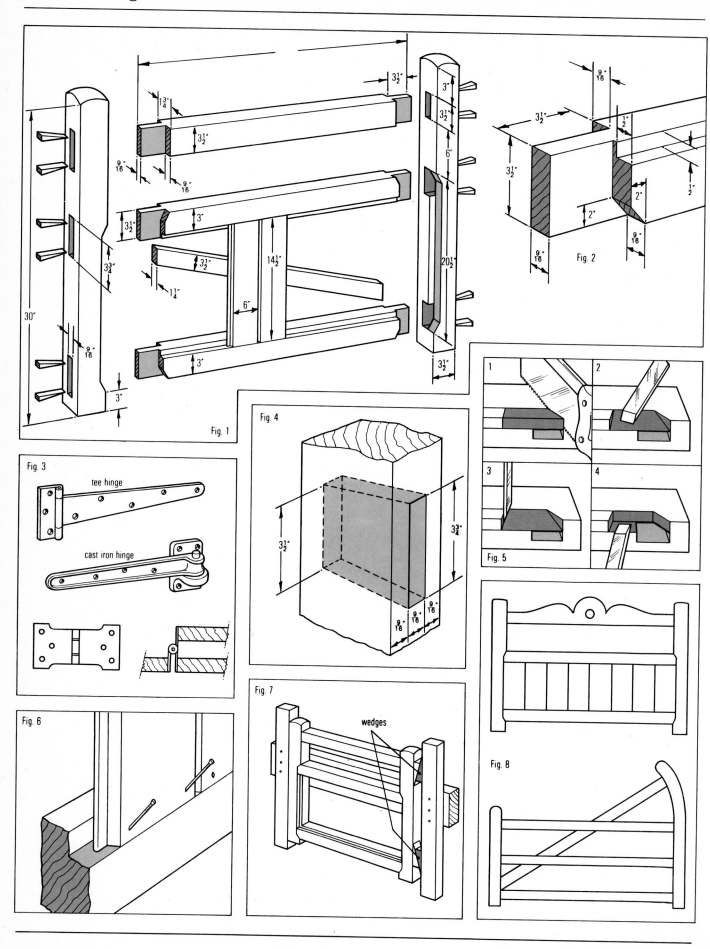

Fig. 1

Fig. 2

Fig. 3

tee hinge

cast iron hinge

Fig. 4

Fig. 5

Fig. 6

Fig. 7

wedges

Fig. 8

the timber.

Cut the mortise by first drilling it out making as many holes as close together as you can, using a bit the same diameter as the width of the mortise hole. The mortise is then squared up with a chisel. Turn the timber over to square up the mortise from the other side and chisel the extra $\frac{1}{8}$in (3mm) marked on the outer edge of the stile. Taper this off to nothing just inside the inner edge.

Now take the rails and place them together flush at each end, hold them with a small cramp if necessary. Mark $\frac{1}{4}$in (6mm) for waste at one end and then from that mark measure the width of the stile through which the tenon has to pass. This second line will be the shoulder line of the tenon. To mark the shoulder line at the other end of the rails, take the width of the gate less the width of both the rails and measure this from the shoulder mark you have just made and square a line across the timber at the other end. You will then be left with the width of the stile plus about $\frac{1}{4}$in (6mm) waste.

Separate the timbers and square the shoulder lines around each piece. Take the gauge that you used for the mortises and scribe a line along the edge of the rails from the shoulder line right over the end-grain and back to the shoulder line on the other side of the timber. Do this from both faces of the rail and at both ends. The tenons may be cut by hand with a tenon saw or a bench-mounted circular saw if this piece of equipment is available.

Do not cut the middle or bottom rail tenons yet as they have to be adjusted to fit into the rebate which will be cut in the stiles for the close boarding at the bottom of the gate.

The front inside corners of the stiles between the middle and the bottom mortise holes are rebated to take the T&G boarding. The bottom front corner of the middle rail and the top front corner of the bottom rail are also rebated. These rebates are $\frac{1}{2}$in $\times$ $\frac{1}{2}$in (13mm $\times$ 13mm).

The ends of the rebates on the stiles are mitred – cut at an angle of 45° – so

Figs 1—8. The basic construction details and designs of garden gates. The mortise and tenons are unusual because they have to be modified to accommodate the rebates, required in the stile, to accept the tongue and groove boarding. This should, however, present no problems.

that the rails can fit into them neatly. Mark out the full extent of the rebates accurately, using a bevel for the mitre, and make a short tenon saw cut up each end along the line of the mitre (see Fig. 5). This cut will not go to the full depth of the rebate because it only cuts across the corner of the wood, but it gives you a starting point for chiselling out the rebate end. Make a similar cut 4in (102mm) further along the rebate, at both ends or however far you need to go to clear a space for the body of the rebate plane. Then chisel out the wood between each pair of cuts, working slowly and accurately to keep the rebate straight and level. As wood comes away from the ends of the rebate, chop down deeper past the saw cuts, with a chisel held vertically to expose more end surface. When all the wood is chiselled out, finish the rebates with the plough plane.

Finishing the parts

When the rebate is finished in all the timbers you should check its depth as the tenon shoulder will have to be adjusted to fit into it. On the side of the middle rail and bottom rail on which you have made the rebates, measure $\frac{1}{2}$in (13mm) (the depth of the rebate) from the existing shoulder line towards the end of the tenon, thus shortening the tenon by $\frac{1}{2}$in (13mm). Now put the rails in a vice one at a time and saw down the waste side of the tenon lines. Take care when cutting the shoulders that you only cut as far as the new line on the rebate side. It is a good idea to shade the waste on that side of the tenon so that it will remind you.

Having cut the tenons you will have to make a small mitre cut on the long shoulder to match the mitre on the end of the stile rebate. Chisel these mitres carefully taking off a little at a time until the mitres fit neatly. Make a trial fitting of all the joints and make the gate up dry. When you are happy with the fit of all the joints, paint all the parts after first giving the knots a coating of shellac or proprietary knotting.

You can then glue the joints and cramp the gate driving the wedges home in the mortises. If you have no sash cramps and cannot hire any, you can make a cramp by fixing two battens to the ends of a length of timber so that they will span the gate but leaving enough space to insert pairs of wedges (Fig. 7). When you cramp the gate measure the diagonals to ensure that the frame is square.

Carefully measure the distance between the rebated front edges of the two lower rails. Cut the T&G boards slightly over this measurement, and plane them to the exact length. This should ensure that they fit neatly into their rebates without a gap.

The boarded area on the front of the gate is unlikely to be made up of an exact number of board widths. To give the gate a symmetrical appearance, the edges should be planed off both outside boards to bring the boarding down to width. This process also removes the tongues and grooves, which are not needed because the outside edges of the boarding fit into the plain rebates on the stiles. The boards must not be too tight a fit between the stiles because you need to allow for expansion in wet weather.

The only job that remains in the construction of the gate is to make the diagonal brace. This has to be made after the rest of the gate has been completed, because its exact length controls the squareness of the frame. Saw and plane its ends to the right length and angle by measuring them against the frame itself. The brace does not need a mortise-and-tenon joint to hold it in place, because it is compressed when the gate is hung. But you must put it in the right way round, with its lower end next to the 'hanging' stile to which the hinges are attached.

Form a slightly domed top on the two stiles (and the gate posts, if you are replacing them) to stop rainwater from collecting on them and rotting the wood. This is best done with a spokeshave or similar tool, working from the edge of the post to the centre to avoid snagging the tool on the grain. Also saw off the ends of the tenons which protrude through the mortises.

Insert the T&G boarding in the rebates. To avoid splitting the ends of the boards, use oval nails set end-on with the grain of the wood, and drive the nails into the rebates in the rails at an angle, as shown in Fig. 6. Use two nails for each end of each board if the gate is to be painted, but only one for an unpainted hardwood gate, to allow the boards to widen in wet weather.

When the glue is dry, take the gate out of the cramps and turn it over. Put the diagonal brace in from the back, making sure that it is the right way round. Glue it to the frame at each end, hold it in place with two temporary nails, and then turn the gate front upward again and

Garden gates

nail all the boards to the brace. This keeps both the brace and the boards from warping. No other form of fixing is necessary.

When you have completed the priming coat of paint, screw the hinges to the gate and place it between the gateposts. Raise the gates on blocks or bricks to the height required, then get a helper to hold it steady while you screw the other part of each hinge to the gatepost.

If you are installing new gateposts, they should preferably be set 24in (610mm) deep in concrete, and at least a week should be allowed (more in cold weather) before putting any weight on them. Posts set in hardcore alone tend to sag unless the hardcore is rammed down with considerable force.

The only things that remain to be done are to fix a latch on the gate and give it its final coats of paint.

Other gates

If you find the design of the gate given here too plain, there are many variations on the basic gate that do not make it any more difficult to build. For example, for the top rail, you can substitute a piece of 6in × 2in (152mm × 51mm) timber cut to any shape with a jig saw (see Fig. 8). The boarding can also be cut into decorative shapes.

The farm-type gate also shown is made in the same way as the basic gate, but the diagonal brace runs the other way, so that the weight of the gate stretches it. As a result, the brace must be firmly anchored with mortise-and-tenon joints at each end, strengthened by screws. This type of gate looks best without boarding, so the braces should be as thick as the rails and stiles. Angled halving joints should be made where the brace crosses the rails – it is best to make these while you are actually assembling the frame, to ensure that the angle is correct. The curved stile to which the brace is attached is cut out of a piece of 8in × 2in (203mm × 51mm) timber, using a jig saw. If you can find a board with a grain that naturally follows the curve you are going to cut, the stile will be much stronger.

If you are prepared to be more adventurous with techniques, the only limit on the designs you can build will be set by your imagination.

Above: A farm gate with diagonal bracing.

Top and right: A pair of simple wicket gates and a creosoted farm-type gate suitable for a wide drive.

Solid wood: Cutting list

	standard	metric
Frame	240 × 4 × 2	6096 × 102 × 51
Diagonal brace	48 × 4 × 1½	1219 × 102 × 38
T&G boarding	132 × 6 × ½	3352 × 152 × 13
Gateposts	120 × 3 × 3	3048 × 76 × 76
Gateposts (alternative)	120 × 4 × 4	3048 × 102 × 102

You will also require:

Knotting. Primer. Undercoat. Paint. Sherardized or galvanized oval nails 1½in (38mm). Black japanned screws. Hinges.

Tree house

Tree house

Fig 1. The frames for the tree house are built to this pattern.

Fig 2. Front and side elevations of the tree house showing the guys and rails.

The basic construction of the tree house is quite simple. It consists of two timber triangles, stood on the apex and bolted together through the short side of the triangles – the top member in the finished construction. The apex of each triangle is fixed to a concrete block, set into the ground. The structure is braced by metal cables, fixed to the top member of the triangles and running to the ground, where they are attached to hooks set in concrete blocks.

A look-out platform is placed between the timber members and the metal guy ropes, about half-way up the height of the tree house. One end of the platform has a rectangular opening – this acts as a kind of trap door to the platform. At the opposite end there is a triangular wall, with an opening in the base of it which acts as another door. Nylon ropes are strung around the tree house timbers and the metal guys. These act as 'safety rails' around the platform.

The platform is reached by means of 'rope ladders' – in this case made from nylon rope with timber rungs. These are securely fixed at the top and bottom.

Planning consideration

The tree house will occupy an area in your garden measuring 9ft × 9ft 8in (2.7m × 2.9m). It is worth drawing a scaled plan of your garden to help you position the tree house correctly – it can be moved after it has been erected, but planning will save you the trouble.

The best position for the construction is near to the house where you can keep an eye on the children. Do not build the tree house near an outhouse or tall trees – children are likely to use the tree house to climb into higher, and more dangerous, places. Build the tree house on a lawn so that if your children do fall out of it they will land on a fairly soft surface.

No cutting list has been included for this project, it being a simple matter to extract the wood sizes required from the illustrations.

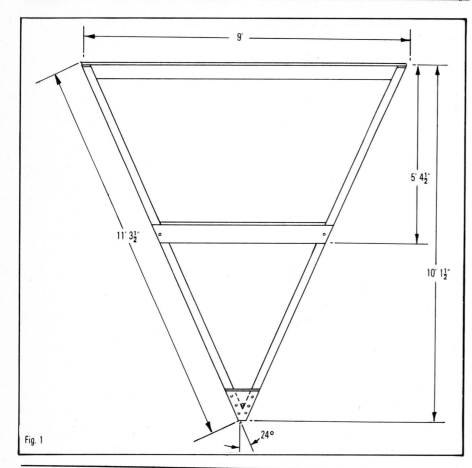

9′

5′ 4½″

11′ 3½″

10′ 1½″

24°

Fig. 1

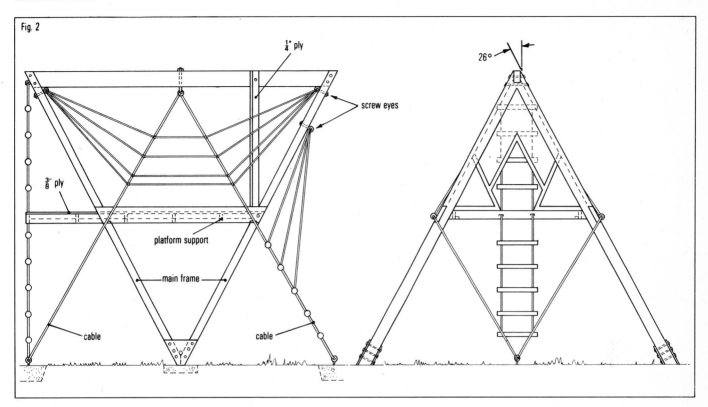

Fig. 2

¼" ply

screw eyes

⅜" ply

platform support

main frame

cable

cable

26°

The triangular frames

The triangular frames are made from lengths of 4in × 2in (102mm × 51mm) timber to the shape shown in Fig. 1. The timber that forms the long sides of the triangle is jointed to that which forms the short side with housing joints. At the apex of the triangle the two long sides are butted. The joints are strengthened by plywood fillets bolted in place over the apex of the triangle on both sides of the timbers.

Cut the long sides of the triangle a little overlength using a circular saw and combination blade. On the ends of these timbers, mark an angle of 156° on the narrow edge of the timbers. You can mark this with a bevel gauge, setting the angle with a protractor. Cut through the timbers, down the marked lines.

Now mark the finished length of the timbers, referring to Fig. 1 for dimensions. From the point marking the finished length, mark an angle of 156° on the wide edge of the timbers. Cut through the timbers, down the marked lines. The next step is to cut, in the newly cut slanted ends, a 1in (25mm) housing to take the ends of the short sides of the triangle.

Cut the plywood fillets that cover the apex of the triangle. These fillets are shown in Fig. 1. Bolt these in place over the apex of the triangle with 5in (127mm)

coach bolts. You now have two V-shaped constructions. Cut the short sides of the triangles overlength and lay them between the arms of the V, set into the housing. Direct mark the length of this side of the triangle. Cut it to length and nail it to the two arms of the V-shaped constructions. This gives you the two triangular frames.

The next step is to cut housings in the frame members for the two timbers that form the side members of the look-out platform. The position and all the necessary dimensions of these are shown in Fig. 1. Nail these side members in place in the housings.

Now bolt the two triangles together through the short sides. Use 7in (178mm) coach bolts for this, spaced about 12in (305mm) apart along the timber. At the end use two coach bolts, one underneath the other. The top one should be 7in (178mm) long, the bottom one 10in (254mm) long.

The concrete bases

With the two triangles bolted together, you can now determine the exact position for the concrete bases for the legs and guy ropes. To do this you will have to hold the construction up in its finished position – you will need at least two helpers.

With the helpers holding the triangles upright, mark round the point on the ground where the legs of the tree house

rest. The guy ropes run to points on the ground almost underneath the ends of the short sides of the triangles (see Fig. 2). You can estimate the position of the blocks here or mark out the ground plan with wooden pegs.

Once you have determined the position of the bases you can dig the holes for the concrete blocks. These should be about 12in (305mm) deep. The holes for the guy rope blocks should be wider at the bottom than at the top – the strain exerted here is an upward pull, whereas the pressure exerted by the legs is downwards – the blocks for these can, therefore, be straight-sided. All four blocks stand proud of the ground by 4in (102mm) so you will need some simple formwork.

As a fixing for the guy ropes, a metal hook with a 1in (25mm) diameter eye on top is set into the block. You can make these yourself from lengths of 10in × ⅜in (254mm × 10mm) mild steel rod. They are bedded in the block so that just the eye stands proud. The fixing for the timber legs of the tree house is 12in (305mm) of 1½in (38mm) diameter pipe, bedded in concrete to a depth of 6in (152mm). A flange joint is slipped over the pipe so that it sits on the top of the block.

Pour the concrete for the blocks and push the fixings into it. Leave the concrete to set.

Tree house

The look-out platform

This consists of a framework of 3in × 1in (76mm × 25mm) PAR (planed all round) timber, boarded over with ⅜in (10mm) plywood. The platform is bolted to the inside edge of the long sides of the triangles, at the points where the side member of the platform wall are housed into the triangular frame members. The platform has a rectangular opening at one end to act as a door to the platform. Construct the platform to the shape and dimensions shown in Fig. 3.

To bolt the square-sided platform to the sloping sides of the triangles, you will first have to cut four wedges. Lightly nail these in place on the triangle members. The platform is bolted in place with 8in (203mm) fence stretchers – these are bolts with an eye at the head. These also give a fixing for the guy ropes that are positioned later. Bolt the platform in place.

Use ⅜in (10mm) plywood for the side wall of the look-out platform. This is nailed to the platform and to the side members fixed earlier. Before you do this though, cut an opening at the base of the panel to be used for the side wall – this acts as another door. The shape of the opening and the position of the extra timbers that frame it are shown in Fig. 2.

The rigging

The rigging that runs to the two concrete blocks set in the ground is ½in (13mm) steel cable, known as Bowden cable. You must use steel cable rather than rope or nylon – you cannot run the risk of children cutting through these essential supports.

You will need four lengths of cable, each about 11ft (3.3m) long. These run from an eye bolt and ring fixed through the top member of the two triangles, in the centre of their length. They then pass through the eye of the fence stretchers on the sides of the look-out platform and round the triangle member to the concrete blocks. At the top the cable itself is attached to U bolts or Bowden clips, and at the bottom to cable stretchers.

Drill a 1½in (38mm) hole up through the bottom of the timber legs. Do this with a brace and expansive bit. These holes allow the legs to be fitted over the metal pipes set in the concrete. Drill a ½in (13mm) hole in the bottom of the plywood fillets also – this will allow rain-

Fig 3. The completed tree house viewed from below.

water to drain out of the base of the legs.

The safety rail

This consists of nylon rope, strung from the ends of the top member of the triangles and fanning out to plastic fittings on the guy ropes. The arrangement of the nylon rope is shown in Fig. 2.

Erecting the tree house

Again you will need two helpers for this. First, attach the guy ropes to the fixing in the top triangle member and thread them through the eyes of the fence stretchers in the platform sides. Get your helpers to lift the tree house in place, with the timber legs over the metal pipe fittings. Attach the cable stretchers on the end of the guy ropes to the eye fittings in the concrete blocks. Tighten the guy ropes.

The rope ladders

The rope ladders are made from lengths of 12in × 8in × 1½in (305mm × 203mm × 38mm) timber, strung on to nylon ropes. Drill ½in (13mm) holes through the 1½in (38mm) edge of the timbers, about 1in (25mm) from their ends. Take a length of

nylon rope. Tie a knot in it. Do the same with another length of rope. Repeat this process, spacing the rungs every 9in (229mm) until the ladders are complete.

Both ladders are fixed at the bottom to the guy ropes, 9in (229mm) from the ground. Fix them to the guys with the plastic eye clips used to fix the nylon safety rail to the guys above the platform. One ladder is vertical and runs through the opening in the platform floor. At the top, about 12in (305mm) from the top triangle member, the two lengths of rope are tied to size 14 screw eyes. The other ladder runs up to the opening in the platform wall. It is tied to the side of the platform, through size 14 screw eyes.

Finishing

You can coat all the timbers with a wood preservative, or paint them in the colour of your choice. This will weatherproof the timbers. Decoration of the tree house – decking the guy ropes with coloured pennants for example – is up to you and your children.

The tree house will last for years, and give your children hours of fun.

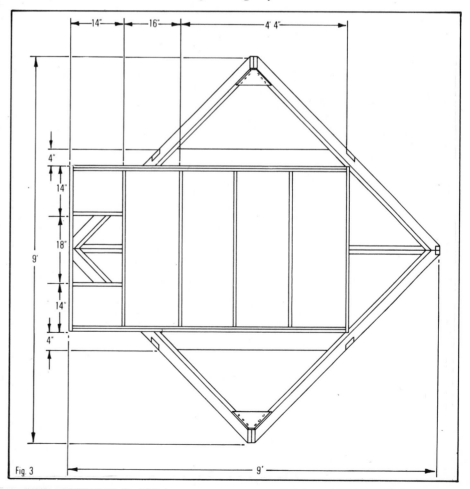

Fig. 3

Climbing frame

The climbing frame shown here is simple to construct and will provide hours of fun. If space is limited, the design may be modified to suit your own garden.

This play area has been designed so that it can be altered to suit the dimensions of any particular garden. It consists of a climbing frame, slide, and sand-pit, any of which could be scaled down in size or omitted if you do not have enough room. Refer to the cutting list for the lengths of timber which you will need for each section of the project.

The main feature is the climbing frame, and as this will be used by children of differing ages, platforms of varying heights have been incorporated. A slide has been included because it is one of the most popular playground items. And any timid types who do not wish to climb the rungs can make use of the stepped ladder which hooks on to one of the platforms.

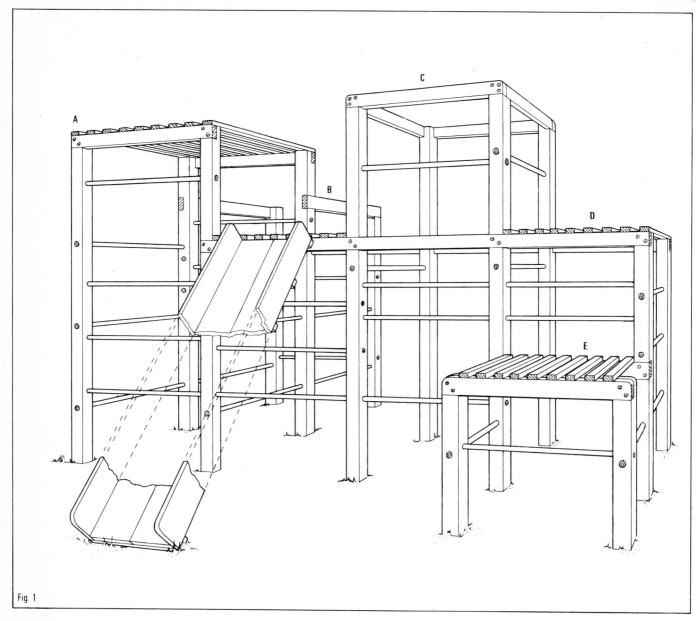

Fig. 1

Fig 1. The completed climbing frame. The construction is very simple and should present no problems.

Fig 2. The uprights are cut to the dimensions shown here.

The frame consists of towers made up from 2½in (64mm) square uprights in modules of 2ft 4in (711mm), the highest towers being 6ft (1.8m) and the lowest platform 2ft (610mm). The towers are joined by 2½in × 1in (64mm×25mm) cross members, and dowel rods 1⅛in (29mm) in diameter. These rods also provide the rungs for climbing.

Planning the project
It is not essential to follow the exact layout of the frame described here, as long as the structure is stable and strong. But various factors should be taken into account when planning the unit.

Safety is the main consideration. As the frame is likely to be used by several children together, a tower must be placed at the rear, and another at the front of the frame. These act as stabilizers, preventing the frame from toppling over if all the children happen to be playing on one section of it.

Your garden may not have enough

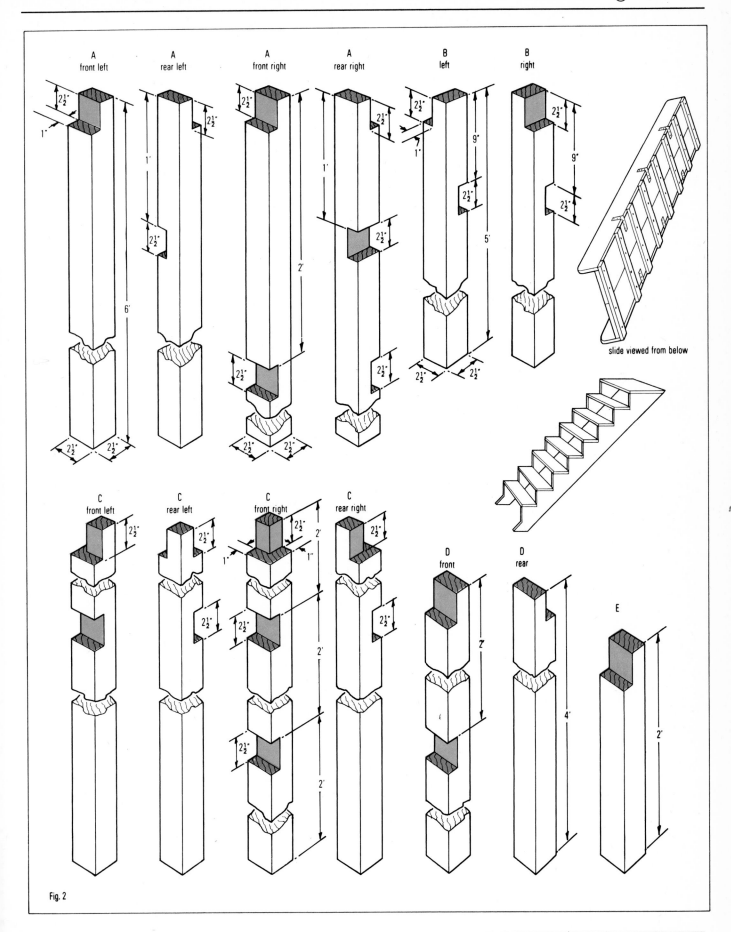

Fig. 2

level space for the design shown here. In this case you will have to limit your frame, or vary the tower legs to allow for irregularities or sloping ground.

Hardwood is an expensive item, and this too may well limit the size you decide on.

At the planning stage you should consider the placing of the feet of the frame. By placing them on concrete slabs you will be able to keep the grass from growing untidily against the uprights.

If you are altering the design of the structure, do not try to eliminate the dowelling that spans two modules. Dowelling that is inserted through three uprights makes for a stronger structure than dowelling through two uprights. Also, make sure the bottom rung is high enough to provide clearance for a lawnmower, as in the original frame described here. Otherwise you will have an untidy patch inside.

Materials
Materials needed for the climbing frame are in the cutting list. The eight 6ft (1.8m) lengths are for towers A and C, and the two 5ft (1.5m) lengths are for tower B. The two 4ft (1.2m) lengths are for the two legs at the right end (D) of the frame, and the shortest lengths are for the lowest jumping platform, E, which acts as a front stabilizer.

Tower B is a stabilizing structure at the rear of the frame. The two 5ft (1.5m) uprights have joints cut at the top of each, to take the bearers which connect it to tower A. Additional joints 9in (229mm) down are cut to take a cross member.

Tower C is a hollow climbing frame (it has no platform on the top). It consists of four uprights, 6ft (1.8m) in length, held together at the top by bearers.

The addition of tower D is made by two 4ft (1.2m) uprights, which join to the main cross members linking towers A and C. These members also act as bearers for the platform battening on the top of tower D.

The front of the structure is stabilized by tower E, the low level jumping platform. This consists of two 2ft (610mm) lengths which act as uprights, joined by a bearer on the front, and at the back to the bearer on the front of tower D.

Cross members and bearers
These are used to connect the three main towers as well as to strengthen the tower tops. (Cross members are horizontal timbers used to strengthen a structure: bearers both strengthen and support a load – in this case, the platform battens.)

For safety alone it is important that all cross members and bearers fit snugly at the joints and are securely screwed and glued. Several children weigh a considerable amount.

Constructing the frame
Plane all timbers to a smooth finish to prevent splinters. Sand all surfaces, then mark out the joints as indicated in the diagrams. Each upright is described as though looking at the front of the frame – that is, the face to which the slide is attached.

The joints are all of the simple halving type, which makes the unit particularly easy to assemble. But take care to mark the joints on the correct faces. It will be a great help if you pencil an identification on each upright. Countersink all screws, using a countersink bit in your drill.

The two main bearers are the 6ft 3in (1.9m) lengths at the front and rear. Tap these into the joints of the uprights, drill holes for screws, then screw and glue to the front uprights. Assemble the rear uprights and tower B in the same manner. This allows the top bearers to be screwed and glued into place, and the battens to be screwed in place between towers A and C to form the platform access between ladder and slide. Allow a gap of 1in (25mm) between the battens. Then screw the battens for towers D and E in place, and fix the top of tower C with the four bearers [two of 2ft 4in (711mm) two of 2ft 2in (660mm)].

Fitting the rungs
Once the main frame is screwed together, the next step is to mark out the centres for boring the holes for the dowelling.

It is essential to work out with care the spacing of the dowelling. The rungs should not be too close to one another, as this takes the fun out of climbing. Also, where two dowels are to be inserted through an upright in different directions (at right angles) the holes should not be bored too close to each other as the upright will be weakened and might split.

First, mark out the centre line on the uprights with a try square. Then mark a line half way at right angles to produce a cross, the middle of which will be drilled for the dowel.

Secure the dowelling jig so that the

guide hole is right over the mark, then drill the holes with a No.8 bit on the power drill.

When you have drilled all the small No.8 holes, thread a string line through them. This will indicate whether the line is running correctly, at right angles to the uprights.

Now insert in the brace a bit the same size as the dowelling, and bore out the holes. Do this fairly slowly. As soon as the point of the bit shows through the pilot hole, stop and drill from the opposite direction, using the pilot hole for centring. This will prevent the edges of the hole from splintering.

Now clean up around the inside of each hole with a round wood rasp.

You are now ready to tap the dowels through with the mallet. It helps to have someone to give some support to the upright when knocking in the first few dowels. Any spare dowelling which sticks out should be left until the frame is well and truly squared up. Then the spare bits can be cut away.

Making the slide

Place the two 7in (178mm) planks side by side and secure them with the eight battens (Fig. F). You must allow the battens to overlap the edges of the planks by 1in (25mm) on both sides.

To form the sides of the slide, place the 4in (102mm) planks on the overlapping battens so that they are at right angles with the slide planks. First screw the sides on to the edges of the slide, then screw the battens to the bottom of the side planks.

Secure the three steel L brackets down each side for additional support.

Plane any corners on the top of the sides and the top and bottom of the slide itself – to half round, so that no nasty angles protrude. Also check that no screw points protrude anywhere.

The method of attaching the slide to the frame depends on whether you want it to be screwed in a semi-permanent manner, or hooked on so that it can be detached quickly. An L bracket could easily be bent to fit, and screwed to the underside of the slide, while a simple hook-and-eye provides an easy slip-on fitting.

Cutting the ladder steps

The ladder is secured to the side of the tower opposite the slide. It is made out of two 4ft 6in (1.3m) lengths of

timber, with shorter planks providing the steps.

Recesses for the steps are cut out by sawing uniform V sections along one side of each plank. This requires nothing more than a measuring rule, a pencil and saw.

To mark out the step positions, begin by fixing one side of the ladder temporarily in place to establish the correct slope. Next, use a builder's level and pencil to mark one horizontal guide line across the board. (This is to ensure that the steps are level.) Remove the ladder side and lay it flat while you do the rest of the marking out. For this, you will need a cardboard or hardboard triangle, whose shortest side is 3in (76mm) and whose longest side matches the slope of the steps. Simply by sliding the triangle along the board you can mark each successive step on the face side. Use the try square to carry the marks across the edge of the board, and the cardboard triangle to mark the other side. Finally, mark out the second board so that it matches the first.

Saw along the zig-zag lines to cut out the outline as in Fig. F. Screw the steps in position and round the edges with the plane. The ladder may be attached to the frame in the same way as the slide.

Polyurethane varnish should now be applied to all woodwork. In view of the fact that this unit will spend its life outdoors, two coats are recommended.

The sand-pit

The area of this sand-pit is approximately 6ft by 4ft (1.8m×1.2m).

Dig the pit to a depth of 2ft 6in (762mm) and line it with any old planking that you can get. Creosote the planking well. Secure the planks at the corners by simple square stakes driven into the ground, and then back-fill them. When the top edge of the planking is level – a visual sighting is sufficient for this – nail through the stakes into the planks.

For this pit, ornamental, square, concrete slabs are laid round the edge, giving a slight overhang which provides an on-site seating arrangement, and a firm base for building sandcastles. The slabs also make it easier to sweep the surround free of excavated sand. If possible, obtain slabs with rounded edges – these are kinder to children's legs.

To assist drainage, line the bottom 6in (152mm) of the pit with gravel and ram it down well. Finally, fill the pit with sand (of the non-staining variety if possible).

Cutting list	standard	metric
Solid wood		
Timber for uprights		
8 lengths	72×2½×2½	1829×64×64
2 lengths	60×2½×2½	1524×64×64
2 lengths	48×2½×2½	1250×64×64
2 lengths	24×2½×2½	600×64×64
Timber for cross members and bearers		
2 lengths	75×2½×1	1905×64×25
9 lengths	28×2½×1	711×64×25
2 lengths	26×2½×1	660×64×25
Timber for platform battens		
37 lengths	28×2×1	711×51×25
Hardwood dowelling for rungs		
11 lengths	28½×1⅛ dia.	724×28 dia.
23 lengths	54×1⅛ dia.	1372×28 dia.
Timber for slide (Parana pine planks)		
2 lengths	96×7×1	2438×178×25
2 lengths	48×48×1	1219×1219×25
Battening for underside of slide		
8 lengths	16×2×1	406×51×25
Timber for ladder		
2 lengths	54×4½×1	1372×112×25
8 lengths	12×3×¾	305×76×19

You will also require:

A quantity of No.8 screws 2in (51mm) long: some of 1½in (38mm); some ¾in (19mm). Nails. 6 steel L brackets 3in (76mm) max. Steel strips or hooks. Wood adhesive.

Gazebo

The 'gazebo' or octagonal greenhouse, can be built largely of softwood or entirely of hardwood. The lower 'cheeks' of the greenhouse sides are timber clad, but plastic cladding could be used here.

The greenhouse is largely prefabricated, then assembled on its foundations. The main structure consists of eight equal panels, forming the octagonal shape when assembled.

Site preparation

Select a position for the greenhouse which makes the best use of sunlight, yet gives ready access. Next, level the overall site areas, using pegs, a straightedge and a spirit level. It is a good idea to provide a slight fall in the level of the ground so that water does not collect around the base of the greenhouse.

The footings are then marked out. Find the overall depth of the structure, from front to back (in the case of the greenhouse illustrated it is 5ft [1.5m]), and mark this, using a measured string line. Place a marked peg at each end of the line. Find the centre position and then take the string across to form a cross; place pegs at each end. Measure between the four pegs to find the half-way points and put in four more pegs, the same distance as before from the centre position, but this time in the form of a letter X. This gives a roughly octagonal shape (Fig. 1). Now mark at right angles with a spade, at the top and bottom and the side pegs of the cross, the width of the frames which form the greenhouse sides. Join up these marks diagonally. This gives an accurate octagonal profile.

Mark out with the spade the line of the footings. Do this by marking slightly in front of the octagonal outline, and also slightly deeper than the greenhouse side frames, giving a total width of about 6in (152mm). The foundations need to be slightly wider overall than the structure to provide a firm bearing.

Excavate a trench to a depth of about 4in (102mm) and place timber shuttering in this, proud of the ground by about 3in (76mm). It is important to raise the foundations slightly above the surrounding earth, to prevent rotting of the greenhouse timber.

The shuttering should be even throughout in height, since the top of this is the top of the concrete. Use a straightedge and spirit level to check the shuttering levels.

Once the trenches are filled with con-crete, this is well tamped down and allowed to set. Shuttering is then removed, leaving the 'footings' with an upstand.

Finally, lay 4½in (114mm) damp-proof bituminous felt on top of the footings, to prevent damp rising into the timber framework.

As an alternative to concrete footings, the greenhouse can stand on raised paving or brick. The main requirements are that these footings are both firm and level, otherwise it will not be possible to assemble the greenhouse accurately on site.

Timber preparation

Dependent on the type of timber you use, and the climate in which you are building, some pre-treatment of the timber may be necessary to prevent it rotting. In some circumstances, every joint in the timber – particularly end-grain – must be given a thick coat of priming paint as the joints are assembled. When you buy your timber, ask your timber merchant for advice on this point.

Building the wall frames

The first stage is to make up the four opposed square frames (Fig. 2). Frames A and B are made up in the same way, except that the former uses a doorstep section in place of the bottom rail (Fig. 3). Frames are made from 3in×2in (76mm ×51mm) planed timber, joined together by 4in (102mm) nails inside the uprights of each frame. For all construction use non-rusting sherardized, galvanized or aluminium nails.

Half-lap joints are cut, preferably with a circular saw, at an angle of 45° in the top rail sections before assembly. Nails are then driven through these joints into the top ends of the side stiles (Fig. 4). Details of the joint are shown in Fig. 5.

Sections marked 'triangle X' on Fig. 4 are sawn from 3in×3in (76mm×76mm) softwood to the desired height of the window sills. This is simply a matter of deciding how much window area above these you want.

Next, cut the base rails (plates) C and place a piece of section X at the end and draw the angle. The V section is formed by returning the angle at 45°. (A piece of section X can be used to help scribe this.) The wedge is then cut out as shown in Fig. 7. This procedure is followed at both ends of rail C.

The X and C sections are nailed together as shown in Fig. 6. In Fig. 8,

B, C and X are seen butted together.

The completed framework is assembled on the damp-proof felt (Fig. 3) and joined together by nailing through the triangle X sections into adjacent uprights of frames A and B. Additional support can be given by fixing angle brackets to the internal edges of floor rails B and C and doorstep A.

The top rails C1 (Fig. 9) are angle cut to 45° and lapped. These are slotted into the lapped sections of frames A and B and nailed downwards into the uprights.

Angle brackets can be screwed to the internal side of the top rails to provide added strength.

Cladding and window sills

Unless you have a fair amount of experience with horizontal boarding (Fig. 10), this material is tricky to work with. The boards must be mitred at 22½° at both ends, because cutting one board to 90° and the adjoining one to 45° would throw the vertical joints off the true line of the corner. Two things will help you get a snug fit: (1) cut the mitres just a fraction too 'sharp', so that no gaps show at the outside edges when they are joined and (2) as you fix each row of boards, butt them against a temporary vertical stop (mitred lengthwise at an angle of 22½°) so that the ends of all the boards align accurately with one another.

Vertical boarding is much simpler, since only the boards at each end of any particular wall need to be mitred – that is, you make two mitre cuts per wall, instead of a dozen or more. Start by vertically mitring a pair of boards a 'whisker' sharper than 22½°, and fix them around the angle farthest from the door. Then work progressively back towards the door. Whichever type of board you use, fix it with non-rusting rails.

Once all the cladding is in place, the window sills can be fixed. Try to buy the type which has a flat base. Other patterns with angled bases are more difficult to work with.

Each length of sill must be cut away at the back (Fig. 11) to fit around the vertical members of the greenhouse frame. At its outside edge, it must be cut accurately to 22½° to meet the adjoining length of sill. If, when fitting the sills, two adjoining pieces are found to be slightly overlength, this can be adjusted by running a saw cut through the joint – but be careful not to score the panelling beneath.

The roof struts W are cut from eight

Gazebo

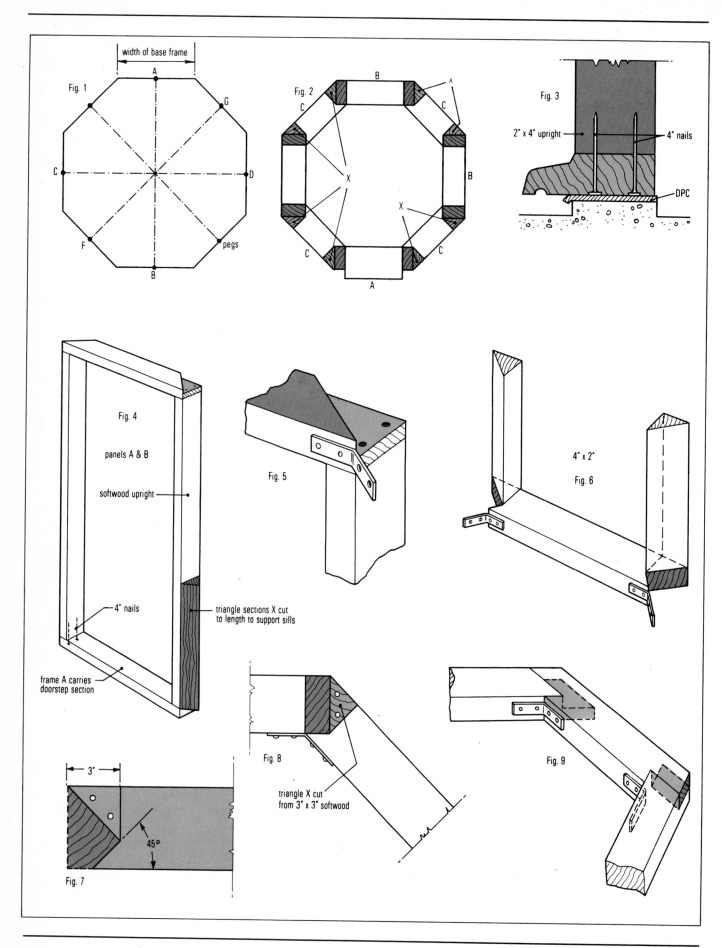

Fig. 1
width of base frame
A
G
C
D
F
B
pegs

Fig. 2
B
C
C
^
X
X
B
C
A
C

Fig. 3
2" x 4" upright
4" nails
DPC

Fig. 4
panels A & B
softwood upright
4" nails
frame A carries
doorstep section

Fig. 5
triangle sections X cut
to length to support sills

Fig. 6
4" x 2"

Fig. 7
3"
45°

Fig. 8
triangle X cut
from 3" x 3" softwood

Fig. 9

Fig 1. Ground plan of the gazebo. Pegs are used to mark out the site before cutting the trench for the foundations.

Fig 2. Plan view of the gazebo. Note the doorstep section which replaces the bottom of one of the frames A.

Fig 3. Section through the frame A showing the doorstep and dampproof course.

Fig 4. Construction of the frames A. The pieces X are sawn from 4in x 4in (192mm x 102mm) softwood.

Fig 5. Detail of the top corners of frames A showing the angle iron used to strengthen the joint.

Fig 6. The lower edge of the frames showing the joint between pieces C and X.

Fig 7. Detail of the corner joint between pieces C and X. A piece of triangular section timber is used to scribe the cutting line on piece C.

Fig 8. The completed joint. Note the angle iron.

Fig 9. Detail of the top end of the construction showing piece C1 and the method used to join it to the frames A.

pieces of 4in × 1in (102mm × 25mm) softwood and pitched at an angle of 10° to converge at a centre point (Fig. 17). The convergent top ends are mitred to $12\frac{1}{2}°$, and trimmed back to make a flat platform of about $5\frac{1}{2}$in (140mm) square. At the lower end they are cut to a 'birdmouth' to fit over the top rails A, B and C1 – a cardboard template will help get the angles right – and slightly oversail the sides to take rainwater clear. Detail of the roof structure is shown in Fig. 12.

Next, cut eight sections of triangular timber diagonally from 4in × $1\frac{1}{2}$in (102mm ×38mm) softwood (Z) (Fig. 16). These are cut 1in (25mm) shorter than the overall length of the octagonal sides and are nailed to the top rails of frames A, B and C1, fitting tightly between roof struts W. The ends of the sections are mitred to an angle of $22\frac{1}{2}°$, the angle at which the roof struts converge.

An octagonal capping piece is fixed to the roof struts at the point of convergence, with an octagonal patrice beneath them (Figs. 12 and 13). These are cut from hardwood and screwed into the struts with brass screws to form a water cover to carry away water from the open joint beneath the capping. They also add extra strength to the structure. The pieces are made from 6in × 1in (152mm × 25mm) blocks of hardwood – beech oak or mahogany. A block plane is used to shape the sections to produce the eight upper faces; the corners are cut away to form an octagon (Fig. 14). The capping piece is bedded on mastic; this is not necessary for the patrice on the underside (Fig. 15).

Cut glazing strips S (Fig. 16) from 2in × 1in (51mm × 25mm) softwood and nail these to each side of roof struts W between the triangular sections Z and the centre point of the roof. The top surface edge of S should form a continuous line with the top surface of Z, to provide support for the glass roof (Fig. 16).

Eight pieces of glass, cut to the triangular shape of the roof, are required, each to overhang the outer edges of Z by about 1in (25mm). The panels are bedded down on to putty spread over the top edges of S and Z.

Eight sections of hardwood R, shaped like an inverted L, are cut to fit to the exact lengths between roof struts W. Hardwood angle section could be used here. The top edges should be rebated to receive, later, the ends of the glass panels Y. Sections R are pinned and glued to

the roof struts W and screwed through the centre of R to top rails B and C1. Bed putty between the glass and rebate after fixing.

Cut sixteen hardwood fixing patterns T to the length of struts W and fix them together to form a flush top surface (Fig. 17). Putty should be bedded between the glass and under the edge of section T.

Outward-opening pivot windows can be fitted if desired. It is a sensible provision to provide greenhouse ventilation; two or three windows would do.

The windows are made up to size using rebated timber. The choice of joint to make the frames is a matter of personal preference. The frames are hinged to swing open from the top and can be kept open by fitting conventional window stays at the bottom.

Figs. 18 and 19 show glazing details. The glass is fixed in position by pinning in place window glass-fixing heads H at the rear. The glass is lightly bedded in putty or mastic.

The fixed lights are similarly bedded and fixed in position by four fixing beads. The lower front one K is angled forward slightly to allow water to run down.

The fixing beads in the angled windows between the main frames are chamfered to an angle of 45° (Fig. 20).

It is possible to make the door, but a suitable whitewood one may be picked up 'off the shelf' from a timber supplier. The door should be suitable for full or partial glazing – again, a matter of personal choice. If the garden greenhouse is built to the small dimensions shown, a 2ft (610mm) door may have to be ordered. A standard 2ft 6in (762mm) door, however, should be easy to obtain from stock.

Fixing the door

The door should be fixed to open outwards, to give the maximum space in the greenhouse and permit staging to be fitted inside.

The long rails, or stiles, have protruding ends, known as horns or joggles, which you have to saw off. These are to protect the door in transit and storage. The door may have to be planed to fit well, but first it should be tried against the opening.

Planing should start from the edge on which the hinges are to be fitted, known as the hanging stile. You should aim to make this stile as good a fit as possible to any curves or variations in the frame. A jack plane is best here, since this will give

Gazebo

Fig 10. The method of fixing the cladding and window sills. The ends of the cladding need to be mitred at $22\frac{1}{2}°$. Accuracy is necessary in order to make a good job of this part of the construction.

Fig 11. The window sills require careful fitting in order to produce a professional appearance.

Fig 12. Details of the roof construction.

Fig 13. The centre of the roof of the gazebo showing the patrice and the method of fixing it to the rafters.

Fig 14. The capping piece is marked out as shown and cut to shape using a block plane.

Fig 15. Detail of the centre of the roof showing the capping piece, which is bedded in mastic to make the joint watertight.

Fig 16. Detail of the roofing at the lower end of the rafters.

Fig 17. Plan view of the roof of the gazebo showing the method of joining the rafters and pieces T.

Fig 18. Section through a window showing the method of hinging and the position of the surround.

Fig 19. Section through the fixed lights showing the beading which holds the glass.

Fig 20. Section through the vertical frames. Note the shape of the beading above the pieces C between the frames A.

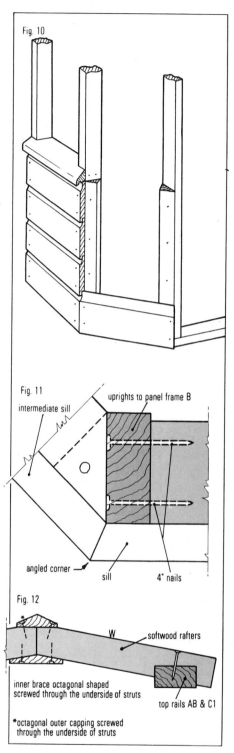

Fig. 10

Fig. 11

intermediate sill

uprights to panel frame B

angled corner

sill

4″ nails

Fig. 12

W

softwood rafters

inner brace octagonal shaped
screwed through the underside of struts

top rails AB & C1

*octagonal outer capping screwed
through the underside of struts

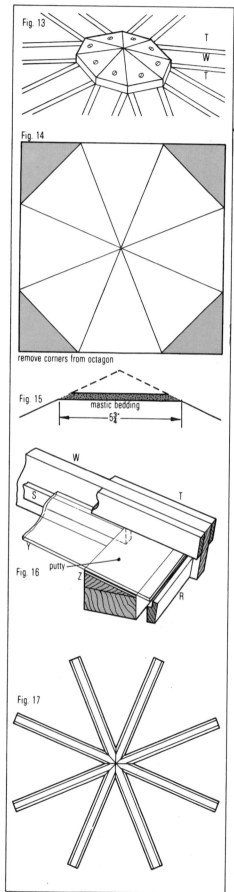

Fig. 13

T
W
T

Fig. 14

remove corners from octagon

Fig. 15

mastic bedding

$5\frac{3}{4}″$

W

S

T

Fig. 16

putty

Z

R

Fig. 17

a truer edge. If the edge is planed to a slight bevel, this will give slight extra clearance without increase of the visible gap.

Once the hanging stile is fitted accurately to the jamb, plane the opposite stile. This must have a slight bevel, of about $\frac{1}{16}$in (1.5mm) for a satisfactory fit. A top and edge clearance of about $\frac{3}{32}$in (2.4mm) should be left for painting.

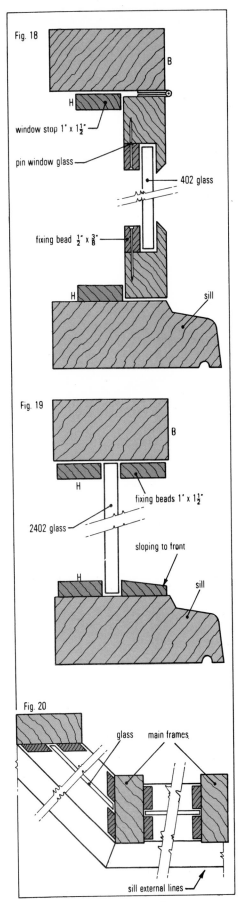

Fig. 18

window stop 1" x 1½"

pin window glass

402 glass

B

H

fixing bead ½" x ⅜"

H

sill

Fig. 19

B

H

fixing beads 1" x 1½"

2402 glass

sloping to front

H

sill

Fig. 20

glass   main frames

sill external lines

When trying the head of the door, allow a little less clearance above the lock stile, since doors tend to drop slightly as hinges wear. The bottom rail should have a clearance of about $\frac{3}{16}$in (4.8mm). Allowance must be made for any weather board fixed across the bottom of the door, which must be 'throated' on the lower edge to throw water clear of the step. The board must, of course, project beyond the step to throw the water clear.

Hinges and latches

Cast-iron hinges or butts can be used to hang the door, though brass or plastic are suitable. Pressed-steel butts are not as strong as cast ones and may rust, unless you can buy galvanized. The door may be hung on two hinges, though three would spread the work load and prevent possible middle distortion. Use three 3in (76mm) pressed-steel hinges or two 3½in (89mm) or 4in (102mm) cast butts.

The depth of each leaf is marked on both the door and the door frame. Each leaf is recessed to this depth. Using a chisel, make a series of cuts across the grain as deep as the gauge line, then pare with the grain to remove the waste (Fig. 21). The hinges can now be screwed to the door which is then fitted into the frame opening. Slide a wedge underneath and a piece of $\frac{3}{32}$in (2.4mm) packing at the top to line up the door in position. The edge positions of the hinges can then be pencilled on to the frame, squared into this using a try square and marking gauged to leaf depth. The recesses are chopped out in the same way as those of the door.

Try the door by inserting one screw in each hinge. Provided no adjustments are needed, a second screw can be inserted and a further check made. Should any recess be too deep, use a piece of card to pack and adjust this. Before final hanging, it is advisable to remove the door and give the bottom edge one or two coats of paint.

Door stops, are made of $\frac{1}{2}$in × 1in (13mm × 25mm) timber, nailed around the door frame $\frac{1}{16}$in (1.5mm) from the inner face of the closed door.

The door 'furniture' can now be fitted. The height for this is optional, around 3ft (914mm) though this will look best if it lines up with any glazing bars in the doors or any other features such as the height of the sills.

The latch is fitted by squaring a line round the stile at the required height with try square and marking knife, and measuring the distance from the stile edge for the latch spindle. Bore a $\frac{1}{2}$in (13mm) hole for this. Now make a similar hole in the edge of the door, the size of which will depend on the size and shape of the latch barrel. Gauge the face of the barrel on to the face of the stile and drill a hole or a series of holes in line (Fig. 22); chop these out to accommodate the barrel. Fit this to the depth of the front plate and mark this on the stile. The depth of the plate can then be chiselled out. The latch spindle and plate and handles can then be fitted.

To find the position of the striking plate, close the door and mark on the side the position of the latch tongue. Next, put the plate in position on the door edge and mark round this. Chop a small mortise in the centre to accommodate the tongue. Bend the lead-in part of the plate backwards slightly and recess it.

Glazing

You may wish to cut your own glass, but usually a glass supplier can do this for you. You should use 24oz (3mm) glass.

There is a special variety of glass suitable for greenhouses which admits plenty of light yet keeps down the temperature.

To cut glass, a steel glass wheel is satisfactory for most work and works out cheaper than the traditional glass cutter's diamond. You need a large flat surface to cut glass. A felt-tipped pen can be used to mark guide lines on the glass. A long straightedge (a yardstick) or a home-made tee square) is needed to guide your cutter accurately along the line.

First, clean the glass. To cut, use a firm stroke, holding the cutter vertically. Never back track, since the glass is unlikely to break along the cut line. After the surface has been scratched, put a strip of wood, or the yardstick, beneath the glass under the score line. Place your fingertips as closely as possible to the line and on both sides and press down slowly and firmly. You should get a clean break. If you have to trim surplus from the glass, scratch a further line and gently break off the waste in small bites with a pair of pliers with emery cloth held in the jaws.

Before glazing, apply pink or white lead primer to all timber rebates to prevent oil in the putty from being sucked out. The putty should be rolled in the hand until malleable. Use linseed oil to

Gazebo

Fig 21. The method used to mark and cut the recesses for the hinges.

Fig 22. The method used to cut the hole for the door latch.

Fig 23. The construction of the staging for the interior of the gazebo. Note that the sills and cladding have been omitted from the drawing for clarity.

Fig 24. Plan view of the gazebo showing the construction of the staging and position of the uprights which support it.

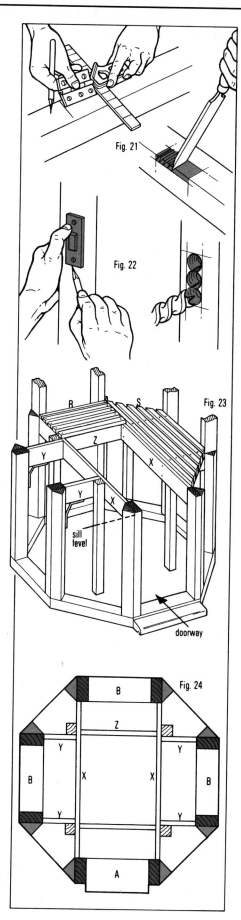

Fig. 21

Fig. 22

Fig. 23

sill level

doorway

Fig. 24

soften it if necessary. Next, line the rebate with bedding putty by 'rolling' this in a thin strip from a ball in the hand. Now press the pane into place at the edges. Never press at the centre. This will squeeze out surplus putty leaving a bed to a depth of $\frac{1}{16}$in to $\frac{1}{8}$in (1.5mm-3mm). Cut off the surplus with a putty knife. Once glazing is completed the glazing beads can be tapped in to hold windows firmly in place.

Glazing presents little difficulty, although a few general points in glazing are: all four beads should be inserted before any of them is finally fixed in place; and pins should not be inserted too near the corners.

Also note when smoothing putty round newly glazed areas, it sometimes tends to stick to the putty knife. This can be avoided if the knife is kept moist with water, providing a smooth finish. In some putties, there is a tendency towards excess oiliness and oversoftness of the material, particularly if it is bought in a polythene or plastic wrapper. To remove the excess, the putty should be wrapped in newspaper, which will absorb the oil.

Staging and finishing

Staging can be fitted to choice in the greenhouse. The following is a suggested arrangement to meet average needs. This provides shelving racks at all levels, consisting of a 4in × 1in (102mm × 25mm) framing with 2in × 1in (51mm × 25mm) decking (Figs. 23 and 24).

Framing is screwed by non-rusting metal brackets to the greenhouse frame uprights. Fixing of the cross members is through the face of the main cross bearers into the ends of the members which butt at right angles (Figs. 23 and 24). Non-rusting rails are used to make the fixings. Where heavy pots have to be carried on the staging, timber centre legs can be fitted.

The level of the shelf rail should be 1in (25mm) below that of the sill level so that the decking is at this height. Paving stones can be laid inside the greenhouse to walk on, leaving the earth at the sides free for planting.

Finally, the finish, inside and out, is a matter of choice. Hardwoods and cedar will not rot, but a preservative or clear varnish will prevent discoloration from weather. The timber can be painted or finished with a polyurethane varnish. An attractive effect can be achieved by using a polyurethane woodstain varnish.

Index

If a page number in this index appears in *italics*, an illustration accompanies the text on that page.

bandsaw 28, 29
    table 29
beds, designs for
    bunk *123*, 124, *125*, 126, 127
    four-poster *141*, 142, 143, 144
    platform *128*, *129*, *130*, 131, 132
    sofa *66*, *67*, *68*, 69, 70
bench *91*, *92*, 93, 94, 95, 96, 97, 98
    garden *150*, 151, *152*, 153
    gazebo 180
    see also workbench
bending wood *see* kerfing
bevel 31, 32
    sliding 10
bit sharpener *22*
bits
    auger *9*, *21*
    countersink *9*, *21*
    dowel *21*
    flat *21*
    Forstner *21*
    hole saw *21*
    Jennings *21*
    masonry 21
    plug cutter *21*
    rose *9*
    spear-point *21*
    trepanning 21
    twist *9*, *21*
    see also grinding, sharpening
brace, rachet *9*
bradawl 10

chair, designs for
    dining *99*, *100*, 101, *102*, 103, *104*
    see also bench, living room suite, studio couch and chair
chisel 10
    blade sharpening 38, 40 ,41
    carpenter's 10
    see also lathe (tools)
circular saws 17, *27*, 28, *29*, 30, *32*, *33*
    bench table 27, 30, *31*
    blade types *28*
    hand held 27, 28, *29*
clamping 17
    see also G - cramp, Gripmate
climbing frame, design for *169*, *170*, 171, 172, 173
couch, design for *see* sofa
crosscutting 29, 30
cupboard, designs for *105*, 106, *107*, *119*, *120*, 121, *130*, 131, 133
cushions *see* upholstery
cutting wood 78, 79, 88, 120, 121

door construction 112, 115, 122, 136, 177, 179
dowelling 24, 80, 81
drawer construction 112, 115, 139, 140
dresser (fitted), design for *137*, 138, *139*, 140
drill
    hand 9
    power *20*, *21*, 22, 23
    rotary hammer action 20, 21
    see also bits
drill stand 22, *23*, 24
drilling techniques 24, 80

fence *see* guides
finishing 50, 58, 82, 90, 96, 98, 104, 107, 127, 136, 140, 149, 168, 180
    pre-assembly 72
firring 31, 32
foam, use of 69, 82, 83, *84*, 101
    see also upholstery

G-cramp *9*, 17, *96*
garden projects
    garden seat–planter *154*, *155*, 156, 157, 158, 159
    see also bench (garden), climbing frame, gate, gazebo, tree house
gate *160*, *161*, *162*, 163, *164*
gauge
    honing 10
    see also marking gauge
gazebo, design for *174*, 175, *176*, 177, 178, 179, 180, *181*
glazing 179, 180
glueing 88, 93, 146
grinding 37, 38, 40, 41
    bench grinder *37*
    see also sharpening
Gripmate 17
guard 28
guides 29, 30, 31
    mitre guide 30, *31*
    rip fence 30, *33*

hacksaw, junior 10
hall stand, design for *46*, *47*, 48, 49 50
hammer
    claw *9*, 10
    Warrington pattern (cross pein) *9*
honing 36, 38

jig 31

dowelling 24, 77, 78, *79*
jigsaw 34, *35*
  blades 34
jointer *36*
  blade sharpening 38
joints 11, 12, 13, 14, 15
  box *15*
  bridle *14*
  butt *11*
  cogged *15*
  dovetail *15*, 124, *126*, *127*, *146*,
    147, *149*
  dowelled *11*
  halving *11*, 12
  housing *12*, 32, *33*
  lapped *13*
  mitred 11, 124, *126*, *127*
  mortise-and-tenon *13*, 124, *126*,
    127, *161*, *162*, 163
  scarfed *15*
  stopped-dado *12*
  tenon *14*, *33*
  tongued-and-grooved *13*

kerfing 32
kitchen unit, designs for *108*, 109,
  110, *111*, *112*, 113, 114, 115, *116*,
  117, 118, *119*, *120*, 121, 122
knife
  handyman's 10
  scriber marking 10

ladder *123*, 127, 132, *172*, *173*
laminate, cutting technique 65, 120
lathe 39, 40, 41, 42
  safety precautions 41
  speeds 41, 42
  tools (gouges, chisels and scrapers)
    40, 41, 42
  see also wood-turning
levelling (legs) 58, 98
linen chest, design for *145*, 146, 147,
  148, 149
living room suite, design for 76, 77,
  78, 79, 80, 81, 82, 83, 84, *85*, 86

mallet, carpenter's 10
marking gauge
marking knife (scriber) 10
mitre 32
mitring 30

oilstone 10, 36
oven unit construction *115*, 116, 117

painting 65
  spray *43*, *44*
pencil, carpenter's 10
pincers (shoulder) 10
plane
  bench 10
    fore 10
    jack 10
    jointer 10
    smooth 10
    try 10
  block 10
  Surform 10
punch
  centre 10, 41
  nail set 10

radiusing 79, 80
rebates 32
right-angle changer 22, 23
routers 36, 37
rules 10

sander
  disc 26
  drum 26
  orbital *25*, *26*
sandpaper 25, 26
sand-pit, design for 173
saw, types of
  back *9*
  handsaw *9*, 28
    crosscut 9
    rip saw 9
  tenon *9*
  see also circular saw
saw blades 28, 29
  coated 28
  combination *28*
  cross-cut *28*
  flooring 28
  planer 28
  rip *28*
sawhorse 16, 17
saw table 30
sawing
  power 27-36
  techniques 30
  see also circular saw, jigsaw
screwdriver
  cabinet 10
  Pozidriv 10
sharpening 37, *38*, 40, 41
  see also grinding, honing
shelving 109, 110, 111, *112*, 115, 122,
  135, 136, 139

slide, design for 173
sofas, designs for
  see bed sofa, living room suite,
    studio couch
spray painting *see* painting, spray
square, carpenter's 10
studio couch and chair, design for *71*,
  72, 73, *74*, 75

tables, designs for
  coffee 59, 60
  dresser *137*, 138, *139*
  fold-down *105*, 106, *107*
  round 87, 88, *89*, 90
  rural looking *91*, *92*, 93, 94, 95, 96,
    97
  telephone *51*, *52*, 53, 54
templates 77, 78
timber buying 72, 76, 151
tray, Victorian butler's, design for 55,
  56, 57, 58
tree house, design for *165*, 166, *167*,
  168
trolley (dinette), design for *61*, 62, 63,
  64, 65
turning, wood 42
  see also lathes

upholstery 69, 73, 74, 75, 82, 83, 84,
  85, 86, 101, 103

vise 16, 17
  drill stand 22, *23*

wall fixing 122
wardrobe (fitted), design for *133*, 134,
  135, 136
window sills 175, 176, 177, *178*
wobble washer 32, *33*
wood preservation 151, 155, 175
wood turning 28, 39, 40, 41, 42
workbench 16, 17
Workmate 16, 17
work top construction 113, 117

Pictures supplied by
Peter Bell 137, 139
Harry Butler 45, 108, 112, 119
Roy Day 174, 181
Alan Duns 71
Nelson Hargreaves 8, 66/7, 70, 79, 80, 114,
  165, 166
John Hovell 164
Paul Kemble 154
R. Locke/Roy Flooks 169
Nigel Messett 51, 76, 85, 91, 105, 141, 145,
  148
Derek Metson 133
John Price 7, 16, 17, 18, 20, 22, 23, 25, 26,
  27, 29, 31, 33, 34, 36, 37, 43, 44
Richard Sharpe 55, 61
Tubby 46/7, 87
Colin Watmough 128/9

Illustrations
Tri-Art 99, 104, 150
All other diagrams by Bob Mathias